Digital Research Confidential

Digital Research Confidential

The Secrets of Studying Behavior Online

edited by Eszter Hargittai and Christian Sandvig

The MIT Press
Cambridge, Massachusetts
London, England

© 2015 Massachusetts Institute of Technology

All rights reserved. No part of this book may be reproduced in any form by any electronic or mechanical means (including photocopying, recording, or information storage and retrieval) without permission in writing from the publisher.

MIT Press books may be purchased at special quantity discounts for business or sales promotional use. For information, please email special_sales@mitpress.mit.edu or write to Special Sales Department, The MIT Press, 1 Rogers Street, Cambridge, MA 02142.

This book was set in Sabon by Toppan Best-set Premedia Limited. Printed and bound in the United States of America.

Library of Congress Cataloging-in-Publication Data is available.

ISBN: 978-0-262-02988-9

10   9   8   7   6   5   4   3   2   1

To our families for teaching us to appreciate the details.

The Microbe

The microbe is so very small
You cannot make him out at all,
But many sanguine people hope
To see him through a microscope.
His jointed tongue that lies beneath
A hundred curious rows of teeth;
His seven tufted tails with lots
Of lovely pink and purple spots,
On each of which a pattern stands,
Composed of forty separate bands;
His eyebrows of a tender green;
All these have never yet been seen—
But Scientists, who ought to know,
Assure us that they must be so...
Oh! Let us never, never doubt
What nobody is sure about!

—Hilaire Belloc (1912)

Contents

Preface

Eszter Hargittai and Christian Sandvig

The premise of this book and its precursor (Hargittai 2009) is that we need more frank, first-person, behind-the-scenes talk about research methods. While "research methods" often sound boring or scary to students, there is no denying that how a research project is planned and executed is one of the foundations of research. Must methods be boring or scary? We think not. With several years of experience teaching courses about how to research digital media, and after engaging in such research ourselves, we are well aware of the many challenges such projects can face. But they can also be some of the most exciting work in which scholars can engage today! They need not elicit anxiety or fear, nor should they be associated with tedium or ennui. However, when details are left out of research write-ups (as they often are) and when challenges are not explicitly acknowledged in formal outputs (as they often are not), it is understandable that newcomers to such domains may be at a loss, confused and frustrated about how to proceed or about why their approaches are not working as expected. The goal of this collection is to articulate in detail the realities of doing social science research in our digital age so as to offer readers guidance on how to proceed with their own projects.

Whether the Internet is the object of study or it is a means to gather data about more traditional questions of interest—or both—many social science research projects in the 21st century require new methodological considerations. While digital media offer opportunities for social scientists, they come with their own set of challenges. The chapters in this volume are not shy to invite the reader into the delicate specifics of what happens backstage during research projects. The goal is to help researchers, from those starting out to those with decades of experience, appreciate what is new and exciting, and also what requires careful thought and consideration, as they embark on studying what is of most interest to them in our digital social world.

The first chapter, "How to Think about Digital Research," by Sandvig and Hargittai, frames the problem of new research methods in a larger historical context. It explains how this domain has evolved in scholarship and why it is intellectually important. The remaining chapters report on the nuts and bolts of specific projects covering a wide range of method-ologies. The two chapters "Read/Write the Digital Archive: Strategies for Historical Web Research" by Ankerson and "Flash Mobs and the Social Life of Public Spaces: Analyzing Online Visual Data to Study New Forms of Sociability" by Molnár and Hsiao each reflect on the experience of try-ing to compile or access archives of online materials and the challenges that come from the ever-shifting nature of Web content and the search tools available to find it. "Making Sense of Teen Life: Strategies for Cap-turing Ethnographic Data in a Networked Era" by boyd and "The Ethno-graphic Study of Visual Culture in the Age of Digitization" by Leonardi both report on ethnographic research, one chapter is focused on the dif-ficulty of conducting one-on-one interviews with teens about behavior online, the other considers how to study workers' use of digital visual artifacts in a major automotive firm. In "Social Software as Social Sci-ence," by Gilbert and Karahalios and "Hired Hands and Dubious Guesses: Adventures in Crowdsourced Data Collection" by Shaw, we are offered two reports of studies that used online platforms, the former developing its own research software in-house, the latter employing a worldwide crowdsourcing system. In "How Local is User-Generated Content?" Hecht and Gergle share how a seemingly simple research question about Wikipedia can mushroom into years of work on millions of data points. With "The Art of Web Crawling for Social Science Research," Shumate and Weber reflect on the challenges associated with gathering network data about Web site linkages. Also dealing with network data, but from a very different perspective, the chapter "Big Data, Big Problems, Big Opportunities: Using Internet Log Data to Conduct Social Network Analysis Research" by Foucault Welles describes the hurdles associated with studying friendships using an automatically-generated data set of interactions in a virtual world. Finally, Bruckman, Luther, and Fiesler ask, "When Should We Use Real Names in Published Accounts of Internet Research?" The authors address new ethical questions regarding online research and offer some challenges to traditional notions of respondent confidentiality and the role of participants in research projects.

While it is unlikely that any one researcher will use all of the methods addressed in this volume, the lessons learned from one project often generalize to other types of studies. The feedback that the precursor to this volume, *Research Confidential,* continues to receive suggests that people, especially students, appreciate hearing about the struggles associated with projects even if said projects are not exactly in line with their own. Reading about studies not directly tied to one's work will also help scholars appreciate the efforts of their peers. And it will help advisors steer enthusiastic students in realistic directions as they mentor a new generation of scholars about how to study social behavior in our digital world.

References

Hargittai, E., ed. 2009. *Research Confidential: Solutions to Problems Most Social Scientists Pretend They Never Have.* Ann Arbor, MI: University of Michigan Press.

Acknowledgments

The editors are grateful to Margy Avery for her interest in the project and to the staff at MIT Press for their help in bringing the book to fruition. They thank the contributors for their willingness to write up their methodological experiences. Eszter Hargittai is grateful to her graduate school peers and mentors, as well as her current students and colleagues for many inspiring and instructive methodological puzzles and conversations. Christian Sandvig would like to thank the past students of the doctoral seminars "Unorthodox Research Methods" and "Culture as Data," as well as co-instructor Karrie Karahalios.

1

How to Think about Digital Research

Christian Sandvig and Eszter Hargittai

"Bench science" has come to connote *routine* scientific labor as opposed to exceptional events. Work done in the natural sciences is sometimes distinguished by the prefix "lab," "bench," "field," or even "wet" when an author wants to emphasize that the scientific labor under discussion has a hands-on relationship with the physical world. This is a way of differentiating "everyday science" from a discipline's finished products and from news coverage that glamorizes new findings. "Bench science" is the process; it is what actually happens among the reagents and enzymes; it is the workaday job of feeding the lab rats, cleaning the fume hood, and keeping the cultures alive. With the exception of the ethnographer's word "fieldwork," social researchers do not have an equivalent phrase. There may be no phrase like "bench social science" because social scientists do not often highlight their own everyday work.[1] But they should. This book argues that social scientific research about digital media and the Internet is a key area of social inquiry where routine research labor is quickly being transformed. Digital media research processes deserve our attention because they are producing new methods, new opportunities, and new challenges for understanding human behavior and society. To appreciate this transformation, we must reconceptualize our everyday research work. This chapter and the essays that follow are reflections by practicing researchers describing "bench" social research with and about the Internet and digital media. They are specific accounts of what actually happened to people doing hands-on work during particular projects. These firsthand accounts should be useful not only to anyone new to the area who wants to learn how to conduct research themselves, but also to those already involved in such work as a way to investigate and consider this transformation in method, with both its opportunities and pitfalls.

Research Methods as a Creative Act

It is difficult to learn about "bench social science" without experiencing it. Detailed, first-person narratives about research methods are hard to find.[2] As scholars, our most common means of written communication is the research article, a kind of writing that originally developed its format from the correspondence between gentleman scientists. All research articles were once written in the first person, as letters (and were required to begin with the salutation "Sir,"; see Swales 1990). The scientific letter was partly a way to update the reader on the process of research, but the research articles that developed later became an end rather than a means. The article is now a final product, and scrutinizing one of them gives the reader few clues as to how the research reported in it came about. Just as the business letter has a formal structure of sender, date, addressee, and body, the genre of the research article evolved to differentiate introduction, method, result, and conclusion.

Yet the research work itself may not divide neatly between compartments like "methods" and "results." And in fact the ideal for many methods sections has become what linguist John Swales has termed the "clipped" style of academic writing (Swales 2004: 220), a kind of writing that intentionally excludes details and omits justifications. The clipped methods section does not explain why a particular process was chosen over alternatives—or even what the other choices were. Due to space constraints, or perhaps the assumption that methodological details are boring, clipped final write-ups of projects do not include enough detail about how studies were actually conducted on the ground to allow for their replication. Yet without knowing certain aspects of a study, such as exactly how the researchers obtained their data, it is impossible to know whether a project is sound enough for its findings to be taken seriously, and readers have no guidance that would help them employ a similar method in their own research. In some traditions of qualitative work, method is never written about at all: indeed, some authors feel that methods should be entirely hidden in the service of narrative and readability (for an overview of this issue, see Iverson and Byler 2012).

To the more jaded eye, there are reasons that explain this state of affairs in writing about method. To the cynical reader, descriptions of methods are not helpful because they are not meant to be so. They are written down in order to report successes and perhaps to build methodological empires. The methods section in a research article is no recipe, because, rather than hoping to instruct the reader, it aims to defend the author from the reviewers or the dissertation committee. Genre analysis of scholarly research articles describes their dominant literary device as the *defensive hedge* (Swales 1990).

The methodological appendix in books is hardly better. Similar to most writing about research methods, it has evolved to be a series of gestures toward procedures the reader is supposed to know already. It exists more as a rear-guard action against the critics than an educational addendum. The motive of authors who write explanations of their methods can even be sinister. The clipped style of writing might be preferable to them not because everyone in the field agrees about the procedures involved (therefore the author may be brief) but because everyone *disagrees* about the procedures involved (therefore all the better to be brief, hide the embarrassing details, and act as though the choices made were too normal to merit more comment).

Contrary to the norms of open science, researchers have built careers by monopolizing new data sets and new research methods, creating incentives against ever sharing the complete details of what they did and how they did it. Methods sections can differentiate among partisans for or against a particular procedure but they can also act to demarcate the expert from the nonexpert. "In practice," economist Deirdre McCloskey explains, much of the function of methodological writing is of this type. "Methodology serves chiefly to demarcate Us from Them," proving that social scientists are more than a group of opinionated people who like to talk a lot about what other people do (McCloskey 1985: 26). The methods in social science say: "What you have here is more serious than just what I think."

Even a methods textbook, which is usually conceived of as a set of instructions, leaves out much of what actually happens during research. Most textbooks prefer to impart a rigid procedure rather than a genuine discussion of process, and since there is little professional incentive for textbook authorship, the writing is often of poor quality. This led famed anthropologist Clifford Geertz (1989) to recommend that graduate students simply avoid all textbooks: they would be better off, he suggested, if they just read finished research and tried to imitate it. This technique is how we often excuse the poor state of writing about research methods with vague talk of a doctorate as an "apprenticeship."

We would at least expect the research methodology literature to help readers interested in research methods, but the methodology literature can be far from inviting. Articles there revel in technical detail and jargon, while the common tone of the writing is closer to reprimand than to advice. McCloskey wrote that the definition of a methodologist is someone who fancies himself the judge of the practitioner (indeed, most self-proclaimed methodologists are men), while the genre of the methodological paper "is to scold [researchers] for not allowing it to interfere more" (McCloskey 1985: 22). In areas of methodological controversy and innovation, methodology can take the form of an insular debate among guild members (methodologists), each armed with a variety of secret handshakes.

With this context in mind, in the area of digital media research we hereby call for a friendlier and more accessible approach. This requires a positive conceptualization of method as a creative act. While it is easy to see methods as boring tools or even as a necessary but unpleasant step on the road to results, genuine discussion of the research process is ultimately as much about grand ideas as it is about nitpicking; and as much about design as it is implementation. A discussion of method is a discussion of the labor to which we have dedicated our research lives. Ultimately this is also about knowledge, understanding, and even beauty.[3]

To get there, a first step is to open a space for frank discussions about the research process. Instead of deploying talk of methods as a defensive gambit, much can be gained by revealing and reflecting upon our struggles, dramas, and even disasters. This is particularly true as we stumble through the process of inventing a new area of research: the study of digital media and the Internet. Although it is invigorating to adopt a radical tone, this call for an elaborated method continues a trend that has been building in some quarters for decades. A few examples will make this case. The ethnomethodologists in 1960s sociology asked that an expansive definition of method be diffused throughout all sociological writing, and even subsume theory (Garfinkel 2002). Similar impulses appeared decades later in human-computer interaction (Dourish and Button 1998). In the 1970s and '80s, feminist theorists argued that adding more detail in order to reveal the researcher's own subjectivity ("standpoint theory") produced stronger quantitative analyses and a new form of objectivity (Harding 1987). Actor-network theorists in science and technology studies recently claimed that abandoning the jargon of social science is the way forward, and that researchers should think of themselves as writing detailed "travel guides" rather than aping the conventions of the natural sciences (Latour 2007: 17).[4] Regardless of your position on these specific ideas, the overall point is that we are now a long way from the gnostically confident social scientific writing of the 1950s. In sociologist Steve Woolgar's phrase, researchers can agree that "the fact that all our analyses are essentially flawed is better celebrated than concealed" (Woolgar 1982: 494). With this volume, following up on Hargittai (2009), we hope to create such a space, where researchers can reveal the messy details of what they are actually doing, aiming toward mutual reflection, creativity, and learning that advances the state of the art.

Two Forms of Transformation in Digital Media Research

The need to improve our writing about what actually happens during the research process is consequential because so many new things are happening in Internet and digital media research. At the moment, this research is not even adequately named as an area, despite the fact that it is not a young field anymore (Dutton and Jefferys 2010: 6). Here we call it "digital media," but the topic can include Internet research, e-research, mobile media, new media, computational social science, cyberinfrastructure, information science, social informatics, and more. It is a "trading zone" between disciplines (Collins, Evans, and Gorman 2007). It includes work being conducted by people with degrees ranging from English to sociology to physics (see Jones 1998, Ess and Consalvo 2002, Urry 2004, and Hendler et al. 2008). There is widespread interest in it, although no one is sure exactly what it is, what it is called or should be called, who should do it, or how exactly it ought to be done. While our approach to the topic is inclusive of this diversity, it is helpful to distinguish two different senses of "digital media," which can help to chart the important transformation in research to which we allude above: digital media as instrumentation and digital media as an object of study.

In the first sense, digital media is exciting as a new research tool. Important methodological ferment has come from the exciting potential uses of digital media in the research process. Basic, longstanding questions about humanity that may have been inaccessible to researchers in the past may now be possible to study thanks to the spread of computing and the Internet. In many parts of the world, scores of newly computerized transactions now leave "digital traces that can be compiled into comprehensive pictures of both individual and group behavior, with the potential to transform our understanding of lives, organizations, and societies" (Lazer et al. 2009: 721). At the same time that computing has helped collect these data, it has also provided a wide array of new means to analyze them. We now have advanced visualization tools, new chips for geolocation,[5] new software for natural language processing, and so on—all now possible at a scale that before would have been prohibitively expensive or even impossible. In this first sense, digital media is a new kind of microscope: it represents an unprecedented tool we can use to see ourselves. We call this sense of the topic *digital media as instrumentation.*

In our second sense of the topic, traditional research methods or even new ones are being applied to *digital media as a new object of study.* Digital media themselves produce and are the site of remarkable new situations, combinations, and kinds of human activity. Research innovation in this second sense is not concerned with developing new research methods—instead it encompasses the challenge of taking our existing research methods and questions about human behavior to this new terrain. If the first sense pointed out that old questions can now be answered in new ways, this second sense instead asks what the new questions are, or at least what new contexts have emerged to reinvigorate the central questions of our scholarship. In this vein, researchers consider what social interaction through specific new digital platforms actually entails. Researchers revisit the classical problems of social science like inequality, the allocation of scarce resources, identity, learning, culture, power, and so on—but do so in the context of digital media and the Internet. (Sometimes this second sense is referred to by others as "Internet studies.")

In other words, our second sense of transformation involves the challenges facing humanists and social scientists who practice longstanding research traditions like ethnography, history, or survey research when they ply this craft in an unfamiliar digital media context. It is true that all research is about studying unfamiliar objects—the very term "research" itself derives originally from hunting, and means "to seek." In this sense digital media are the quarry—the object of the hunt. But when dealing with this second sense of our topic, which we call digital media as an *object of study*, pointing an existing method at a new object often raises difficult intellectual questions related to method. Even if the procedure of a method is relatively unchanged, its meaning might be wholly transformed. Alternately, an existing method's applicability in the first place might be a point that a researcher has to defend, as when a study design employs paper-and-pencil surveys to study Internet use, or an author claims to be performing "an ethnography" without geographically visiting any research sites or speaking to interlocutors in person.[6]

These two forms of potential transformation—as *instrumentation* and as *object*—constitute frames for how to think about research involving the Internet and digital media. They are not exclusive. It is certainly possible that research projects both investigate new phenomena and use new tools and methods to do so. We will now consider the implications that these frames provide when considering the intellectual problems surrounding discussions of method.

The Internet as Instrument

Let us consider digital research as *instrumentation* first. As described by noted physicist and historian of science Derek J. de Solla Price (1986), much of natural science during the era known as the Scientific Revolution can be explained by the fortuitous discovery of a series of new instruments. These were always borrowed from some other endeavor. The first pumps were created for firefighting and mining, but they led to the realization that air is a gas. The cloud chamber was an attempt to create artificial clouds built by a mountaineering buff, but it then became the way to visualize atomic particles. The telescope was first marketed as a novelty, then as a military device, and then Galileo used it to discover that the moon had mountains. De Solla Price calls this era of science the period of "instrumental revelation" (247), writing that:

For the first time in history, [Galileo] had made a discovery not available to other people and by a process that did not involve deeper and clever introspection. Galileo had discovered what was effectively a method of artificial revelation that promised to enlarge what was to be explained by science. (245)

As we noted above, some now believe that the Internet and digital media are instruments that could enable a similar revolution of revelation for the social sciences (Lazer et al. 2009). In this view, online games like World of Warcraft were created by private companies to allow people to pretend to be night elves (or more accurately, for the company to make money from what people spend on subscriptions allowing them to pretend to be night elves). Yet these games might hold the potential to answer basic questions about the networked structure of human interaction. Social network sites like Facebook were developed through private investment with the goal of making money through advertising, but they may allow us to answer basic questions about human behavior.

So far, the most-trumpeted successes of the digital media instrument have been outside of social science. Much of the excitement has surrounded "big data." Consider two of the most well-known examples. First, monitoring Google search queries for the frequency and location of terms like "flu" produced a new way for epidemiologists to monitor influenza outbreaks. Analyses of big data suggested that this could work 1–2 weeks faster than the current method: a weekly survey of doctors conducted by the Centers for Disease Control (Carneiro and Mylonakis 2009; Ortiz et al. 2011). Second, financial engineers found that an automated sentiment analysis of posts on Twitter could predict stock market returns 1–2 days in advance, something not possible with any other method (Bollen, Mao, and Zeng 2011). However, these success stories quickly became controversies. First, Google flu prediction proved to be strongly confounded by media coverage of the flu. Since media coverage of the flu does not accurately reflect the prevalence of the flu, this led to Google flu-prediction errors that could have cost millions of dollars in erroneous vaccine procurement had anyone relied on the Google model and not the traditional CDC surveys of doctors (Butler 2013). Second, systematically watching and tracking Twitter for stock market information quickly made Twitter an unreliable source for that information. A hedge fund managed by Twitter sentiment analysis closed (Leinweber 2013). Stock market prediction using Twitter posts subsequently proved to be susceptible to manipulation, and some of the observed macro-level Twitter trends may in fact be the result of intentional manipulation (Melendez 2013; Messias et al. 2013). In these areas it seems that the digital research revolution is not here yet, or at least the value of these techniques is still being tested and refined.

Within the social sciences and humanities, the novelty and success of digital media as a research instrument has so far been the most celebrated in the context of large-scale digitization projects like Google Books. In the most prominent example, Michel and colleagues argued that large-scale digitization enables a "new kind of science" called "culturomics ... the application of high-throughput data collection and analysis to the study of human culture" (2011: 181) that would subsume traditional methods in the sciences and humanities. Culturomics research has been publicized by promoting a variety of topically disconnected results with claimed relevance for fields like history, English, linguistics, communication, media studies, political science, and law. A sampling of these touted findings reads like a list copied from a manual of cocktail party conversation ideas. The findings include a new estimate of the size of the English lexicon (much larger than was previously thought), a new method to evaluate the scope and impact of government censorship, the fact that the longevity of personal celebrity has been decreasing over time (in other words, the duration of an individual's fame is decreasing), and that for reasons that are not explained, the phrase "ice cream" lost about half of its popularity from 1950 to 1970, and in the years since has almost regained it (Michel et al. 2011).

These claims from the authors selling "culturomics" are relevant here because they demonstrate both the pitfalls and potentials of a possible transformation in instrumentation brought about by digital research, and they do so more clearly than Google flu trends or Twitter stock market prediction. It is tantalizing to imagine that digital research enables the revelation of new facts across such a broad domain from celebrity to ice cream, and bombastic media accounts have even argued that new digital processes of discovery will lead to a new scientific method or "the end of theory" (Anderson 2008). Yet the ability to unearth these facts does not in itself constitute a new science or even perhaps a "finding" in the sense that researchers usually mean the term. Simply participating in fields of endeavor like medicine and finance means that *ipso facto*, the prediction of influenza or the stock market are important, yet the utility of facts unearthed by "culturomics" without a clear research question is not so obvious.

In response to the announcement of the above "culturomics" findings in the journal *Science,* an English professor (Morse-Gagné 2011) apologetically noted that while culturomics provided a new estimate of the size of the English lexicon, this number is not really useful for anything. History professor Tim Hitchcock, commenting on the culturomics findings purporting to be relevant for history, writes that the presentation of these facts "simply misunderstands" history itself:

These large-scale visualisations of language may be the raw material of history, the basis for an argument, the foundation for a narrative, the evidence put in the appendix in support of a subtle point, but they do not serve as a work of history. (Hitchcock 2011)

De Solla Price's earlier description (quoted above) of the telescope providing "instrumental revelation" to Galileo was astute: he wrote that the telescope's revelation was to "enlarge what was to be explained by science" (1986: 245). This was done by adding new facts, such as the existence of unexpected mountains on the moon. Culturomics does present us with new facts to be explained. We could ask ourselves: "What caused the dramatic shift in the popularity of the term 'ice cream'?" But answering that question is sensible only if a fact can be situated in an intellectual frame and context that makes it evidence for a debate of some importance. We could also ask ourselves: "Who cares?"[7]

The telescope also provided Galileo with facts as evidence to support a controversial existing theory—heliocentrism. This led to a paradigm shift in astronomy and physics and to Galileo's eventual conviction by the Catholic Inquisition for heresy. While the scientific revolution in de Solla Price's account was dominated by pivotal developments in instrumentation and apparatus, this does not appear to have been paralleled by any decline in or absence of theory. Indeed, by providing a new source of evidence, instrumentation shaped the codification of the scientific method as we know it today and changed what was meant by "theory." This change could be seen as a much more explicit codification of the role of theory and of the relationship between theory and evidence. We expect the same trajectory for digital research.

In contrast with the high expectations for "big data" projects like the three profiled above (Google Flu Trends, Twitter stock market prediction, and Culturomics), we do not expect that a switch will be flipped and the answers to all research questions will automatically appear, or that with the appropriate software in place, theory will end (see also Crawford 2013). Popular accounts have focused attention on a few large-scale digital media or Internet projects as a research revolution. All of these involve corporate data sources and a great deal of hype. We instead see that the actual revolution in digital research instrumentation is going on now, all around us, in smaller, "ordinary" research projects. We see it in the use of crowdsourcing to replace traditional pools of research participants (see Shaw, this volume); the use of hyperlink networks as a new source of data to study the relationships between organizations (see Shumate and Weber, this volume); or in the idea that writing your own Web-based application is now a viable data collection strategy (see Gilbert and Karahalios, this volume). Just as in the earliest period of "instrumental revelation" in science, these instruments are providing new sources of evidence. Since the historian de Solla Price diagnosed "instrumental revelation" 400 years after it occurred, so we must wait for the ultimate judgment of future generations as to whether our era is engaged in revolutionary social science. Yet it feels exciting to its "ordinary" practitioners, and it feels exciting to us.

The Relationship Between Instrument and Theory

If the history of science is any guide, the excitement surrounding digital media and the Internet as a new kind of instrumentation is likely to take some time to translate into new bodies of knowledge. We foresee some immediate challenges for those who embrace these new digital research methods. Sociologist and philosopher of science Harry Collins (1985) popularized the concept of *the experimenter's regress* to explain one of the crucial difficulties faced by empirical researchers with new instruments when they are working in an area where the theoretical expectations may not be clear. Paraphrasing Collins, the experimenter's regress functions this way: To answer an empirical research question correctly, we must build a good instrument that measures something. But we do not know if we have built a good instrument until we have tried it and obtained the correct answer to a research question. But we do not know what the correct answer to a research question is until we have built a good instrument … and so on *ad infinitum* (84). The experimenter's regress explains how investigations with new tools can quickly become stuck, controversial, and intellectually unproductive. In a deeper way the regress, like our earlier discussion of the telescope, is a reflection on the relationship between theory and evidence. As Collins writes, "the experimenter's regress can only be avoided by finding some other means of determining the quality of an experiment" beyond its own results (85). This can be a paradoxical proposition because "a criterion must be found which is independent of the experiment itself" (85).

To illustrate the regress in the context of our topic, if a social scientist used a previously unobtainable source of digital research evidence to obtain a very surprising result, a process related to the experimenter's regress would apply.[8] Imagine that a new method for the large-scale quantitative analysis of Facebook profiles produces an extremely sensational and unexpected fact (say, "92% of married Americans are polyamorous," or "The homeless are the most influential group in matters of public opinion"). The more unexpected the fact, the more the methodological innovation would be called into question ("It must be false! The new method is mistaken!"). If a new method gives us new evidence, we can only make sense of it by comparing it to our existing theories. When a new method produces surprising results, this is as likely to be a problem as it is a success, as it invalidates the method rather than proving its worth. In contrast, in what we might call *the methodologist's lament*, when a new method proves its correctness by delivering a completely obvious result ("poor people are less likely to have high-speed Internet access at home than rich people") the method also damns itself ("If a new method cannot deliver new information to us, of what value is it?" "Why switch to a new method?"). This may explain why methodological changes in day-to-day research practice tend to make their first inroads when methods offer an incremental savings of money or time rather than a bold new way to measure or conceptualize the world.

In a third situation, a new method might deliver evidence about which we have no expectation at all. Imagine that at the dawn of Facebook, a researcher developed a new method to sample and crawl Facebook profile pages. The results suggested that the fewer favorite books a user listed on their profile, the more likely they were to use the Facebook "poke" feature. In this situation the method is also proven worthless, as the result is not interpretable at all. Before asking, "How could those two things be related?" many readers would have been stumped by the things themselves ("What is the 'poke' feature? " or even "What is Facebook?"). This illustrates the peril of using a new method to deliver facts that are disconnected from a research question or a theoretical frame. In this way the phenomenology of research is always entangled with the epistemology of instrumentation and evidence (see Davis 1971).

It is new ideas, concepts, and models that we ultimately want, not just new facts. Despite the difficulties listed above, the ultimate promise of new instrumentation is in fact to escape the experimenter's regress and also to do more than simply perform the same research process faster, cheaper, or with a different tool. As a way to expand the available evidence and kinds of evidence, digital research instrumentation has the potential for far-reaching consequences reaching beyond method and into theory. This is an important point, because despite extensive, required doctoral-level training in both theory and method, the relationship between the two is often a topic unconsidered by graduate education.

As theory and method are normally presented they seem independent of each other, like two different *á la carte* menus from which the student can select a main course and dessert. Of course this cannot be the case. Sociologist Howard Becker (1986), writing about the research process, takes pains to emphasize the link between the two. He writes that as a research project proceeds, each decision about method forecloses a potential theoretical perspective. That is, he argues that in graduate education it is often thought that theory is something that can be bolted onto a research project after the empirical work has been completed. He points out that the choice of theory has already been made—at least partially—when the methods are chosen due to the observations that were not made, the interview questions unasked, and the sites not visited. Within a broad problem area—inequality, education, well-being, and so on—if an empirical study has already been done, what was studied and how it was examined severely narrow the potential explanations that can be fit to the data later. The idea of digital media and the Internet as instrumentation has profound consequences for theory as well as method.

The use of a method constrains theory. If a study is undertaken without a theory in mind, it may well produce results that are off the theoretical map and cannot be explained at all—they might not fit into any narrative that is comprehensible as research. This applies to every method presented in this book and in every methods book—every procedure comes with a set of theoretical commitments, whether or not they are stated explicitly. We therefore need to ask ourselves with what hidden theoretical baggage digital media instrumentation is burdened. We might also ask what older theories digital media and the Internet as instrumentation might allow us to escape. Rather than conceiving of theory and method as separate menus from which the researcher can choose, Becker might prefer the simile that combining theory and method in a research design is like combining two chemicals—with the wrong combinations, they explode and are unable to provide the desired results. Some combinations just will not work in a productive way.

Becker's point is certainly true and important, but Becker takes the linkage of method to theory as always a liability. This presupposes a research universe where theory is finished; in Becker's scheme, the scholar's duty is only to select from what explanatory apparatus already exists. Contrary to Becker, we can just as easily state that each empirical step opens possibilities for the creation of new theories as well as foreclosing some that already exist. Each step of procedure, in this view, has the chance to produce new data and new kinds of data that can be explained inductively. This chance for new theory is the goal of many methodological movements. For instance, "grounded theory" in the qualitative sociology of the late 1960s explicitly tried to link new methods to the production of new theory. This impulse was born in an environment where sociologists worried that their research had become too descriptive (and too dependent on a few "great man" theories of society; Glaser and Strauss 1967).

By pointing out that method has hidden links to theory even when the theory is left unstated, then, we are not arguing for atheoretical work, or saying that theory need not be mentioned because it is already implied. In fact, we mean to recognize explicitly what already happens: research is a messy and exploratory process and there is value in focusing on methods and technique as a means of producing new puzzles that can be solved. Like it or not, in "bench" social research, sometimes theory comes later. To be clear, this is not meant as a justification for data mining without any a priori ideas about what one might uncover and without any link to existing relevant literature. Rather, we want to acknowledge that methods can be usefully discussed by themselves and their theoretical frames deferred, as long as theory is not put off forever.

De Solla Price pointed out that "lab," "craft," or "apparatus" work is often delegated to a professional class of laboratory assistants and tool-builders in science who live a parallel but demeaned existence. In opposition to the received wisdom that science advances thanks to the cogitation of the noble scientist, de Solla Price argues forcefully that the cause of most progress in science should be properly attributed to instrumentation and method, and he asks us to reconsider pragmatically the unwarranted prestige of theory. "In social standing, the people with brains in their fingertips are regarded as servants of the ... people with theoretical training" (252). Yet "the dominant force of the process we know as the Scientific Revolution was the use of a series of instruments" (246). His prescription for science policy is that the surest way to produce new, important knowledge in a domain is to invest in research tools, technical knowledge, apparatus, instrumentation, and the like without a particular theoretical frame or question in mind, and from this new theories and questions will also be born. This follows chemist Homer Adkins's famous adage, "Basic research is like shooting an arrow into the air and, where it lands, painting a target." Digital research methods are the pump, the cloud chamber, or the telescope of today, and there is promise in where this new instrument could lead us.

The Internet as an Object of Study

In our second major sense of digital research and its potential for transformation, we consider digital media and the Internet as an *object of study*. It is worth spending some effort unpacking what role an "object of study" entails in the grammar of research. In their classic review of "oddball" social scientific research designs, *Unobtrusive Measures* (1966), Webb and colleagues framed the interaction between a research question and the way that question is studied by arguing that researchers should be drawn to new sources of evidence that can be studied in pursuit of some invariant underlying question. "Science," they wrote, "opportunistically exploits the available points of observation" (Webb et al. 1966) to allow multiple chances to get at the truth of a particular issue. They argued that by relying on just one source or on a narrow range of evidence, social scientists had severely and unnecessarily constrained their view of knowledge, of the total possible findings and scope of all research. Most social scientists, in their view, simply did not really consider creativity in method and were thus constrained in what manifestations of a phenomenon they explored. They instead investigated their substantive question of interest through the method with which they were already familiar, and encouraged their students to do the same. In the logic of the book, the average researcher who claimed to be studying "politics" in 1966 was actually revealed to be studying things people wrote on an exit poll survey, or to be studying voting records kept by the county election department. Politics in some other context was not open to consideration because the political scientist in question habitually only looked at exit polls and voting records.

Webb and colleagues strongly implied that most social science findings of the day were probably wrong for this reason—because researchers visited only one "outcropping" of a phenomenon and employed only one narrow lens at a time to study it. They asked: if a researcher is studying media use and wants to measure the audience for radio stations, why rely solely on the survey questionnaire as the "obvious" research method? Instead, why not go to the auto mechanic and sample the radio presets of cars brought in for repair? While all methods have biases, by triangulating the source of information we scrutinize, Webb argued, we are most likely to gain a complete picture of the phenomenon under study. When one begins to consider digital media and the Internet as an object of study, it complicates this picture further. While the radio station example posits the auto mechanic sampling as a new instrument (just as we discussed in the previous section), at the same time we can go beyond Webb and colleagues to point out that there may be a new way to listen to the radio in cars. The radio in a car may have some important difference from listening to radios in the kitchen or at the beach. It may be that the object of study produces new phenomena that should be studied, or highlights boundaries and limits to the older phenomena, defamiliarizing them.

In the view of *Unobtrusive Measures*, the questions of social science are fixed, but the sources of evidence, the settings for these questions, and the designs, instruments, and methods designed to measure them within those settings may vary. Webb and his colleagues often employed geographic metaphors; they wrote of using "outcroppings" to "triangulate." In the dictionary definition, triangulation uses angles to identify a location, and an outcropping is the visible projection of invisible subterranean bedrock. In the radio audience example, devices in cars are one particular outcropping of the phenomenon under investigation: media use. In a similar vein, Webb and colleagues might feel that behavior "on the Internet" should then be like a rock outcropping to a geologist. The geologist should visit this new outcrop to get a more complete picture of what lies beneath, unknowable, about the particular social scientific question of interest. There is no sense, in this view, that one outcropping is more or less important to the geologist than another, that is, that studying gender dynamics by observing behavior in a school yard is more insightful than doing so in an online context. Any research context is of value: "If we want to understand nature, if we want to master our physical surroundings, then we must use all ideas, all methods, and not just a small selection of them" (1966). Similarly, if we want to understand social behavior, we should triangulate our sources of evidence and include online manifestations to gain a better sense of the overall picture.

Webb and his colleagues were so confident about their formulation of triangulation and the value of diversity that they closed their book with Cardinal John Henry Newman's epitaph. Cardinal Newman was a prominent Anglican academic in Victorian times who now exemplifies both principled doubt and scholarship—Newman converted to Catholicism after he conducted historical research on Anglican theology and found it untenable. Newman was buried beneath the epitaph "*Ex umbris et imaginibus in veritatem*" (out of shadows and pictures into truth). To Webb and colleagues, then, it seems digital media and the Internet could serve as just one more "place" or setting where truth is accessible. Researchers interested in politics will want to supplement traditional offline studies with studies of politics online because it is a new "outcropping" (in Webb et al.'s term) of political action that can help shed light on existing understandings of political behavior. At the same time, studying the Internet can help us understand what may be changing in light of this specific new online context where people engage in the political process. More than just instrumentation, digital media and the Internet offer a view of a potentially new politics. Digital research is more than a different route to the same destination.

To continue the geographic metaphor, unlike Webb and colleagues, we suspect that the outcrop of the Internet may be part of a wholly different subterranean mountain than the others. We suspect that climbing it informs all mountaineering. We recognize that some outcroppings might be more valuable than others. We might value methodological diversity, but we also value the particular contribution that studying online phenomena may bring. That is why the chapters covering Internet settings in the rest of this book deserve to be included in a conversation about methodological transformation. These authors should not be seen as researchers who happen to have brought their existing research questions and methods to the Internet. There is more going on than that, as we will explain.

If the Internet and digital media are important in their own right, this begs the question, "What is research about the Internet about?" Other authors have cataloged and classified research about digital media and the Internet from 2001 to 2013 in an attempt to answer this question. A sampling of these review essays shows a surprising amount of agreement about recurring emphases (see particularly DiMaggio et al. 2001; Silver 2000, 2006; Dutton 2013).[9] Reviews identify the six most frequently recurring themes in research about the Internet as identity, community, inequality, politics, organizations, and culture (adapted from DiMaggio et al. 2001), with some reviews arguing that identity and community have received disproportionate attention even within this subset of topics (Silver 2006). This list of major themes may seem broad; however, it excludes a number of topics that loomed much larger for other social scientists and humanists. For example, the concept of "empire" is arguably one of the most important ideas in the humanities in the last few decades (Hardt and Negri 2000), organizing and informing a great deal of scholarly work. Yet compared to the themes of Internet research listed above, empire has simply not had a great deal of conceptual intersection with research about the Internet. Initial Internet research has also excluded topics that loomed larger in the study of earlier communication technologies, such as journalistic practice or the effects of televised violence on children, although as the field matures, an exploration of these topics is moving to the online realm as well.

A key justification for studying digital media and the Internet given by practitioners is that these constitute something beyond "just one more place," communication channel, or platform where researchers gather to investigate central research questions. While of course inequality on the Internet is an example of the broader phenomenon of inequality, the

Internet probably has to be more exceptional in some way, or at least offer us some new information or other benefit, to justify studying it in depth. This assumption is a little controversial. As the use of the Internet and digital media has become more popular and mainstream, scholars have argued that there is a "developing [area] of consensus" that researchers should "move away from any strict duality between ... the real and the virtual" (Dutton 2013: 8) and stop treating the Internet like a distinct place. Yes, the Internet is not "strictly" separable from other parts of life, and should not be continually reified as an exceptional object. At the same time it is likely that Internet scholars (us included) implicitly still believe in some Internet exceptionalism, since it justifies their existence. A number of researchers have explicitly taken up this challenge and argued for the uniqueness and importance of the Internet as an object of study.

The Internet as an Exceptional New Object

Dutton (2009) provides one compelling approach to the Internet, describing it as a distinctive and exceptional domain that produces its own new phenomena and research problems. He argues that the Internet is the "fifth estate." While it is commonly known that the term "the fourth estate" refers to the press or the media, many wrongly think that the term is meant to reference the three constitutional branches of government in the United States. In fact, the term probably references the three "estates of the realm" that were seen as the institutional sources of power in the societies of the Middle Ages and formed the inspiration for the organization of the English government. These three estates in the Middle Ages were the clergy (sometimes analogized today to public intellectuals), the nobility (sometimes analogized to the government), and the burghers or bourgeoisie (sometimes analogized to the business classes).[10] In the 18th century, Edmund Burke (as reported by Thomas Carlyle) identified the press as a new "fourth estate," implying that the printing press and the development of journalism had established a new source of political power beyond that of intellectuals, government, and business (Dutton 2009: 2). Dutton extends this further by naming the Internet the fifth estate. He writes,

Many of those who acknowledge that some aspects of the Internet compose something distinctive also have a limited notion of new digital media as being essentially a complementary form of news publishing—a[n] ... online digital add-on to the mass media. (4)

Or, alternately, Dutton writes, they focus limited emphasis "on techno-logical novelty" that they believe will be a passing fad (4). Instead, Dutton sees the institutional, cultural, and technological complex that we call "the Internet" as a configuration that has been able to produce a new source of power. Drawing from evidence about the Internet's ability to allow new routes and kinds of communication that change the outcome of politically charged debates in a variety of contexts, he argues that the Internet is not a new location to study politics, but rather a new kind of politics.

Many other writers have taken up this thread—Dutton's "fifth estate" is only one well-named example. Benkler, in contrast, argues that the Internet is instead a "networked fourth estate" (2011) in order to empha-size its continuity with other institutions (i.e., the press) and secure for the Internet the protection of laws originally written to apply to the press. But elsewhere, Benkler makes a strong case for Internet exceptionalism of his own in *The Wealth of Networks* (2006). He writes:

It seems passé today to speak of "the Internet revolution." In some academic cir-cles, it is positively naïve. But it should not be. The change brought about by the networked information environment is deep. It is structural. It goes to the very foundations of how liberal markets and liberal democracies have coevolved for almost two centuries. (1)

Benkler identifies the technological and institutional framework of the Internet as a source of radically distributed production processes (such as Wikipedia and open-source software). These processes, Benkler asserts, can lead to innovation, new efficiencies, and most importantly, a new form of radically distributed authority. Benkler portrays the Internet as locked in combat against those with a vested interest in traditional pro-duction. He explains that a critically important focus for researchers in this environment is this struggle between the old and the new.

Justifications for Internet exceptionalism are too extensive to be listed here exhaustively. For instance, Dutton's "fifth estate" and Benkler's "wealth of networks" were heavily influenced by the earlier work of Castells (1996) and others. Castells is part of a longer research tradition theorizing and studying the consequences of new information and com-munication technologies. (For a complete review, see Webster 2006.) Our point is that there is ample justification for the premise that the Internet is worthy of consideration as an object of study in its own right, and not simply as another example of an existing phenomenon. In closing, we will now turn to the implications of this situation for all research methods—our central topic in this book.

The Internet Transforms Traditional Methods

With both senses of the Internet and digital media (as instrumentation, as object of study) now in hand, we conclude with observations about their interplay and their future implications for method and knowledge. We end this chapter by arguing that one important lesson to be drawn from the new digital methods described in this book is that they help us to reconsider and transform older, nondigital methods. To recap, above we explained that as instrumentation, the Internet and digital media may promise bold new forms of evidence and "instrumental revelation," yet these seem likely to appear at some time distant in the future. Today, the Internet may offer more efficient, cheaper, or otherwise superior itera-tions of our existing research methods. Even though these changes seem minor, they can still subtly ask us to reconsider and revise the theoretical assumptions that are linked to our methods. We argued that theory and method are inextricably linked, even when theories are left unstated. We posited that practitioners of new digital methods may often encounter a variation on the *experimenter's regress* (Collins 1985)—epistemologically unable to make bold new contributions to knowledge because of the non-traditional nature of their instruments, which calls their new findings into question. As an object of study, we explained that the Internet promises us new phenomena to research. It asks us to consider the Internet as a new "outcropping" (Webb et al. 1966) where existing research questions can be examined, but also as a way to interrogate our existing questions in light of new and exceptional facts. While some scholars see the Internet as just another context where social phenomena occur, others have argued that the Internet is an exceptional new "fifth estate" (Dutton 2009) allow-ing people to practice a new form of politics, that networked social pro-duction allows us to redistribute power in topographies that were previously unknown (Benkler 2006) and that are deserving of study in their own right. This tradition of work sees the Internet as a domain of new and exceptional social action, not as an additional, slightly refined example of what came before.

Elaborating on this last point in conclusion, we assert that even if a researcher takes an ostensibly conservative view and visits the Internet looking for answers to the same old questions about identity, community, inequality, politics, organizations, culture, or other areas that they know from nondigital research, and they try to answer them using the traditional nondigital social research methods they already employ in other work, this experience can leave both their methods and their concepts quite changed. By watching this encounter, it is possible to understand how the practice of "bench social science" evolves and methods come to take new forms and meanings.

Research like Ankerson's study of the recent history of the Flash programming language (this volume) demonstrates that claiming a continuity in method is an interesting intellectual move. Claiming a continuity in method does not, in fact, keep the details of research method fixed for writers like Ankerson, because the Internet as a new object of study reopens concepts for consideration that in traditional settings for research are closed and taken as a given. For instance, even though both pre-Internet history and Ankerson's work on Internet-related topics count as *history*, performing archival research to understand the development of the Flash programming language on the Internet quickly unsettles the fundamental historiographic concepts of "archive," "preservation," "reference," and even the notion of a historical record and how it functions. Reflections by Molnár and Hsiao (this volume) on their searches of online video archives suggest similar experiences. In projects that bring existing methods to the Internet, trying to exercise existing research procedures can unintentionally and unexpectedly produce new research practice and force the researcher to clarify and extend what is meant by their traditional method. In another example of this phenomenon, Bruckman, Luther, and Fiesler (this volume) describe performing a study of an online creative community (Newgrounds) using the research method of the interview. Even though they intended their use of the interview method to be "standard" (their term), the context of the Internet led them to question what they thought they knew about privacy, anonymity, and ultimately "human subjects" and "research." These are terms that they end up putting in quotes, yet they were probably not worrying concepts that they expected to put in quotes when they began their research project.

This implies that our ideas about the continuity provided by a "stable" method over time or "the same" research method in two different studies might require a great deal of intellectual labor to maintain. In our closing example, the notion of continuity in method as an ongoing challenge can be seen most clearly by contrasting two ethnographies of the Internet that were produced about a decade apart.

In 2001, anthropologist Daniel Miller and sociologist Don Slater coauthored the very influential ethnography *The Internet: An Ethnographic Approach*. It consisted of a long-term multisite ethnography performed to understand modern Trinidad in the context of the Internet and vice versa, and it was one of the first works of ethnography about the Internet. It combined the area studies expertise of one author who had a longstanding interest in Trinidad (Miller) with one author who had previously studied the Internet (Slater). The object and often the instrument of this research were both the Internet, yet the writing often emphasized the value of the Internet as an instrument. Miller and Slater used the Internet to reach diasporic Trinidadians that a traditional ethnography would not have been able to consider. The researchers used screen captures of Trini websites as texts that were diagnostic of Trini culture generally and were not just about the Internet. They proudly published supplemental images on a website, an innovation at the time. The book conveys a sense that the Internet can benefit traditional ethnographic methods and vice versa, and in the book these procedures were framed as methodological innovations.

To both compare and contrast, 10 years later anthropologist Tom Boellstorff published the excellent ethnography *Coming of Age in Second Life: An Anthropologist Explores the Virtually Human* (2010). (The title is a reference to Mead's 1928 book, *Coming of Age in Samoa*.) Boellstorff's book is an ethnography of the commercial virtual world Second Life developed by the company Linden Labs, analogizing this digital media platform to be a place, as do its creators and users. Obviously digital media is the object of study, and while it must necessarily be the instrument as well, this notion is often downplayed by Boellstorff, who denies any innovation in method. Although an ethnography of a virtual world is still an unusual idea to some (for an overview, see Beaulieu 2004; Hine

2005), Boellstorff emphasized in the book that he "engaged in normal anthropological methods" (Boellstorff 2010: 4). In a later coauthored methods handbook developed after that project, Boellstorff and colleagues (2012) stated this even more strongly: "the ethnographic research paradigm does not undergo fundamental transformation or distortion in its journey to virtual arenas" (4). Maybe so, but at the same time the "bench social science" or the practice of ethnographic procedure has been entirely transformed from Boellstorff's first book to this one. Describing in detail what a researcher actually does on a day-to-day basis when conducting an "ethnography" of Indonesians in Jakarta would be quite a different description from that of an "ethnography" in the virtual world of Second Life—so much so that Boellstorff and his colleagues wrote a whole book explaining how to do the latter, for people familiar with the former (2012), all the while arguing that the two conditions are fundamentally equivalent.

The above comparison makes it clear that a claimed continuity in method is often quite the opposite; it is a way to enlarge and refine the definition of traditional research methods while still receiving full credit for rigor and tradition. This is not a bad thing. However, this clever maneuver illustrates the way that research methods evolve as a complicated mixture of the new and the old, all the while maintaining their impressive power to define the everyday experiences of our research work. The following chapters contain more examples of "bench" social researchers attempting to puzzle out new procedures that might transform their research. We have come to see it as a process of small steps with big implications—implications for our procedures, for our working life, for the future of scholarship, and, ultimately, for knowledge itself.

Notes

1. Important exceptions include Becker (1986), Clifford and Marcus (1986), and the reflexive sociologists of science dedicated to understanding the everyday practices of science (e.g., Latour and Woolgar 1986).

2. A precursor volume to this book (Hargittai 2009) was one attempt to include them.

3. "When I am working on a problem, I never think about beauty … but when I have finished, if the solution is not beautiful, I know it is wrong." —R. Buckminster Fuller

4. Latour writes that we should even abandon "the pompous Greek name of 'method,' or even worse, 'methodology'" (2007: 17).

5. Geolocation refers to discovering the geographic location of something. New geolocation capabilities in mobile phones, for instance, have allowed new forms of research about human mobility.

6. This last example of "virtual" or Internet ethnography has been contentious for a number of years. For a review, see Beaulieu (2004) and Hine (2005).

7. The authors of the paper claim this fact is important in the field of "historical gastronomy," (Michel et al. 2011: 181), a claim we are not qualified to judge.

8. This discussion of "surprising" results is extrapolated from Davis (1971) and extended to apply to methodology. On the conservatism of science, compare Kuhn's concept of the "paradigm" (1962). Although Kuhn stated that he did not intend the "paradigm" to apply to social sciences, the word is widely applied there.

9. Reviews of the topic that disagree (Ess and Consalvo 2012) tend to do so because they take a more inclusive view and have a longer list, not because they think the things on our list are not central.

10. The third realm is also called the commons, but this is confusing as it typically does not refer to the peasantry or populace as a whole but to those who rise to influence without nobility or ordination.

References

Anderson, C. 2008. July. The end of theory: The data deluge makes the scientific method obsolete. *Wired.* http://archive.wired.com/science/discoveries/magazine/16-07/pb_theory

Beaulieu, A. 2004. Mediating ethnography: Objectivity and the making of ethnographies of the Internet. *Social Epistemology 18* (2–3): 139–163.

Becker, H. 1986. *Writing for Social Scientists: How to Start and Finish Your Thesis, Book, or Article.* Chicago: University of Chicago Press.

Benkler, Y. 2006. *The Wealth of Networks: How Social Production Transforms Markets and Freedom.* New Haven: Yale University Press.

Benkler, Y. 2011. A free irresponsible press: Wikileaks and the battle over the soul of the networked fourth estate. *Harvard Civil Rights-Civil Liberties Law Review* 46: 311–397.

Boellstorff, T. 2010. *Coming of Age in Second Life: An Anthropologist Explores the Virtually Human.* Princeton, NJ: Princeton University Press.

Boellstorff, T., B. Nardi, C. Pearce, and T. L. Taylor. 2012. *Ethnography and Virtual Worlds: A Handbook of Method.* Princeton, NJ: Princeton University Press.

Bollen, J., H. Mao, and X. Zeng. 2011. Twitter mood predicts the stock market. *Journal of Computational Science 2* (1): 1–8. doi:.10.1016/j.jocs.2010.12.007

Butler, D. 2013. When Google got flu wrong. *Nature* 494 (7436): 155–156. doi:10.1038/494155a.

Carneiro, H., and E. Mylonakis. 2009. Google Trends: A Web-based tool for real-time surveillance of disease outbreaks. *Clinical Infectious Diseases 49* (10): 1557–1564. doi:.10.1086/630200

Castells, M. 1996. *The Rise of the Network Society*. New York: Oxford University Press.

Clifford, J., and G. E. Marcus, ed. 1986. *Writing Culture: The Poetics and Politics of Ethnography*. Berkeley: University of California Press.

Collins, H. 1985. *Changing Order: Replication and Induction in Scientific Practice*. Chicago: University of Chicago Press.

Collins, H., R. Evans, and M. Gorman. 2007. Trading zones and interactional expertise. *Studies in the History and Philosophy of Science Part A 38* (4): 657–666.

Ess, C. and Consalvo, M. 2012. What is "Internet Studies"? In *The Handbook of Internet Studies*, ed. M. Consalvo and C. Ess, 1–8. New York: Wiley-Blackwell.

Crawford, K. 2013. May 9. Think again: Big data. *Foreign Policy*. http://foreign policy.com/2013/05/10/think-again-big-data/

Davis, M. S. 1971. That's interesting! Towards a phenomenology of sociology and a sociology of phenomenology. *Philosophy of the Social Sciences 1* (1): 309–344. doi:.10.1177/004839317100100211

De Solla Price, D. J. 1986. *Little Science, Big Science ... and Beyond*. New York: Columbia University Press.

DiMaggio, P., E. Hargittai, W. R. Neuman, and J. P. Robinson. 2001. Social implications of the Internet. *Annual Review of Sociology* 27:307–336.

Dourish, P., and G. Button. 1998. On "technomethodology:" Foundational relationships between ethnomethodology and system design. *Human-Computer Interaction 13* (4): 395–432.

Dutton, W. H. 2009. The fifth estate emerging through the network of networks. *Prometheus 27* (1): 1–15. doi:.10.1080/08109020802657453

Dutton, W. H. 2013. Internet studies: The foundations of a transformative field. In *The Oxford Handbook of Internet Studies*, ed. W. H. Dutton, 1–24. Oxford, UK: Oxford University Press.

Dutton, W. H., and P. W. Jefferys. 2010. World wide research: An introduction. In *World Wide Research: Reshaping the Sciences and Humanities*, ed. W. H. Dutton and P. W. Jefferys, 1–17. Cambridge: MIT Press.

Ess, C. and Consalvo, M. 2012. What is "Internet Studies"? In *The Handbook of Internet Studies*, ed. M. Consalvo and C. Ess, 1–8. New York: Wiley-Blackwell.

Garfinkel, H. 2002. *Ethnomethodology's Program: Working Out Durkheim's Aphorism*. New York: Rowman & Littlefield Publishers.

Geertz, C. 1989. *Works and Lives: The Anthropologist as Author*. Stanford: Stanford University Press.

Glaser, B. G., and A. Strauss. 1967. *The Discovery of Grounded Theory: Strategies for Qualitative Research*. New York: Sociology Press.

Hargittai, E. ed. 2009. *Research Confidential: Solutions to Problems Most Social Scientists Pretend They Never Have*. Ann Arbor, MI: University of Michigan Press.

Harding, S. 1987. Is there a feminist method? In *Feminism and Methodology*, ed. S. Harding, 1–14. Bloomington: Indiana University Press.

Hardt, M., and A. Negri. 2000. *Empire*. Cambridge, MA: Harvard University Press.

Hendler, J., N. Shadbolt, W. Hall, T. Berners-Lee, and D. Weitzner. 2008. Web science: An interdisciplinary approach to understanding the Web. *Communications of the ACM 51* (7): 60–69.

Hine, C. 2005. Virtual methods and the sociology of cyber-social-scientific knowledge. In *Virtual Methods: Issues in Social Research on the Internet*, ed. C. Hine, 1–16. Oxford: Berg.

Hitchcock, T. 2011. June 19. Culturomics, big data, code breakers and the Casaubon delusion. Historyonics. http://historyonics.blogspot.com/2011/06/culturomics-big-data-code-breakers-and.html.

Iverson, S. D., and D. Byler. (2012). Introductory essay: Literature, writing, and anthropology. *Cultural Anthropology* [virtual special issue]. http://www.culanth.org/?q=node/587

Jones, S., ed. 1998. *Doing Internet Research: Critical Issues and Methods for Examining the Net*. Thousand Oaks, CA: Sage.

Latour, B., and S. Woolgar. 1986. *Laboratory Life: The Construction of Scientific Facts*. Princeton: Princeton University Press.

Latour, B. 2007. *Reassembling the Social: An Introduction to Actor-Network Theory*.Oxford: Oxford University Press.

Lazer, D., P. Pentland, L. Adamic, S. Aral, A. Barabási, D. Brewer, N. Christakis, 2009. Computational social science. *Science 323*:721.

Leinweber, D. (2013). Mining Twitter Sentiment For Stocks Dies in London, OK at the SEC, Scary in the Market. *Forbes Wall Street*. http://www.forbes.com/sites/davidleinweber/2013/04/24/so-much-for-fund-mining-twitter-sentiment-for-picking-stocks-but-ok-at-the-sec

McCloskey, D. 1985. *The Rhetoric of Economics*. Madison, WI: University of Wisconsin Press.

Mead, M. 1928. *Coming of Age in Samoa: A Psychological Study of Primitive Youth for Western Civilization*. New York: William Morrow.

Melendez, E. D. 2013, February 1. Twitter Stock Market Hoax Draws Attention of Regulators. *The Huffington Post*. http://www.huffingtonpost.com/2013/02/01/twitter-stock-market-hoax_n_2601753.html

Messias, J., L. Schmidt, R. Oliveira, and F. Benevenuto. 2013. You followed my bot! Transforming robots into influential users in Twitter. *First Monday 18* (7). doi:.10.5210/fm.v18i7.4217

Michel, J., Y. K. Shen, A. P. Aiden, A. Veres, M. K. Gray, Google Books Team, J. P. Pickett, . 2011. Quantitative analysis of culture using millions of digitized books. *Science 331*:176–182. doi:.10.1126/science.1199644

Miller, D., and D. Slater. 2001. *The Internet: An Ethnographic Approach*. Oxford: Berg.

Morse-Gagné, E. E. 2011. Culturomics: Statistical traps muddy the data. *Science 332*:35.

Ortiz, J. R., H. Zhou, D. K. Shay, K. M. Neuzil, A. L. Fowlkes, and C. H. Goss. 2011. Monitoring influenza activity in the United States: A comparison of traditional surveillance systems with Google Flu Trends. *PLoS One* 6:4. http://dx.doi .org/10.1371/journal.pone.0018687

Silver, D. 2000. Looking backwards, looking forward: Cyberculture studies 1990–2000. In *Web.studies: Rewiring Media Studies for the Digital Age*, ed. D. Gauntlett, 19–30. London: Arnold.

Silver, D. 2006. Introduction: Where is Internet studies? In *Critical Cyberculture Studies*, ed. D. Silver and A. Massanari, 1–14. New York: New York University Press.

Swales, J. M. 1990. *Genre Analysis: English in Academic and Research Settings*. Cambridge: Cambridge University Press.

Swales, J. M. 2004. *Research Genres: Explorations and Applications*. Cambridge: Cambridge University Press.

Urry, J. 2004. Small worlds and the new "social physics.". *Global Networks 4* (2): 109–130.

Webb, E. J., D. T. Campbell, R. D. Schwartz, and L. Sechrest. 1966. *Unobtrusive Measures: Nonreactive Research in the Social Sciences*. Chicago: Rand McNally.

Webster, F. 2006. *Theories of the Information Society*. 3rd ed. New York: Routledge.

Woolgar, S. 1982. Laboratory studies: A comment on the state of the art. *Social Studies of Science 12* (4): 481–498.

2

Read/Write the Digital Archive: Strategies for Historical Web Research

Megan Sapnar Ankerson

When I was in the very early stages of my dissertation research, I spent one memorable summer working on a pilot digital-access project for a historical archive. The Wisconsin Center for Film and Theater Research, home of some of the oldest and most extensive collections of research materials relating to film, theater, radio, and television entertainment industries in the United States, was embarking on an initiative to digitize a selection of primary source materials and make them available online alongside scholarly research and analysis of these materials. Working with the center's director and head archivist, we chose a collection to feature and spent several weeks pouring through boxes of letters, memos, photographs, and scripts, searching for and scanning the juiciest nuggets that revealed the tangled behind-the-scenes negotiations informing the production of some of Hollywood's classics.

"It's a wonder any film ever gets made," I remember remarking after reading some particularly bitter correspondence between a director and a writer. I could hardly believe all the potential deal-breakers that might cause a film to be scrapped or the final concessions that helped usher it through to the box office. Of course, to film scholars, these behind-the-scenes negotiations are crucial for historicizing the complex relationships between individual films, the institution of American cinema, and the economics of Hollywood filmmaking. My experience with the center's collections made me eager to see what juicy tidbits I would dig up while researching my own dissertation topic: the historical development of a commercial Web industry in the 1990s and the accompanying digital cultural forms and aesthetic sensibilities that were produced and circulated during the dot-com era.

I came to my dissertation project as a graduate student invested in critical, humanities-oriented approaches to the study of media and communication technologies and had chosen a graduate program that emphasized the social, economic, political, and historical contexts of media institutions and media texts in order to ground my interest in new media studies historically and comparatively. In class, I read engaging accounts of the development of film, radio, and television as cultural industries and popular forms (e.g., Schatz 1988; Hilmes 1997; Douglas 1987, 1999; Boddy 1993; Anderson 1994). It was clear that these media benefited from detailed historical investigations of their institutions and representational practices, aesthetics and style, technology, creative labor, and managerial strategy. But while there is a growing body of work that investigates the history of software, video games, and computer systems (e.g., Campbell-Kelly 2003; Montfort and Bogost 2009; Ceruzzi 1998), there are few comparable inquiries that focus on the Web. Historical Web-studies research is still in its nascent stages; it is a tiny subfield of Internet studies that is just starting to garner more scholarly attention (see, for example, Brügger 2010; Park, Jankowski, and Jones 2011; Aspray and Ceruzzi 2008).

Yet, the majority of digital media scholarship looks forward, not back. I hoped to address this gap by providing similar historical context for understanding the development, discourses, and logics at work when the Web became commercialized and a new cottage industry of start-ups exploded in cities like New York, San Francisco, and London to meet the demand for professional interactive services. Specifically, I aimed to historicize the semiotics of the Web interface by connecting industrial negotiations, financing, and ideological struggles with the rise and fall of dominant visual styles that were expressed as an evolving set of discursive "rules" formed for thinking about the production of a "quality" Web site during a period of rising speculation in Internet stocks. In short, I wanted to examine how and why the look and feel of the Web changed during the dot-com era. This was a time when vertiginous stock valuations for young Internet companies reached breathless heights (see Cassidy 2003 for specific examples). Accusations of "irrational exuberance" persisted alongside impassioned pronouncements of a "New Economy" that claimed the old rules governing business, economics, and social relationships no longer applied in the Internet age (Shiller 2000; Kelly 1998). This project interested me personally because I worked as a Web designer during this period and wanted to situate some of my own experiences within a larger historical context of technological, industrial, and social change.

But as soon as I began my research, it became clear that historical Web-studies work is an uphill battle, and I longed for the orderly world of the traditional archive. Sure, there is a very particular system of protocols and customs governing access to archival materials that at first seems confusing and elaborate (for a useful overview, see Gallo 2009). Nonintuitive finding aids must be mastered. Little paper call-slips specifying box numbers and shelf locations are submitted for each request. Hours are spent combing through boxes before finding something particularly revealing (if one is lucky). Pens, those unforgiving ballpoint ink bombs, are strictly forbidden. Adorable white cotton gloves are available for handling the most fragile of documents. Yes, there is a system. A wonderful, orderly system, and once you become adept at navigating it, a whole world of audio-visual and primary source materials is suddenly at your fingertips.

Of course, the prevalence of such archives is no guarantee that media historians can actually access the texts and documents they are looking for, either due to copyright, legal issues, ideological priorities governing collection, or because deposited materials have somehow managed to escape cataloguing (see Wilson 2009 for more on the elusive nature of media archives). All archives have their biases and omissions. Yet these preexisting institutional archives provide a sense of something stable, something that looks the same to us today as it did to those who viewed it contemporaneously. There are several useful and impressive resources available to new media historians, but there are few parallels between the traditional archive and the Web archive. How I managed to navigate this transition to the digital archive is the subject of this chapter. My journey involved not just acquiring a new form of digital literacy as I learned to read the Web archive and write my own personal one; it also meant attending to the ways that the production of knowledge is reorganized.

For my project, I wanted to know more about the complexities of interaction design but had no access to the letters, memos, or files of inter-active agencies and design shops that might offer some perspective on the key issues framing the production context. From my own background, I had some sense of the negotiations between designers, art directors, programmers, and clients, but I knew little about the production of a large-scale commercial site or the way advertising agencies and interactive shops managed the creative process. Were there arguments between designers and account managers that rivaled those disputes between film artisans? Were there different arguments between developers and creatives, working at various levels across these organizations? How did these new Web specialists negotiate different understandings of expertise and categories of "quality" professional interface design? How did the criteria for "good site design" change and evolve? How did technological conditions shape textual possibilities? These were just some of my questions, but there were no company inboxes to pore through, no heated correspondence records to reference, no fantastic gems tucked away on donated hard drives.

My questions were informed by my experiences studying the histories of other media; but unlike television, radio, or film, the institutional preservation of new media records (at least the kind I was imagining) was not yet in place.[1] As a result, both my questions and my methods for answering them shifted over the course of the project. The graduate seminars I took on historical methods raised important questions about the nature of truth, the role of power, the claims that could or could not be made from different types of evidence, the particular exclusions and biases that might be identified, and the ideological values that inform research questions and preservation decisions. But all were geared toward the historical study of traditional media, where state, regional, or national institutions managed access to donated, indexed, and cataloged records and personal papers. I needed to balance my critical orientation with new methodological approaches that would, by necessity, demand some improvisation. I wanted to examine a variety of early commercial websites, long gone from the live Web, in order to understand their design, tone, modes of address, functionality, content, and overall organization. But I was also on a quest to track down and analyze as many relevant primary source materials as possible, looking for anything that could help me understand the contours of creative practice and industrial negotiations in this heated moment of dot-com exuberance.

In the fields of library and information sciences, where digital preservation efforts demand constant attention, I first discovered the world of Web archiving—a topic now jointly addressed by librarians, researchers, and preservationists (Brügger 2008, 2009; Brown 2006; Masanès 2006;

Schneider and Foot 2004; Dougherty et al. 2010; Dougherty and Schneider 2011; Meyer, Thomas and Schroeder 2011).[2] This new terrain required familiarizing myself with a particular vocabulary ("snapshots," "time skew," "Web crawlers") and a set of concerns that were very different from the way I was accustomed to thinking about archives and archival research. Yet, because of my background in Web design, I was not entirely without a digital compass. Though my production skills were rusty, I could not shake the sense that feeling my way around this new realm was not unlike the process of building my first Web site back in 1996, a do-it-yourself practice that required figuring out what worked as I went along. What I found was that the character of these artifacts and the methods I employed for understanding them prompted me to rethink my analytical framework. Ultimately, it was my journey through the Web archives—a process that began as a methodological undertaking—that produced an epistemological change in the way I thought about Web historiography.

In this chapter, I discuss the processes and considerations that relate to the work of doing Web history and using sources like the Internet Archive's Wayback Machine. In many ways, Web archives are unlike any other type of archive that has previously existed. Traditionally, items are removed from circulation and placed in archives for preservation; Web archives, however, contain neither objects removed from circulation nor exact duplicates of original sites (Dougherty and Schneider 2011: 257). They are, as Brügger (2008, 2009) notes, artifacts that are created by the archival process. I describe the challenges and limitations of writing Web histories based on this type of archival evidence and reflect on the new modes of temporality that are enacted by this practice. I then detail the process I used to work around these constraints by triangulating sources and building my own personal archive, compiled in order to address my specific research questions. This is a necessity when the materials you hope to analyze are either not available or not publically accessible. Finally, I describe the methods I used for going "behind the scenes" in Web production work by examining the discourses surrounding the multimedia production software Macromedia Flash (now Adobe Flash). Turning to the application itself as a primary source helped illuminate the ways that software functions as an ideological expression of cultural discourse.

As highly dynamic networked forms that are continually rewritten and updated according to the whims of creators, Web sites are notoriously unstable artifacts. Web production software, however, bundles updates in specific release versions and often comes packaged with documentation. This affords a sense of stability, an anchored reference point from which to examine how changes to features, algorithms, interface components, tutorials, and help files speak to the particular values, assumptions, and "best practice guidelines" that accompany Web production in different historical moments.[3] In the process of forging new analytical techniques for historicizing digital visual culture, I looked for ways to bring insights from critical media studies to bear on the slippery, ephemeral world of digital objects created for outdated browsers, reliant on long-lost proprietary components, and designed to run on obsolete operating systems.

The digital realm is messy, dynamic, and unstable. But at the same time, these limits also underscore the importance of thinking through the materiality of digital media, leaving a mark not only on the objects or texts we hope to recover, but also on the types of questions we might ask and the methods we employ for answering them.

The Great Opportunities and Serious Limitations of Web Archives

The largest and most prominent archive of born-digital materials is the Internet Archive (www.archive.org), an initiative founded in 1996 by computer engineer Brewster Kahle to preserve the Internet's digital cultural heritage. Kahle (along with Bruce Gilliat) actually founded another for-profit company at the same time called Alexa Internet, which is responsible for amassing the materials that make up the Internet Archive's collection of archived Web pages. Alexa was initially established to provide a navigation system for the Web that offered an alternative to search engines (see Livingston 2008: 275). The company produces a toolbar that can be installed as a browser extension, providing background information about a site as well as other relevant "links of interest" as users moved around the Internet.[4] To do this, the toolbar tracks users' traffic patterns and usage trails in order to determine which sites are most popular. "Links and clicks [are] essentially votes on the value of a given page," explained Kimpton and Ubois (2006: 204) of the Internet Archive. Alexa's "Web Crawler," an automated computer program that roams publicly accessible Web pages by following hyperlinks and downloading the files it encounters along the way, uses this information about popularity and traffic patterns to direct its Web crawling efforts, prioritizing which sites would be archived first (Kimpton and Ubois 2006).[5] This type of archiving strategy is known as a "snapshot" approach (as opposed to an event-based or selective strategy), where a huge swath of pages are archived at various moments in time (Brügger 2011).[6] Gathering roughly 1.6 tera-bytes of content per day, it takes about two months for the Alexa crawl to complete a snapshot of the Web.[7] Although Alexa's crawler started archiving sites in 1996, the resulting snapshots were not made available to the public until 2001, when programmers at Alexa created the "Way-back Machine" as an interface to the archive (Kimpton and Ubois 2006: 207). This interface allows users to enter a URL and view a series of snap-shots the crawler saved on particular dates.

Although at the time I had no idea how it worked, my early awareness of the Wayback Machine helped me sketch out the boundaries of my dis-sertation. I knew I wanted to write about "old" Web sites that were no longer online, and I figured that the Wayback Machine would serve as my digital time machine, a window through which I could turn back the clock and, as the Wayback Machine promised, "surf the Web as it was." My initial willingness to believe this premise was undoubtedly due to what Wendy Chun characterizes as the persistent "conflation of memory and storage that both underlies and undermines digital media's archival promise" (2008: 148). In other words, there are assumptions built into discourses of the digital that depend on the idea of memory as something stable, lasting, and therefore capable of preserving the past in storage. I marveled at pictures of the "petabox," the Internet Archive's custom-built storage unit capable of processing a million gigabytes of data. I imagined (quite ridiculously, I know) that inside that box, the Web of the past was safely contained. There was a politics to this storage that made the links to memory quite clear: the Internet Archive claims to be "exercising our 'right to remember,'" and was thereby, as Stewart Brand puts it, curing our amnesiac civilization by offering a "complete, detailed, accessible, searchable memory for society."[8] Such powerful testaments!

But I had barely begun my research when I started to notice some dis-parities between the site I saw in the archive and representations of the same site from the same time period that I encountered elsewhere. One particularly puzzling example was the Zima Web site, launched in the fall of 1994 by Coors Brewing Company and developed by the interactive marketing company Modem Media. The first snapshot in the Internet Archive is from October 1996; there are two more from December 1996. Four snapshots were saved in 1997, indicating the site was taken down sometime after July of that year. But no snapshot caught the site's most talked-about features: a serialized narrative about the adventures of Duncan, a tech-savvy Gen-X Zima-drinker, and an online affinity group called "Tribe Z" that provided members with access to some specialized content (see Turow 1997: 120). Web guides published between 1995 and 1997 use the site as an example of how to create community, encourage user contributions, and use sound effectively (short audio clips—"cool aural earwacks"—were offered as free goodies for visiting.) A 1995 *FrontLine* documentary, "High Stakes in Cyberspace" (Krulwich et. al. 1995), shows the host, Robert Krulwich, visiting Modem Media's offices and browsing the site with Modem founder G.M. O'Connell (figure 2.1). The site's navigation scheme features an interactive refrigerator stocked with digital content that doesn't appear in the otherwise seemingly complete archive: there are snapshots on the Wayback Machine with no missing images or other indicators of errors as the site was being crawled (figure 2.2). Nor do the archived images match up with screenshots printed in design guides that were published at the time (figure 2.3). The archived site shows three content sections ("Diversions," "Earwacks," and "Icons") but the other sources show nine different categories,

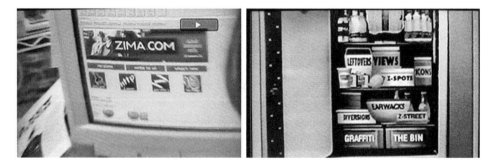

Figure 2.1
Images of the Zima website featured in the Frontline documentary *High Stakes In Cyberspace* (aired 31 Oct. 1995). Source: PBS.

Figure 2.2
Zima website snapshots from Wayback Machine (dated 12 Oct 1996). Source: Internet Archive.

Figure 2.3
Screenshots of Zima website printed in design guide. Source: *Web Publisher's Design Guide for Windows*, 2nd ed. (published 5 Jan. 1997).

including "Leftovers," "Views," "Z-Spots," "Z-Street," "Graffiti," and "The Bin."

Now, it could be that Zima decided sometime in 1996 to recreate their site with over half of the content excluded (it was no secret that the Zima brand was struggling). Other trade accounts, however, continued to reference the contents of this "cool site" through 1997. Perhaps the extra content was only available to registered "Tribe Z" members and could not be accessed by the crawler. Despite significant detective work, I never discovered a reason for these inconsistencies. As I came to understand better, the Wayback Machine is certainly an invaluable source of rich information about the early Web that would otherwise not be available. But in order to be useful, Internet researchers must be familiar with the process of automatic crawling and the way it affects the archived snapshot.

The Internet Archive is undoubtedly the largest and most popular archiving effort to date, but there are also a number of national initiatives devoted to archiving portions of the Web. Depending on the topic area, researchers might find that the Web archive of a particular national library has a more thorough collection of relevant sites.[9] The biggest advantage of the Wayback Machine, however, is the breadth of sites that have been crawled: by 2009, 150 billion pages had been archived, amounting to over three petabytes of data—about 150 times the content of the Library of Congress (Mearian 2009). But this great breadth comes at the price of depth, consistency, and accuracy. Rarely are the entire contents of a site preserved, and the snapshots, more often than not, are incomplete: missing images and broken links are commonplace. As anyone who has used the Wayback Machine has probably realized, one must click through countless snapshots of sites with errors and broken images in order to find a version that looks complete. These incomplete pages fix the chronological overlap between present and past in visual form, the result of a condition Chun refers to as "the nonsimultaneity of the new" (2008: 169). In their attempt to stabilize the past, these pages actually proliferate something new—an "enduring ephemeral" that results from the constant degeneration and regeneration of digital content.

Sometimes deficiencies are caused by technological problems during the process of archiving; sometimes they are the result of temporal inaccuracies that arise if a site changes during the process of archiving (Brügger 2009: 126).[10] Although a Web page may look like a single file with its own URL, it is often made up of numerous references to other files—images, style sheets, scripts, dynamic content, rich media—each with a separate URL. Automatic crawlers roam the Web by requesting HTML files and then following each of the references to other linked URLs. Some of this content, including Common Gateway Interface (CGI) scripts, JavaScripts, and multimedia files, cannot be saved properly by the crawler. According to Gordon Mohr, chief technologist for Web projects at the Internet Archive, when an archived page either fails to display properly or does not represent a complete capture of the initial live site, the problem is usually caused by what he calls "time skew." On the Wayback Machine's team blog, Mohr (2010) explains: "Even on a frequently and deeply collected site, all the different independent resources that make up one 'page' may be collected hours, days, weeks, or months apart. The site could change design or ownership over that time, and so the page you see may be a mosaic of disparate elements. Less-frequently or less-deeply-collected sites, or sites that could not be fully collected due to technical limitations (such as crawler-blocking robots.txt), could be assembling resources together from years apart—the Wayback is always doing a 'nearest' date match, but 'nearest' could be years earlier or later."[11]

Since the method the archive uses to fill in the gaps of incomplete sites involves substituting a file with the same name that has the closest available date to the file a user is viewing, links between pages may connect two files that were never actually connected when the site was live. And, since images are external files embedded with HTML links, the Wayback Machine may display a site that combines navigation images from one date with text and content from another. Since the resulting snapshot might contain a Web page that never actually existed, this affected my research greatly. As an example, Mohr describes the following scenario: "[A] page in [the] year 2000 might have tried to use a background image, but had a robots.txt that prohibited crawlers from reading the 'images/background.jpg' resource, so we have no copies of it and can never render the page perfectly. In 2003, the site changes hands, removes the robots.txt, and—by coincidence or design—starts serving a different image under the same name. Now, it can be archived. Finally, in 2010, trying to view the year 2000 page will find the 2003 image as the nearest-match for the needed background, resulting in a mixed display."

Because the process of archiving is reflected in the artifact, Brügger (2008) suggests that the Web archive may be "a new type of historical document." Captured pages, he points out, may be both "incomplete" and also, paradoxically, "too complete," as when "something that was not on the live Web at the same time, the content of two pages or site sections, is now combined in the archive and it is difficult to determine what the site was actually like at a given point in time" (Brügger 2009: 127). The term "snapshot" is a metaphor borrowed from photography and implies a single captured moment in time. When viewing a photograph, one does not see parts of a picture recorded at different times. The chronology of the digital—moving both forward and backward at once—is often masked by tools that help us mistake the nature of what we see.

Indeed, the work of reading Web archives is both interpretive work and technical work. Although the knowledge required to understand the fine details of Web archiving far exceeded my comfort level, basic "digital archive literacy" was essential for using the Wayback Machine for historical research. Conveniently, the Internet Archive also incorporates user-friendly cues in the URL of archived pages to indicate when a file was captured. I learned always to pay close attention to the browser address bar to identify if a mixed display was produced from time skew. The URLs of archived pages use the following format: http://web.archive.org/web/{yyyymmddhhmmss}/{url}. For example, the page located at http://web.archive.org/web/19961230075410/http://www.levi.com/ is the front page of the Levi's brand site, which was archived on December 30, 1996 at 07:54:10 (UTC world clock standard). Since images displayed within this site might have been captured at different times, I had to check every image's URL to make sure each was also captured on this date.[12] Although I could be reasonably sure after examining these files that the site looked as it did on the date it was captured, I could never be entirely certain, so I regarded these archives as "very close approximations" of the historical Web and always looked for other records of a site's design for confirmation.

The Wayback Machine's limitations underscore the need for additional sources for analyzing commercial Web practices. Most significantly, the exclusion of multimedia files and plug-ins was a huge constraint for my project. The widespread alternation of enthusiasm and disdain for various multimedia "bells and whistles" was a major part of the discourse I was following through industry press and discussion boards. As I waded through trade journals, newspaper articles, conference reports, design magazines, and production manuals, the more obvious it became that by late 1996, when the Internet Archive started capturing Web sites, most of the early commercial sites had already launched second, third, or even fourth-generation versions. Those very first commercial sites, created for companies like Zima, Saturn, MCI, Ragu, Molson, and Levi's, could not be accessed in any Web archive, so I would have to turn to a broad range of additional sources and resign myself to the fact that I would be writing about Web sites I would never be able to view online. Media historians, especially those studying early radio and television, have long faced similar constraints, and I turned to this scholarship as a model for thinking through Web historiography and exploring other entryways into the story (see Ankerson 2011).

Triangulating Sources and Creating a Personal Archive

To supplement recovered snapshots from the Wayback Machine, I relied on a broad assortment of supporting materials and used multiple methods to determine what the Web used to look like, how its visual design was talked about, and how the Web industry was configured and financed to create it. This triangulation revealed some of the complex ways visual design methodologies and assumptions responded to social, ideological, economic, and industrial pressures. Since a public archive of the commercial Web was not available to me, I went about assembling my own (for an excellent account of how personal archives are created for historical media research, see Douglas 2010). I collected archived snapshots, news and trade press articles, and scanned screenshots printed in Web design books, magazines, and production manuals. Through the Internet Archive's moving image collection, I downloaded broadcasts of the annual "Webby awards," an Internet equivalent of the Emmy's that recognizes the "best of the Web."[13] I collected 10 years of television news coverage culled from the Vanderbilt TV news archive and located dot-com prospectuses that were filed with the Securities and Exchange Commission in anticipation of a company's initial public offering.

I found that many trade press accounts in business, advertising, management, and technology journals magnified developments and claims of newness and innovation. Sometimes beta versions or planned updates were talked about as if they were already implemented, only to be scrapped months later when technical problems made it hard for ambitious features to work properly. But these sources were useful for creating a detailed timeline that tracked the pulse of Web advertising, the dizzying mergers, spin-offs, and buyouts that accelerated as the Web industry matured alongside the rising fortunes and dips of the stock market. In several cases, I secured interviews by contacting those who were mentioned repeatedly in press accounts of a site's design and launch. I then used a "snowball sampling" method, where I asked those I interviewed for referrals to others who had worked in Web production during the dot-com boom. It was certainly much easier to get responses when I mentioned one of their former colleague's name in my subject line. But there were other times when I faced nothing but dead ends as my emails were either shot down or ignored. After learning from one article that Levi's corporate archivist was present in meetings discussing the launch of the company's first Web site in the fall of 1995 (a gargantuan effort that pulled together a huge team of companies from across the globe), I inquired about the possibility of accessing the site and talking to her about the company's early vision for the Web. "I'm afraid that background on our Web site concepts and marketing is considered proprietary and cannot be shared with students," I was told flatly. Corporate archives like this one were private collections carefully guarded by company historians.

I had more luck with designers, who often willingly shared files and screenshots if they still had them. It is not unusual for creatives to produce working versions of Web sites that can be browsed on a CD-ROM or hard drive so they can be demonstrated to clients without a network connection. Receiving these copies was like hitting pay dirt. Others shared "demo reels," CD-ROMs created to show off an artist's portfolio.

While receiving this material was extremely helpful, it posed yet another challenge. Often such files would only work on Macintosh OS9, an operating system no longer widely in use. Fortunately, I was eventually able to view the files after installing an emulator on my computer called SheepShaver, an open-source program that permits newer Windows or Mac OSX computers to run classic Mac applications in a separate window. This was handy, as it allowed me to run my favorite screen-recording software, Snapz Pro, over the classic environment in order to create videos of myself navigating these sites, which were then annotated and added to my archive.

I examined hundreds of Web design books and magazines published between 1994 and 2003 (HTML manuals, "best of the Web" collections, developer guides, designers' resources, etc.), which I obsessively ordered from Amazon.com for the bargain price of $.01 plus shipping and handling (i.e., $3.50 each). I received a $1,000 dissertation grant from my department and spent the whole thing at Amazon's used marketplace, buying from smaller retailers that provided detailed information about the book's condition. I was delighted to find that many design books included CD-ROMs with additional materials such as sample files, video clips of interviews with various members of Web design teams, and screenshots of profiled Web sites. And from an online forum for Web designers, I was able to find someone in London who agreed to sell me his complete collection of *Cre@te Online*, a UK publication devoted to Web design trends that was not held by my university library or available through interlibrary loan. (I knew what a tremendous resource this magazine was because I had once subscribed to it, but I made the unfortunate decision to throw away my collection as I packed up to move to graduate school. As a result, to this day, I fear discarding anything.)

I looked for interviews with designers and developers that appeared alongside case studies of prominent commercial initiatives in design journals like *Communication Arts, How, Print,* and *Eye.* Many popular interactive shops and their designers were the subject of feature stories and case studies; many published their own books reflecting on their creative process and illustrating their production practices with examples of code, reprints of storyboards, photographs of studio spaces, and mock-ups of designs in development.[14]

As my archive grew, it became clear that two closely related problems continually plagued my research process. First, in my frenzy to recover the Web of the past, I almost forgot that the live Web was changing. Files were being deleted, moved, and amended every day. Bookmarks I saved during my preliminary research turned up Error 404 "Page Not Found" messages just when I tried to revisit them, and I kicked myself for not remembering to store my own copies locally. The irony of losing my own material about the lost material of the Web was almost too much to bear. After losing pages from a Web design discussion board that I remembered for the self-reflective attitudes and heated arguments among participants about changing design sensibilities, I became adamant about using Zotero, the open-source Firefox add-on that helps researchers collect and organize materials. Most importantly for my work, Zotero made it easy to save snapshots (a different type of snapshot than those created by crawlers) of sites, and I vowed never again to lose a discussion thread or online article that might one day be useful.

At the same time, I found that not only would sites disappear, they would sometimes reappear, even if only briefly. This was the case, for example, when Adobe (the software company that acquired Macromedia and its suite of authoring applications in 2005) launched a 10-year retrospective of Flash in 2006, which included a coordinated relaunch of several prominent Flash sites produced between 1997 and 2006.[15] I was pleased that I had used my screen-recording software to create videos of these sites when I did because by the time I started work on my dissertation a year later, many were already gone. Then, just as I was in the final stretch of finishing the dissertation, the fifteen-year anniversary of the first Web banner ad, followed by the ten-year anniversary of the historic NASDAQ plunge that signaled the end of the dot-com bubble, prompted a brief flurry of resurrected images, retrospectives, and personal accounts that I scrambled to include in my analysis. Such instances further reinforce Chun's (2008) notion of the enduring ephemeral as the nonsimultaneity of the new: old things were continually relaunched as new, while new things were already old as soon as they were uploaded.

Dealing with this constant regeneration and degeneration of images on the live Web obviously points to the second problem: knowing when to stop archiving. Since I anticipated turning the dissertation into a monograph, it was very difficult to draw the line—the project would be ongoing until the book was finished. But eventually (aside from the rash of new reflections that accompanied those anniversary moments), I hit a point of "informational redundancy" where I was no longer learning new things from the additional sources that I found (Lincoln and Guba 1985).

At that point, I turned to the project-management software program Scrivener to organize my archive and help me draw connections across multiple sources. Scrivener was designed to help fiction writers keep track of complicated long-form narratives, but I found the index card corkboard scheme useful for mapping the evolution of Internet companies alongside the peaks and valleys of the NASDAQ composite and the changing design paradigms that informed production practices. It helped me visualize a web of connections that were becoming unwieldy. Because the software also allows you to point to images and video files (while storing all files outside the program itself), I used it as a hub for managing and analyzing the files I kept in my archive.

Software as Source: Going Behind the Digital Production Scenes

As I lamented in the introduction, Web researchers do not have access to the same kinds of memos and correspondence files often found in traditional archives. But there was no shortage of discussion, both online and in the countless design books I perused, about the "right" and "wrong" ways to design the Web. As I followed these debates to the climactic finale—the bursting of the Internet bubble in the spring of 2000—and through the immediate years following the crash, I was struck by the discursive alignment of Flash Web sites with "irrational exuberance." Against the rising tide of "usability," which emerged as the new dominant discourse of Web practice after the bust, Flash sites were being talked about as the visual manifestation of dot-com excess, full of self-indulgence, gratuitous animation, and grossly overvalued hype. At the same time, many Flash designers fiercely defended the technology as a means for new forms of creative expression and experimentation. As critiques of Flash Web design escalated, Macromedia launched an ambitious post-crash "usability campaign" to teach designers how to use Flash "responsibly" by publishing tips and whitepapers online and hosting competitions like the "Design a Site for Usability" contest.

But for all of the noisy debates about these divisive sites, Web archives are largely silent when it comes to Flash. Because automatic crawlers are designed to read HTML and follow hyperlinks, they have a hard time handling proprietary multimedia formats, like Flash files. Viewing snapshots of commercial sites through the Wayback Machine between 2000 and 2003 reveals a patchwork of blank squares where Flash had at one time appeared. Sites designed entirely in Flash (and many were in those days) do not show up at all. The images of the Barney's New York site (figure 2.4) demonstrate this well.

Relaunched as part of Adobe's 10-year Flash retrospective, the Barney's site was notorious for invoking passionate feelings among those enamored and alarmed by its aesthetic sensibility. But trying to access this highly visual site through the Wayback Machine reveals only the launch page listing the technical requirements for viewing the site ("Macromedia Flash 4+, Internet Explorer 4+/Netscape 4.5+/AOL 5.0, 800x600 resolution for screen display"). Upon clicking "enter," we see only a solid gray

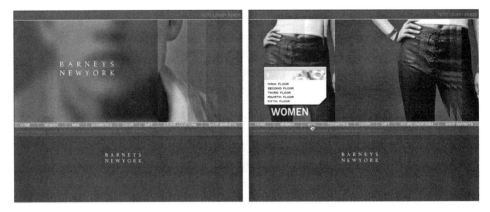

Figure 2.4
Screenshots from the Barney's New York Flash website (launched May 2000).

Figure 2.5
Barney's New York Web page as viewed through the Wayback Machine.

box with no content and no error messages (figure 2.5). Essentially, the Wayback Machine suggests only that a Flash site once existed, but it does not give any indication to the site's content, visual style, or purpose. It is as if the site has quite literally been wiped from the record (for a larger discussion of these implications, see Ankerson 2011).

Most Flash content created between 1996 and 2003 was long gone by the time my research was underway in 2007, and I felt discouraged by this digital black hole. Such is the fate of proprietary technologies, one might argue. But at the same time, Flash calls attention to some of the most contentious debates about commercialism, creativity, and the Web, and was therefore an important part of the story I was trying to tell. Focusing solely on the technological form as the reason why Flash sites are not archived obscures the value systems that play a significant role in determining what is worth saving. Undoubtedly, if the preservation of Flash were deemed a high cultural priority, systems would have been built to archive these sites. Since Macromedia publicly released the .swf file format in 1998 (in a move to let third-party developers create tools that could export Flash movie files), the code for reading Flash has been publicly available.[16] In this regard, the erasure of Flash in the Web archive is not simply due to a proprietary format, but also to the purposes and values that guided the development of crawler software. Most of the Flash content that existed on the live Web during my period of study will likely never be found, so I looked for other entryways that might help me capture the zeitgeist of ambitions, hopes, fears, and anxieties that Flash provoked.

I came to realize that understanding software and its various affordances offers a digital equivalent of the behind-the-scenes negotiations that I first longed to find. Through my experiences navigating the intricacies of automatic crawlers, searching for emulators, adding browser extensions, and selecting applications to help manage my archive and make sense of my data, I could not help but notice the ways my entire engagement with this project was thoroughly organized through software. I had initially modeled much of my thinking alongside critical media studies approaches to film and broadcast history, which was particularly engaged with exploring the connections between cultural industries, textual production, and sociohistorical context. But as I investigated the rise of Web industries and the evolution of Web design alongside the heightened economic context of dot-com speculation, I realized I had been approaching my archive of Web sites as the actual "texts" that were produced. Yet, in very important ways, the materiality of software (Web authoring software, browser software, extensions, server software, etc.) infused those digital objects with certain conditions of possibility that should not be ignored (Fuller 2008). As I knew from my experience making Web sites, however long ago, more than one window was used to view the Web: tweak code, check in browser, tweak code more, refresh.

To get behind the scenes of the Flash debate, I turned to the software application itself as an archive of the discourse circulating around design. After all, software often comes with its own version of personal memos and correspondence records that can be mined for internal conflict and ideological assumptions: the tutorials, support and help files, interface metaphors, icons, dialogue boxes, and marketing materials all present to the user as a "preferred reading" that guides the "appropriate" interpretation and use of technology (Woolgar 1996; Gillespie 2003, 111). As Gillespie (2003) points out in his analysis of the interface metaphors and the "guided tours" within the Macromedia Dreamweaver Web authoring program, digital tools "tell stories" with explicit suggestions to users about what kinds of Web sites the software is designed to produce and what the Web is for (113).

I found that as Flash evolved from its roots as a graphical package for pen computing systems in the early 1990s to a platform for building rich media applications like Flickr, YouTube, and Hulu in the Web 2.0 era, the logic of the production environment embodied ideological meanings about the social life of the Web—how it should be properly imagined, who it should be for, and how it should be appropriately used. By tracing the industrial context and programming logic in which the software was first produced, through its subsequent redesigns and development as a platform for applications and content delivery after the dot-com collapse, I was able to gain some insight into how the tool, its packaging, and its accompanying messages (like the usability campaign) responded to social, industrial, and economic developments while framing particular uses and interpretations as natural or "intuitive." Taken on its own, the trajectory of a single commercial software product like Flash might point to little more than an evolutionary march toward greater technological sophistication or a product's inevitable response to market forces. But read alongside the other evidence I had collected in my archive, I found that attention to the materiality of software and the discourses that surround and construct it can help us historicize the large and small shifts that make up the character of social life in a digital networked culture.

Conclusion

Cultural histories of new media objects and labor can help illuminate the ways digital artifacts (Web sites, software, databases, algorithms, templates, platforms, virtual worlds, etc.) are deeply embedded in their socioeconomic contexts and reveal the often-contested circumstances in which they were imagined (cf. Leonardi, this volume). This can also throw a productive lens on the present, helping us see contemporary networked digital culture not as the obvious outcome of technological progress, social media initiatives, or usability research, but as a moment similarly defined by ongoing struggles to harness the way the Web works, looks, feels, and is talked about.

The logic of software penetrates the Web at all levels, as I repeatedly realized through my first attempts to access its past and somehow see the Web perfectly, uncorrupted by the artifacts of archiving or the creeping obsolescence of its technological forms. When I began this project, I imagined I would use the Wayback Machine to access a stable historical Web, uncovering snapshots buried like time capsules that held the remnants of a lost civilization carefully preserved. I should have known better. The archive will never be a perfect representation of the Web. These assumptions depend on the notion that storage equals memory, but they are also founded on the notion that a "perfect" representation could exist. (What exactly did the Zima Web site look like in the fall of 1996?) The Web confounds this very idea that a single representation is the ultimate form. Zima.com likely looked different to users depending on whether they were members of Tribe Z or not. The site surely looked and felt different based on browser rendering, network connection speed, monitor resolution, and computer operating system. But at the same time, my experience in Web design during the 1990s suggested there *was* a perfect representation: the mock-up that a client signed off on in the planning stages. The technical work of Web design was trying to get the mock-up, often created in Photoshop, to render the same across non–standards-compliant browsers running on computers with varying technical configurations. It could never truly look the same, but we sure worked hard to make it so. To read the Web archive, then, is to engage with both technology and the production context in order to understand how this shapes and structures the way the Web is constructed, consumed, and conceived.

Whether piecing together the obvious gaps left by an incomplete crawl or finding a snapshot that looks untouched by a Web crawler, a general awareness of how the archive works is essential for getting the most out of the sites you hope to analyze. Rather than see these limitations as imperfections, I have found them to be productive reminders of the Web's material form. Facing these absences and instabilities, I turned to a host of surrounding materials that, despite their partiality, helped me write my own archive in order to weave my narrative together. Dougherty and Schneider (2011) refer to archives like mine as "idiosyncratic archives" that embed the questions and motivations of the researcher in the archive itself. The potential is that these archives may someday become available for future researchers and historians to further annotate, remix, or filter in the creation of new iterations of old Web content. Yet, as Lessig (2008) notes, copyright battles designed to protect earlier media continue to plague "read/write culture" in the digital age. These conventions limit and constrain the potential of historical Web archives—not only in terms of the remixed content that will be available for future historians but also in the possibilities for sharing these accrued personal archives. As I was handed valuable Web materials for a number of historical sites, I was reminded by several sources that the copyright circumstances were either unknown or beyond their control. I could look at these files for my own research, but few felt they had the authority to grant official rights to share these publicly, even in cases when the original production studio folded or merged.

I may not have worn white gloves, submitted call sheets, or surrendered my pens before digging through the technical manuals, CD-ROM extras, advertising annuals, interview transcripts, conference reports, public access programs, mailing list archives, "cool site of the day" descriptions, software installers, and so on—but I came to realize that there were a lot of potential entryways to help me understand the shifting meanings and dominant discourses surrounding Web production at the height of the bubble and in the immediate years after its collapse. The next big question to address is how these personal archives might be shared with others in order to further the historical Web research agenda.

Notes

1. I later became aware of The Dot-Com Archive (http://www.dotcomarchive.org), an initiative first launched in 2002 by David Kirsch to collect the business plans and other related entrepreneurial records from dot-com firms that were founded in the mid-90s to commercialize the Internet.

2. The International Web Archiving Workshop series was first organized in 2001 to provide a forum for Web archiving research among librarians, archivists, and

researchers. A number of national libraries formed the International Internet Preservation Consortium in 2003 to facilitate international collaboration for the preservation of Internet content.

3. By suggesting that software products offer a sense of stability that often eludes Web content, I do not mean to suggest that software escapes preservation concerns or exhibits a degree of permanence. Like all digital objects, it depends on the configuration of other software, hardware, and storage media that becomes obsolete with time. However, software releases are more self-contained, and they provide additional contextual evidence and are often easier to date.

4. The Alexa toolbar was one of the first examples of "collaborative filtering," a system for making automatic predictions about users' interests by collecting the preferences from a large number of users. This is the basis of recommendation software that predicts what other content a user might like by matching their taste preferences with data from users who have made similar choices. In 1998 the toolbar came preinstalled on Netscape and Internet Explorer browsers, and in 1999, Amazon.com bought Alexa Internet to take advantage of its data-mining technology. In 2002, Kahle left the company to devote his time to the Internet Archive (Kimpton and Ubois 2006).

5. Crawler data were then used to provide toolbar users with information about the sites they visited (page ranking, connection speed, registrant, number of pages included, how many sites link to it, how frequently it is updated, etc.).

6. An event-based archiving strategy seeks to collect sites related to a particular event (Hurricane Katrina, 9/11 attacks, national elections, etc.) The crawler starts with a number of relevant "seed" URLs and follows links from there. Selective strategies are created when a limited number of sites are hand-selected for archiving based on their perceived significance (Brügger 2011: 31).

7. Alexa Internet, "How and Why We Crawl the Web." Retrieved 11 May 2015. http://web.archive.org/web/20111212173729/http://www.alexa.com/company/technology

8. "About the Internet Archive." Retrieved 11 May 2015. https://web.archive.org/web/20110520214001/http://www.archive.org/about/about.php

9. Australia's Pandora archive, Sweden's Kulturarw3, and Denmark's Netarchive. dk, for example, use snapshot approaches that define boundaries along national domains as well as selective methods that use traditional appraisal techniques to identify a smaller number of "significant" sites that meet particular institutional missions or goals (see Brügger 2011 for an overview). The U.S. Library of Congress's MINERVA archive focuses on collecting sites around a particular event or theme (e.g., the Iraq War, the Papal transition).

10. Because Web crawlers risk overloading servers by continually requesting files, they are designed to adhere to certain "politeness policies" by pausing between page requests and downloading files over a period of time.

11. This explanation was posted by Mohr on the Wayback Machine and Web Archiving Open Thread, September 2010. Web Archiving at Archive.org blog. Retrieved 11 May 2015. https://iawebarchiving.wordpress.com/2010/09/07/wayback-machine-Web-archiving-open-thread-september-2010/#comment-641.

12. The easiest way to do this is to right-click on each image and open it in a new browser, where the dates can be compared in the address bar.

13. The NetCafe collection at the Internet Archive has broadcasts of the Webby awards from the years 1997, 1999, and 2000. See: https://archive.org/details/2000Webb00.

14. For example, see Roger Black, *Web Sites That Work* (San Jose, CA: Adobe Press, 1997); Andrew Sather and Adjacency, *Creating Killer Interactive Web Sites: The Art of Integrating Interactivity and Design* (Indianapolis, IN: Hayden Books, 1997); Hillman Curtis, *Flash Web Design: The Art of Motion Graphics* (Indianapolis, IN: New Riders, 2000); Todd Purgason, *Flash Deconstruction: The Process, Design, and Actionscript of Juxt Interactive* (Indianapolis, IN: New Riders, 2002); Mighty Assembly, *Macromedia Flash: Art, Design + Function* (Berkeley, CA: Osborne/McGraw-Hill, 2002).

15. Although many have since disappeared again, the Flash 10-year retrospective can be found at: http://www.thefwa.com/flash10.

16. In fact, the release of the SWF format to third-party developers spawned a number of "Flash decompilers," code-viewer software that let users see the formerly invisible ActionScript code and timeline of a Flash movie. These tools sparked a huge outcry in 2000 and 2001 among Flash designers, who saw these tools as "illegal" ways to crack (and potentially copy) the recipe of protected creative works.

References

Anderson, C. 1994. *Hollywood TV: The Studio System in the Fifties*. Austin, TX: University of Texas Press.

Ankerson, M. S. 2012. Writing Web histories with an eye on the analog past. *New Media & Society 14* (3): 384–400. doi:.10.1177/1461444811414834

Aspray, W., and Ceruzzi. P., eds. 2008. The Internet and American Business. Cambridge, MA: MIT Press.

Boddy, W. 1993. *Fifties Television: The Industry and Its Critics*. Urbana, IL: University of Illinois Press.

Brown, A. 2006. *Archiving Websites: A Practical Guide for Information Management Professionals*. London: Facet Publishing.

Brügger, N. 2008. The archived website and website philology: A new type of historical document? *Nordicom Review 28* (2): 155–175.

Brügger, N. 2009. Website history and the website as an object of study. *New Media & Society 11* (1–2): 115–132.

Brügger, N., ed. 2010. *Web History*. New York: Peter Lang.

Brügger, N. 2011. Web archiving—between past, present, and future. In *The Handbook of Internet Studies*, ed. R. Burnett, M. Consalvo, and C. Ess, 24–42. Malden, MA: Wiley.

Campbell-Kelly, M. 2003. *From Airline Reservations to Sonic the Hedgehog: A History of the Software Industry*. Cambridge, MA: MIT Press.

Cassidy, J. 2003. *Dot.Con: How America Lost Its Mind and Money in the Internet Era*. New York: Perennial.

Ceruzzi, P. 1998. *A History of Modern Computing*. Cambridge, MA: MIT Press.

Chun, W. H. K. 2008. The enduring ephemeral, or the future is a memory. *Critical Inquiry 35* (1): 148–171.

Dougherty, M., E. T. Meyer, C. Madsen, C. van den Heuvel, A. Thomas, and S. Wyatt. 2010. Researcher engagement with Web archives: State of the art. London: Joint Information Systems Committee. http://ssrn.com/abstract=1714997

Dougherty, M., and S. Schneider. 2011. Web historiography and the emergence of new archival forms. In *The Long History of New Media: Technology, Historiography, and Contextualizing*, ed. D. Park, N. Jankowski, and S. Jones, 253–266. New York: Peter Lang.

Douglas, S. 1987. *Inventing American Broadcasting, 1899–1922*. Baltimore: Johns Hopkins University Press.

Douglas, S. 1999. Listening. In *Radio and the American Imagination*. New York: Times Books.

Douglas, S. 2010. Writing from the archive: Creating your own. *Communication Review 13*: 5–14.

Fuller, M. 2008. Introduction. In *Software Studies: A Lexicon*, ed. M. Fuller, 1–14. Cambridge: MIT Press.

Gallo, J. 2009. Doing archival research: How to find a needle in a haystack. In *Research Confidential: Solutions to Problems Most Social Scientists Pretend They Never Have*, ed. E. Hargittai, 262–285. Ann Arbor: University of Michigan Press.

Gillespie, T. 2003. The stories digital tools tell. In *New Media: Theories and Practices of Digitextuality*, ed. J. Caldwell and A. Everett, 107–126. New York: Routledge.

Hilmes, M. 1997. *Radio Voices: American Broadcasting, 1922–1952*. Minneapolis, MN: University of Minnesota Press.

Kelly, K. 1998. *New Rules for the New Economy: 10 Radical Strategies for a Connected World*. New York: Viking.

Kimpton, M., and J. Ubois. 2006. Year-by-year: From an archive of the Internet to an archive on the Internet. In *Web Archiving*, ed. J. Masanès, 201–212. New York: Springer.

Krulwich, R., Koughan, F., Koughan, M., Marshall, R. 1995. October 31. High stakes in cyberspace [television broadcast]. *Frontline*. WGBH Educational Foundation. Alexandria, VA: PBS Video.

Lessig, L. 2008. *Remix: Making Art and Commerce Thrive in the Hybrid Economy*. New York: Penguin Press.

Lincoln, Y. S., and E. G. Guba. 1985. *Naturalistic Inquiry*. Beverly Hills, CA: Sage.

Livingston, J. 2008. *Founders at Work: Stories of Startups' Early Days*. Berkeley, CA: Apress.

Masanès, A., ed. 2006. *Web Archiving*. Berlin: Springer.

Mearian, L. 2009. March. Internet Archive to unveil massive Wayback Machine data center. Computerworld. http://www.computerworld.com/s/article/9130081/ Internet_Archive_to_unveil_massive_Wayback_Machine_data_center. Retrieved 11 May 2015.

Meyer, E. T., A. Thomas, and R. Schroeder. 2011. Web archives: The future(s). Oxford Internet Institute, University of Oxford. http://ssrn.com/abstract=1830025.

Mohr, G. 2010. Wayback Machine and web archiving open thread. https:// iawebarchiving.wordpress.com/2010/09/07/wayback-machine-Web-archiving-open-thread-september-2010. Retrieved 11 May 2015.

Montfort, N., and I. Bogost. 2009. *Racing the Beam: The Atari Video Computer System*. Cambridge, MA: MIT Press.

Park, D., N. Jankowski, and S. Jones, eds. 2011. *The Long History of New Media: Technology, Historiography, and Contextualizing Newness*. New York: Peter Lang.

Schatz, T. 1988. *Genius of the System*. New York: Pantheon Books.

Schneider, S., and K. Foot. 2004. The Web as an object of study. *New Media & Society* 6 (1): 114–122.

Shiller, R. J. 2000. *Irrational Exuberance*. Princeton, NJ: Princeton University Press.

Turow, J. 1997. *Breaking Up America: Advertisers and the New Media World*. Chicago: University of Chicago Press.

Wilson, P. 2009. Capturing media history through archives. In *Convergence Media History*, ed. J. Staiger and S. Hake, 182–191. New York: Routledge.

Woolgar, S. 1996. Technologies as cultural artefacts. In *Information and Communication Technologies*, ed. W. H. Dutton, 87–102. Oxford: Oxford University Press

3

Flash Mobs and the Social Life of Public Spaces: Analyzing Online Visual Data to Study New Forms of Sociability

Virág Molnár and Aron Hsiao

In 2007, while being on a year-long research leave in Hungary, I[1] accidentally listened to a radio report about a new urban activity, the so-called flash mob, which was apparently spreading like wildfire in cities across the world. Examples of flash mobs discussed in the report included a bunch of youth gathering in a downtown historical square in Budapest, suddenly opening their umbrellas in the sweltering August heat when the bells of the nearby evangelical church began to toll, and disappearing instantly the moment the bells stopped. In another instance, a crowd spontaneously assembled in a flash in a busy square and started blowing bubbles, then abruptly stopped after 10 minutes, and participants dispersed quickly as if they had never been there in the first place. The Oxford English Dictionary codified the definition of flash mobs in 2004 as "a public gathering of complete strangers, organized via the Internet or mobile phone, who perform a pointless act and then disperse again." The "pointless acts" can indeed encompass a bewildering range, from pillow fights, zombie walks, freezing in place to synchronized swimming in a public fountain. Despite the seemingly odd and frivolous character of these gatherings, as an urban sociologist, I became instinctively interested in the phenomenon because to me it potentially indicated the emergence of a new form of urban sociability. Such new forms of sociability usually reflect and thus provide insight into more profound changes in the structure of everyday urban life. However, what I failed to realize at the time was that my budding interest in flash mobs did not simply steer me toward a new research project but also marked the beginning of my transformation into an "Internet researcher."

As I began to trace the evolution of the flash mob, it became increasingly evident that its novelty, appeal, and effectiveness stemmed in large part from the ways in which participants embraced new digital media for organizing as well as documenting the events. I moved to New York City the same year, which further piqued my interest in flash mobs for several reasons. First, I learned that flash mobs originated from New York City. They were apparently introduced by Bill Wasik, an editor at *Harper's Magazine*, who organized the first flash mob in a Macy's department store in Herald Square in 2003 to test viral culture while mocking the "scenesterism"[2] of New Yorkers (Heaney 2005; Wasik 2006, 2009). Second, I realized that the physical intensity of the urban experience in New York is only paralleled by the vigor and intensity with which New Yorkers cling to their mobile digital devices. The first time I bumped into a person on the crowded sidewalk who was busily texting while walking at a breakneck pace, I finally understood what media researchers meant by the term "ubiquitous media." Flash mobs appeared increasingly interesting sociologically because they also forcefully demonstrated that the virtual and the physical were not parallel realms, but continuously intersecting social realities (McCullogh 2007).

By this time, there was a sprawling offline and online media discourse about whether flash mobs were simply pointless pranks, creative public performances, or impromptu mass experiments in community building. Yet academic scholarship had continued to shy away from scrutinizing what it perceived to be the latest manifestation of the self-indulgence of contemporary urban youth culture. Scholars have, of course, investigated the impact of new digital communication technologies (mobile phones, social networking sites, blogs, etc.) on social mobilization processes. But they have focused on "*smart* mobs" (Rheingold 2000, 2003), in which participants were pursuing weighty political causes while digital technology seemed merely to enhance the effectiveness of traditional protest. They also concentrated on examples where the Internet facilitated the diffusion and adoption of traditional political tactics (e.g., petitions, boycotts) for nonpolitical purposes, like the case of "fan activism" (Earl and Kimport 2009). Flash mobs seem to have remained below the radar of academic researchers because the objectives of the gatherings were simply not deemed "serious" enough from a sociological perspective.

By contrast, I—always the enthusiast for topics ignored by the rest of the profession—felt that flash mobs offered an important gateway into understanding how digital media intersects and interacts with physical space, how it changes the experience of everyday urban life, and how it challenges established norms of using urban public and semi-public (mostly commercial) spaces. Over the span of three years, I compiled an extensive database about flash mobs that have taken place globally since 2003, relying on the Internet as my main source of empirical data. I have used these data to argue that the chief social meaning of the flash mob lies in its being a new form of sociability: a form of social interaction that embodies the play form of social association first described by Georg Simmel (1949). In other words, I contend that flash mobs illustrate the inverse of fan activism. In fan activism, political protest tactics are increasingly utilized for nonpolitical causes, partly because the Internet made them easily accessible and applicable to all. In contrast, I argue that flash mobs exemplify an organizational tactic that originally arises as a pure form of sociability, diffuses rapidly, and soars in popularity, which inspires its adoption for political and commercial purposes (Molnár 2014).

My primary objective in this chapter, however, is to share with readers my experience of collecting and analyzing the online data that constitute the empirical component of this research project. As I mentioned, I stumbled on this topic as an urban sociologist, and I had little experience working with online data sources when I began this project. I jumped into Internet research with all the naïveté and enthusiasm of a novice. I was soon to face very real obstacles to systematic, reliable data collection. I found a data universe that is in constant transformation, where the rate of transformation is much higher than what academic research can normally keep up with in a timely fashion. In the remainder of the chapter, I will distill the most important lessons of this exciting but challenging intellectual journey organized around the following themes: First, I will highlight the general aspects of my research on flash mobs that should be of interest to everybody who embarks on collecting empirical data from online sources, not only to those who are captivated by flash mobs. Second, I will outline the construction of the original research design and the data collection process. Third, for the sake of this chapter, I actually decided to engage in a "methodological revisit" analogous to how ethnographers sometimes conduct an "ethnographic revisit" (Burawoy 2003) when they return to the original site of their research a few (or many) years later for a follow-up. I will use this "methodological revisit" to assess whether in retrospect, three years after I originally collected the data, I could have devised better ways to conduct this exploratory research.

How Does Research on Flash Mobs Contribute to Understanding Online Data?

The Internet offers an unprecedentedly vast and rich data source that still remains relatively underexplored by social scientists. This is mainly so because in most cases it is impossible to determine the size of the population of interest in a statistical sense, generate a population list for relevant websites, and sample website content randomly (Earl 2006; Earl and Kimport 2009; Hargittai, Gallo, and Kane 2008). This fundamental shortcoming undermines the representativeness and generalizability of research findings as well as the reliability of the data collection process. In other words, any research that is interested in analyzing the substantive content of online sources is by definition likely to violate the chief criteria used to judge the validity of most (especially quantitative) social science research.

The only exception to this rule is research that approaches the study of the Internet from the point of view of users. Users can be sampled using traditional probability sampling techniques and their online activities studied much the same way in which offline activities would be probed (Ellison, Steinfeld, and Lampe 2007; Hampton, Livio and Goulet 2010; Hargittai 2010). But a lot of times we are interested in not simply *who* is online but *what* is online: what topics are discussed on political blogs, food blogs, design blogs; what avatars do in Second Life; what argot has been invented by hackers, and so on. In these cases, random sampling based on user characteristics (age, gender, ethnicity, educational attainment, socioeconomic status, etc.) does not get one closer to understanding the questions at hand, and one needs to find a way to sample the content of available online information. Because of the challenges mentioned above, the overwhelming majority of content-based research has followed nonprobability sampling techniques that greatly constrain the reliability and generalizability of findings (e.g., Bardzell and Odom 2008; McCaughey and Ayers 2003; Holt 2009).[3]

Flash mobs are a new and elusive social phenomenon, and as such they present an example in which research is motivated primarily by the desire to understand *what* exactly they are about, what is their social significance, and what variations one could find in the range of activities that are denoted as flash mobs. These research objectives entailed that I somehow had to find a way to generate a sample of events (as opposed to users).[4] Therefore, my research design offers a variation on how one can conduct systematic empirical research about online content when probability sampling is not a feasible option for case selection.

Another general and novel aspect of online research highlighted by flash mobs is that the data to be analyzed turned out to be in large part visual. This has introduced a new layer of complexity in addition to the usual challenges of content-based online research that typically operates with textual data. At present, search engines are less reliable in identifying visual information than textual information. Moreover, although significant improvements have been made in locating still images on the Web, indexing video content remains a significant challenge (Hubbard 2011). Many search engines continue to rely on the textual information provided in the tags and captions of videos, which can at times be misleading or intentionally manipulated to yield higher page rankings in a search. Considering the exponential increase of visual data on the Internet due to the proliferation of Web 2.0 applications, including video-sharing and photo-sharing sites, there is a growing need to find ways to analyze this type of data as well.[5] My study on flash mobs offers an interesting preliminary reflection on the limits and possibilities of incorporating visual online data into sociological analysis.

Similarly, research on flash mobs reveals yet another difficulty when it comes to working with online data: namely, using the Internet to compile a longitudinal data set. The overwhelming majority of research that examines online content is either cross-sectional or covers a relatively short time frame, generally ranging from a few months to a year (Bardzell and Odom 2008; Earl and Kimport 2009; Hargittai, Gallo, and Gane 2008; Holt 2009). In contrast, my analysis traces the evolution and global diffusion of flash mobs over a six-year period, from 2003 (the year that marked the "invention" of the flash mob) to 2009. The selection of a longer time frame was dictated by the general research objectives, but turned out to be the most challenging aspect of the data collection process. The Internet is an immense depository of information but is not organized as a historical archive. All the search engines are focused on the present, on delivering real-time information, and search results are skewed by the assumption that more recent information is more relevant to the person who is conducting the search. The effectiveness and reliability of searches can thus dramatically decline when one is trying to find cases of actual past events on the Internet. By this I do not mean searching for historical information, but searching retrospectively for real-time reporting on events as they took place in the past. It is in fact often difficult to even introduce custom time-range filters in certain search contexts.

Fortunately, two distinctive cultural aspects of flash mobs facilitated the design of this study, which is more global in scope than most existing research on online content. First, and most notably, the original English term "flash mob" diffused globally without—as of the time of the study—having been translated into local languages, which made it possible to locate international cases together with cases from English-speaking countries in the same searches. Second, the centrality of the visual component of online data on flash mobs, which I will elaborate on in the next section, required less reliance on linguistic interpretation. Often by watching the videos that documented flash mobs, coders could collect sufficient information about the event, even when it was a foreign event labeled in a language that coders did not speak. Hitherto, the analysis of online content has been chiefly confined to English-language sites simply because of the continuing dominance of English as the lingua franca of the Internet, on the one hand, and because most researchers studying Internet use are based in English-speaking countries, on the other. Flash mobs help us expand our theoretical reach and understand better the process of global diffusion of ideas and forms of social interaction that was enabled by the Internet in the first place.

In Search of Flash Mobs: Designing Exploratory Online Research

Defining key dimensions of interest and locating data sources

Researching online content almost by definition requires one to engage in an analytical process that is closely akin to the construction of grounded theory (Glaser and Strauss 1967; Strauss and Corbin 1990; Corbin and Strauss 1990). Namely, data collection, analysis, and theory construction cannot be neatly divided into sequential phases as in traditional quantitative research; rather, they become interrelated processes. This was emphatically true in the case of flash mobs, which seemed to embody a new form of social interaction, creatively combining online and offline features, and, as such, there was no well-established body of scholarship from which testable hypotheses could be derived to guide the research. In fact, I still know of no systematic empirical study that has analyzed either a large number of flash mob events or offered an ethnographic account of flash mobs. Most commentary on flash mobs has been based on anecdotal evidence derived from a few random cases and has taken place outside of the domain of academic discourse.

The research design, therefore, followed an inductive and exploratory strategy, asking broad questions about the types of practices that were described by the term and other possible clues about the social meaning of this new activity, and began with the collection of empirical data. The main aim of the data collection was to assemble a large number of cases of actual flash mobs that had taken place since the inception of flash mobs in 2003. To understand the interaction between digital media and urban space, between the offline and online facets of the activity, I defined the following dimensions of flash mobs as most relevant, and subsequently set out to collect detailed information on these aspects of specific flash mob events:

1. Precise physical location of the flash mob, including country, city, and location within the city. When the exact location within the city could not be determined, the type of space was recorded: whether the flash mob took place in a public space, commercial space, on a university campus, or some private space.

2. Type of activity (freezing in place, zombie walk, bubble blowing, pillow fight, etc.).

3. Approximate number of participants.

4. Whether the flash mob was part of a simultaneous flash mob event taking place in other cities as well.

5. Organizer(s) of the flash mob.

6. Existence of any visual documentation of the flash mob event (mostly in the form of a video clip).[6]

7. Links to any other sites that included a description or commentary on the specific event.

First, with the help of a research assistant (the second author of this chapter), I started doing simple Google searches for "flash mobs," hoping the results would contain Web sites describing actual events. However, it soon turned out that Google Web searches were not very helpful in this regard, because the hits included all sorts of information on flash mobs, ranging from blog discussions on the novelty of the form, digital copies of newspaper reports, commentary on this new phenomenon, and clearing-house sites that organized and popularized flash mobs to documents of actual events. From this jumble of flash-mob-related discourse it would have been extremely difficult and arduous to select only the pages that contained depictions of specific cases.

But during these preliminary searches, we noted that the official Oxford English Dictionary definition of flash mobs I cited in the intro-duction overlooked an important aspect of flash mobbing. It seemed that it was basically obligatory for participants to document visually—that is, to film—the flash mob and upload a video of it to a video-sharing site, primarily YouTube. In other words, flash mobs might end in physical space with the dispersal of participants, but they have an important after-life in cyberspace in the form of video recordings. This was a very impor-tant discovery that directed us to YouTube, where searches for flash mobs indeed returned videos of actual cases of flash mobs.

Sampling cases

YouTube thus offered us a large pool of flash mob cases, but it still did not get us closer to being able to determine the size of the entire popula-tion of flash mob events. The total number of results that appear for YouTube searches is itself an estimate, not an actual case count, and it can include several videos of the same event as well as false cases that are not really videos of flash mobs but simply use the term in their description or their tags. Therefore, even with restricting our searches to a single video-sharing site, we were still unable to create a population list of flash mobs and hence draw a random sample of cases for the analysis.

Instead, with my research assistant and co-author Aron Hsiao, I decided to search YouTube for flash mobs and sort the results by "rele-vance." The precise definition of "relevance" is hidden in the YouTube search engine algorithm, but it is generally assumed that the "relevance" rankings are determined by combining information on the number of times a video is viewed and a range of other factors including title, description, tags, comments, embeds, age of video, and so on (for a discussion of what factors matter most, see Gabe 2009). We decided to use this list because the rankings suggested some correlation with the broader public impact a given flash mob generated. This was important for our purposes, as we were also interested in the global diffusion of this practice, which was facilitated and accelerated by the public availability of videos by participants of actual flash mobs, encouraging the proliferation of copy cats.

We then started entering the information about the seven key dimensions of interest defined above for individual cases into a database, sorting the cases by year. We reviewed the first 200 results and eliminated the duplicates and false cases, using the definition provided by the Oxford English Dictionary as our definition of what a flash mob is. In cases when the description of the video and viewing of the video on YouTube did not provide sufficient information on the seven dimensions, we conducted simple Google searches for the specific event in question to fill in the missing information.[7] We also saved the results of these searches as well as comments on flash mob videos on YouTube as complementary data to help contextualize the cases and for later analysis. This way we were also able to keep track of "secondary" online discussions on blogs and other Web sites as well. After cleaning the 200 "most relevant" search results, we ended up with 127 cases of flash mobs that exhibited remarkable geographical variation, ranging from Beirut, Lebanon to Tokyo, Japan.

The iterative process of data collection, analysis, and theory building
Following the general principles of grounded theorizing, we began analyzing the data at this relatively early stage to see if there were any patterns emerging that we needed to take into consideration when including additional cases in the data set. I was focusing on examining variation by city, the types of urban spaces in which flash mobs took place, and the types of activities that were performed under the category of flash mobs. As for cities, New York, London, San Francisco, and Berlin were clearly key hubs of flash mob activity. But, surprisingly cities like Bialystok in Poland or Riga in Latvia also appeared to be important centers. Moreover, our data captured cases from 62 different cities from all over the world, not only from English-speaking countries, confirming the truly global spread of the flash mob phenomenon. Looking at the types of

urban spaces, we confirmed that urban public spaces were the most favored locations, but commercial spaces (shopping malls, supermarkets, big box stores) as well as university campuses were important sites as well, providing an important reflection on what places are perceived as "public" in an urban context.

The most interesting patterns, which contributed most significantly to theory building, were revealed through variation in the types of activities that fell under the category of flash mobs. It appeared that all cases shared crucial similarities that justified their labeling as a flash mob: they were organized via instruments of new digital media, participants were generally strangers to each other, participants gathered in an urban public or semi-public space "spontaneously," performed a "pointless" activity, filmed the event, and dispersed shortly afterwards. At the same time, there also seemed to be systematic differences among groups of activities, suggesting the existence of distinct subtypes within the broader category of flash mob. It should be underscored that individual cases were sorted into different subtypes based on conceptual similarities, not on similarities in the actual activity performed during the flash mob. That is, I did not create separate subtypes for "freeze in place" flash mobs, "zombie walk" flash mobs, or "pillow fight" flash mobs. The subtypes implied similarities in the nature of social interaction embodied in the flash mob. As a result of this conceptual sorting, I identified the following four subtypes: atomized flash mobs, interactive flash mobs, performance flash mobs, and political flash mobs.

1. *Atomized flash mobs* were particularly common during the initial phase of flash mobbing. Participants are mobilized through text messaging and emails to meet in a public or semi-public urban space (mostly in a retail store) to perform the same (absurd) activity and disperse within 10 minutes. Participants strictly do not interact with each other and stress the apolitical nature of the gatherings.

2. *Interactive flash mobs* usually take a simple children's game such as a pillow fight, capture the flag, or follow the leader and transpose it into an urban setting with multiple participants. These flash mobs involve interaction among participants and often last longer than 10 minutes, causing considerable disruption in the life of affected urban public spaces.

3. *Performance flash mobs* reinterpret the age-old script of performance art by incorporating the use of new communication media. These pranks also differ from earlier manifestations of performance art by moving out of the insular and exclusionary world of art galleries and theaters to the open space of the city and by involving large groups of strangers, as opposed to a few artists in the role of professional provocateurs.

4. *Political flash mobs* are "related" to "smart mobs" with respect to their intensive reliance on new communications technologies (mobile phones, Internet) to enhance the organization of political protest. But political flash mobs adopt more guerilla type tactics than digitally enhanced but traditional street protests, and they also always incorporate an element of absurdity that distinguishes them from smart mobs.

After I devised this classification scheme, I discussed the definition of the categories with my research assistant, and we both, independently, went through the 127 cases and sorted them into one of the four categories. The research assistant was also asked to evaluate whether cases could easily be classified as belonging to one or the other category and whether he felt the need to introduce new categories that would better describe some of the cases. The categories seemed to capture adequately the differences among the cases, and the intercoder reliability rate was 85%. The conceptual classification scheme thus emerged from the data, pointing to sociability as the underlying theoretical category. The four subtypes emphasized different facets and levels of sociability in public space.

About six months later, in May 2009, we expanded and updated the database by entering new cases. This time we searched for the 300 "most relevant" cases on YouTube and entered the positive cases that were not yet part of our database. In line with grounded theory's emphasis on theoretical sampling (Corbin and Strauss 1990; Dey 2004), we were focusing on whether there were any new cases that did not fit the four categories of flash mobs distinguished in the first search. The number of cases in our database went up to 203, and, indeed, among the new cases we encountered instances that were similar to each other but did not fit the earlier typology. They signaled the need for the introduction of a new category, the advertising flash mob:

5. *Advertising flash mobs* use the flash mob form as a promotional tool.
    Advertising campaigns are organized as a flash mob by a corpora-
    tion to promote a product. One of the earliest and most influential
    advertising flash mob campaigns was commissioned by the German
    cell phone company giant T-Mobile and took place at the Liverpool
    Street train station in London in January 2009. T-Mobile organized a
    "flash mob dance" at the station in as part of its "Life is for Sharing"
    campaign. A single "commuter" suddenly broke into what looked
    like a spontaneous dance on the main concourse of the train sta-
    tion. More and more people joined, until over 300 hundred "strang-
    ers" performed a perfectly choreographed dance routine, drawing
    in unsuspecting bystanders into the show. The ad proved immensely
    popular; it currently counts over 40 million views on You Tube and
    has won a prestigious award at the 56th Cannes Lions advertising
    festival.

The identification of this new type was theoretically relevant as well,
because it suggested that the sociability aspect of flash mobs began to
loosen over time, and that they were undergoing a transformation from a
spontaneous and subversive practice to a mainstream one that was
increasingly appealing to corporations for its potential for commercial
applications. In this sense flash mobs showed a great deal of affinity with
symbolic and organizational innovations that arise from underground
culture, which often get commodified as they draw the attention of the
mainstream. The use of graffiti or elements of hip-hop in advertising and
fashion design also illustrate this process.

At this point, I stopped collecting new data and wrote up the findings
within a theoretical framework that focused on the concept of sociability
(Molnár 2014). It is important to underscore, again, that the analytical
typology and the theoretical categories were developed inductively and
iteratively from the data. If we had proceeded deductively and started with
an exhaustive review of the theoretical literature on social movement theories and on the construction of online communities—the two literatures
that seemed most likely to suggest hypotheses about the social meaning of
flash mobs—we would have probably overlooked the importance of sociability as a central concept. We would have overemphasized the political
and community building aspects, failing to notice the fleeting character of
flash mobs that is so central to this form of social interaction.

The inductive analytical process helped to recognize that the concept of sociability better captures the original social meaning of flash mobs. Namely, in Georg Simmel's conceptualization, sociability represents one of the main forms of social interaction besides exchange, conflict, and domination. Sociability stands for the "play form of association" that in its pure form has "no ulterior end, no content and no result outside itself," and the "free-playing, interacting independence of individuals" takes center stage in the interaction (Simmel 1949: 255). The use of the concept allowed us to demonstrate that sociability was essential to the early history of flash mob activity. We were also able to show how the sociability aspect waned over time as flash mobs became more mainstream and institutionalized.

"Methodological Revisit"

When I agreed to write up the methodological lessons of my research on flash mobs in this chapter, about a year and a half after we completed the data collection for the original project, I thought we would just do a quick update of the database. I thought we would simply see if any new types of flash mobs cropped up that would require us to revise the original typology, much like we did between the first and second phases of the data collection process described earlier. However, it soon became clear that the online conditions of research had changed quite significantly since we had last collected new data. Instead of a quick routine update, there was a need for a "methodological revisit," for a more comprehensive reflection on the data in light of changes in access to the original data sources. I decided to devote an entire section of this chapter to detailing this experience, because it illustrates the principal challenge posed by longitudinal research on online content. The parameters of online data collection change much more rapidly than in traditional, offline contexts, which can often call for a substantial overhaul of the original research design as opposed to just fine-tuning.

In the case of flash mobs, we noticed that there were important changes to how search options were configured in YouTube compared with the last time we had updated the database. Most importantly, it was no longer possible to conduct searches for videos uploaded within a custom time range. This meant that we could not just search for flash mobs that took place since our last update—that is, between 2009 and 2010—and it also meant that we could no longer set a time frame on our search for flash mobs at all. Given the importance of a set time frame in our case, this meant that we could no longer use YouTube directly to update our data, even though hitherto it provided the most convenient data source for our purposes. This example illustrates how the online search environment can undergo sudden and unexpected changes within a relatively short time frame, requiring adjustments in established data collection procedures. In addition to the need to change tactics over time, it suggests that when using online tools for research purposes, it is best to take care of certain logistics in a fairly concentrated time frame to make sure that the tools do not undergo fundamental changes in the middle of one's use of them.

Google gradually made important changes to YouTube's search user interface after it acquired YouTube in 2006, the omission of the custom date range search being one painful example.[8] We believe some of these changes were partly motivated by the intention to reroute all video searches via Google's main search page as opposed to directly searching in YouTube, making Google the main entry point for every type of search. At the same time, Google developed its video search interface to have more search and sort options than YouTube originally did. We decided to relocate our searches to Google Video to see if we could use it as a source to update our data. We began by running searches for flash mobs for 2003–2010 to see if we would find results similar to our previous You-Tube searches. There was significant overlap with earlier cases, although Google Video also included flash mob videos from other video-sharing sites, not only from YouTube.

We concluded once again that despite its more sophisticated user interface, Google Video searches still did not bring us any closer to determining the size of the population. If anything, Google Video searches contribute to illustrating the enormous variation, and hence unreliability, in the figure different search engines return as the total number of cases for flash mobs (figure 3.1).

Nevertheless, it seemed that the Google Video search features could help us refine the longitudinal aspect of the analysis. We decided to break down the searches by year as opposed to searching for the entire time period of interest (2003–2010) as we did in previous phases, and calibrate

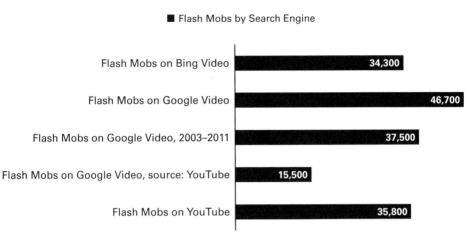

Flash Mobs by Search Engine

■ Flash Mobs by Search Engine

Flash Mobs on Bing Video	34,300
Flash Mobs on Google Video	46,700
Flash Mobs on Google Video, 2003–2011	37,500
Flash Mobs on Google Video, source: YouTube	15,500
Flash Mobs on YouTube	35,800

Figure 3.1
Number of results returned by search engine for the search string "flash mob,"
August 28, 2011.[11]

our sampling strategy by year. We started by checking the total number of
results returned for individual years (figure 3.2).[9] As mentioned above, we
are aware that this number is not a very good approximation of the size
of the population of events. But, in our view, the year-by-year changes in
the total number of cases are still indicative of the overall trend of growth
in the number of actual cases between 2003 and 2010.

For the 2003–2005 period, given that there were relatively few flash
mobs in total, we included all of the positive cases found in the search.
From 2006 on, however, the number of cases soared every year (figure
3.2), and we could no longer include all cases but had to take a sample.
Hence, for the 2006–2010 period, we increased the size of our sample
every year, starting with a sample size of 50 in 2006 and increasing the
sample size by 50 cases every year to adjust our sample size to the overall
trend of growth over the years.[10] My research assistant and I independently went through the search results for every year and eliminated false-
positive cases. We only kept the cases that we both identified as "authentic"
flash mobs. We also compared the cases we found in Google Video
searches with the cases we had in the original database we compiled using
YouTube. For every year between 2006 and 2010, there was a significant

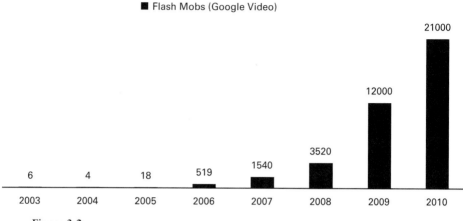

Figure 3.2
Flash mobs by year (Google Video), December 8, 2010.

overlap between the cases, but there were also new cases that were not located by previous YouTube searches, and there were old cases that were not found by the Google Video searches. After comparing these three groups of cases (old cases, new cases, overlaps) for every year, we ended up keeping all those cases in the final data set, as they seemed to increase the comprehensiveness of the sample as a whole. We clearly oversampled earlier years, which was justified from a theoretical perspective, since we were most interested in the emergence, early diffusion, and diversity of flash mob practice.

In fact, when we got to 2009, the new cases revealed that in the second half of 2009 a major shift occurred in the meaning and practice of flash mobs. The year 2009 marked one of the first commercial application of flash mobs, in the form of advertising flash mobs like T-Mobile's "Life is for Sharing" Campaign at London's Liverpool Street train station, which we mentioned earlier. This particular format, a choreographed dance that drew in innocent-looking bystanders, triggered a diffusion of its own and began to crowd out older forms. The diffusion was aided and accelerated by the adoption of this type of flash mob by influential outlets of popular culture. For instance, the popular comedy series *Weeds* started its 2009 season by prominently featuring a flash mob. Similarly, Fox channels' hit musical drama series, *Glee*, featured a dance flash mob in one of its episodes. At around the same time, the *Oprah* show's 24th season started with a monumental kick-off party organized as a flash mob: over 20,000 people took over Chicago's Magnificent Mile and performed a choreographed dance routine to a song by the band Black Eyed Peas. Closely related to these promotional dance flash mobs were the Michael Jackson tribute flash mobs that were organized in the wake of his death in summer 2009 all over the world. These flash mobs generated countless copy cats, and it seemed that by the end of 2009 flash mob activity had come to be dominated by such choreographed and pre-rehearsed dance performances in public space.

With this shift, flash mobs largely lost the spontaneity, absurdity, and subversiveness that characterized the original flash mob. This was a very significant change, but we felt that we could not fully address this latest transformation in the framework of our previous analysis. Therefore, we decided to end the data analysis in 2009 with the emergence of commercial flash mobs and the dance-performance flash mobs they closely influenced, thus focusing on the first, distinctive and "avant-garde" chapter of the evolution of flash mobs as a new form of sociability from 2003 to 2009. The 2009 shift marks a new era in the trajectory of flash mobs, and we will explore the turning point in a separate analysis.

The updated, extended, and refined data set (N=331) we generated as a result of the "methodological revisit" is the closest to what we have to a quasi-random sample of flash mobs, and as such it is worth reporting some descriptive statistics on our data regarding the distribution of flash mob activity by country, city, type of flash mob, and types of urban space (tables 3.1–3.4).

The data confirm the key findings of the previous phase of the research about the cities and countries that are the most prone to flash mobbing as well as the types of urban locations that are used to stage flash mobs. At the same time, the new data help us better capture the changing composition of flash mob activity over time. The dramatic shift toward dance-performance flash mobs inspired by classic advertising flash mobs can be clearly seen in the new data.

The amassed data have also marked out some new directions for further research. The closer study of how the major shift in meaning occurs in 2009 and how the flash mob becomes hijacked by commercial applications is an obvious extension of our research mentioned earlier. Similarly,

Table 3.1

Top 10 cities for flash mob activity, 2003–2009 (N=331)

Cities	Number of flash mobs
New York	23
Gothenburg	20
London	15
San Francisco	12
Bialystok	8
Berlin	7
Austin	5
Cologne	5
Copenhagen	5
Madrid	5

Table 3.2

Top 10 countries for flash mob activity, 2003–2009 (N=331)

Countries	Number of Flash Mobs
United States	75
Germany	31
Sweden	27
Poland	19
Canada	14
Australia	11
Russia	11
France	10
South Africa	8

Table 3.3
Types of flash mobs, 2003–2009 (N=331)

	2003	2004	2005	2006	2007	2008	2009	Total
Atomized	6	1	2	30	20	59	36	154
Interactive	2	1	5	23	32	29	21	113
Performance	0	2	1	3	2	6	32	46
Political	0	2	1	1	4	0	4	12
Advertising	0	0	0	0	0	1	5	6

Table 3.4
Flash mobs by type of urban space (N=331)

Location	Count
Public space (street, square, monument)	165
Semi-public space (shopping mall, retail store, museum, gallery, event)	84
Transportation (train station, transit vehicle)	36
Educational institutions (university campus, school)	33
Unknown	13

we noticed that not only did the number of flash mobs grow significantly over time, but viewers were more likely to leave detailed comments on the videos in later years. These comments are an interesting complementary source of data that can be analyzed systematically, shedding light on the public reception of flash mob activity.

Conclusion

The "methodological revisit" was productive in the sense that it has helped us refine the longitudinal aspect of the analysis and further "randomize" our sample. It also generated some interesting and unexpected new data that signal a significant shift in the meaning of the flash mob and a new chapter in its evolution, which we will definitely explore further. This, again, underscores the usefulness of a grounded theory approach for empirical research on online content. The "revisit" has helped us refine the iterative process of data collection, analysis, and theory building while highlighting that there is not really an alternative to this iterative strategy, given the extreme fluidity and presentism of the online data universe, which raise many epistemological and ontological, not simply methodological, issues. Similarly, our "methodological revisit" highlights especially forcefully the challenges of collecting time-series data on the Internet retrospectively and hence, the importance of gathering data about online phenomena as they occur. With search engines constantly calibrating their search algorithms and modifying their search interface, the replication of searches for past events on the Web proves extremely difficult over time.

In our view, therefore, Internet researchers are better off accepting these conditions of uncertainty and disclosing them clearly in the course of their research. Instead of trying to mimic traditional ("offline") quantitative social science research, Internet researchers have to develop their own canons and procedures, and devise evaluative criteria that are consistent and made explicit but take into account the unique conditions of online empirical research.

Finally, the "methodological revisit" has also confirmed that Google currently has an iron grip on our access to online information, which proved increasingly troubling to us in the course of our research. The reliability and accuracy of online data collection could be hugely improved if only Google provided more information about the key algorithms behind search results, especially those used for determining case counts and page rankings. But Google is, after all, a for-profit corporation while it is simultaneously the most important gatekeeper to the digital information universe. The lack of transparency that results from this situation presents serious difficulties for social scientists who are trying to use online data for academic research, even as the Internet is rapidly becoming a crucial repository of information about almost every aspect of our contemporary social life.

Notes

1. The "I" refers to the first author who started working on this project in 2007 by herself. The second author joined the project later originally as a research

assistant and played a crucial part in collecting and analyzing the empirical data as well as setting the agenda for the "Methodological Revisit" section of the chapter.

2. A "scenester" is somebody who is trying hard to fit the social stereotype of a certain scene (i.e., subculture) by meticulously following the dress, speech, and behavioral styles, and frequenting the places and events associated with, the given scene. In this context the term also refers to the general "insiderism" of New Yorkers, who always claim to be in the know and at the forefront of identifying and adopting the latest trends in everything ranging from music, culture, media, and fashion to food.

3. There are a few recent studies that claim to use "quasi-random" samples of website content as their data source (Earl 2006; Earl and Kimport 2009). But even though these analyses work with very large Ns, they only "simulate" probability sampling techniques and are not based on random samples in the traditional statistical sense of quantitative social science research.

4. Until some representative picture is drawn about flash mob events, we cannot generate information about who the typical participants are either, and this is why user-based sampling was not an option for this research.

5. Social science research that uses visual data is virtually nonexistent. A notable exception is research in progress by Elizabeth Currid that analyzes celebrity networks using Getty Images as a data source, though even she relies exclusively on the textual information in the caption of the images, not the visual information in the images (Currid and Ravid 2009).

6. While at later stages we used YouTube as our main online data source for flash mobs, at the beginning of the research it was not yet clear that flash mob events could best be captured in visual format. As we describe below, we started collecting cases through simple Google Web searches. Including this category helped us identify video-sharing sites (primarily YouTube) as the most useful and comprehensive source of empirical data on flash mob events.

7. We could not always determine the number of participants, but if this was the only piece of information missing about a given flash mob, we still included the case in the database. In general, participant information was the most challenging to find and verify.

8. Another important change was that the ability to sort by the number of views was temporarily eliminated. This move, however, provoked a flurry of user complaints, so Google decided to reintroduce it.

9. It is a crucial feature of this type of Internet research that, since the case count displayed by the search engine only approximates the actual number of cases, the total number of results returned for the same search can change within a matter of a few hours. This again highlights the importance of approaching search results with a grain of salt rather than taking them as definitive.

10. The increase of the sample size is not proportional to the growth of the yearly results returned by Google Video, because that number does not really indicate the population of events, for reasons explained earlier.

11. The 2003–2011 date range for the search for flash mobs on Google Video should include all flash mobs up to the date on which figure 3.1 was created, because flash mobs did not exist before 2003.

References

Bardzell, S., and W. Odom. 2008. The experience of embodied space in virtual worlds: An ethnography of a Second Life community. *Space and Culture 11* (3): 239–259.

Burawoy, M. 2003. Revisits: Outline of a theory of reflexive ethnography. *American Sociological Review* 68:645–679.

Corbin, J., and A. Strauss. 1990. Grounded theory research: Procedures, canons, evaluative criteria. *Qualitative Sociology 13* (1): 3–21.

Currid, E., and G. Ravid. 2009. Celebrity as category and group: An empirical network analysis of an elite population. Unpublished manuscript.

Dey, I. 2004. Grounded theory. In *Qualitative Research Practice*, ed. C. Seale, G. Gobo, J. F. Gubrium, and D. Silverman, 80–94. London: Sage.

Earl, J. 2006. Pursuing social change online: The use of four protest tactics on the Internet. *Social Science Computer Review 24* (3): 362–377.

Earl, J., and K. Kimport. 2009. Movement societies and digital protest: Fan activism and other nonpolitical protest online. *Sociological Theory 27* (3): 220–243.

Ellison, N. B., C. Steinfield, and C. Lampe. 2007. The benefits of Facebook "friends": Social capital and college students' use of online social network sites. *Journal of Computer-Mediated Communication 12* (4): 1143–1168.

Gabe, G. 2009. YouTube SEO—ranking factors—beyond views, titles, and tags. http://www.reelseo.com/youtube-ranking (accessed August 28, 2011)

Glaser, B., and A. Strauss. 1967. The Discovery of Grounded Theory. Chicago: Aldine.

Hampton, K., O. Livio, and L. Sessions Goulet. 2010. The social life of wireless urban spaces: Internet use, social networks, and the public realm. *Journal of Communication.* 60 (4): 701–722

Hargittai, E. 2010. Digital na(t)ives? Variation in Internet skills and uses among members of the "Net Generation." *Sociological Inquiry 80* (1): 92–113.

Hargittai, E., J. Gallo, and M. Kane. 2008. Cross-ideological discussions among conservative and liberal bloggers. *Public Choice* 134:67–86.

Heaney, F. 2005. October. The short life of flash mobs. *Stay Free* 24. http://www.alternet.org/story/26807/the_short_life_of_flash_mobs (accessed May 9, 2015).

Holt, T. J. 2009. Examining the role of technology in the formation of deviant subcultures. *Social Science Computer Review 28* (4): 466–481.

Hubbard, D. 2011. The key to top video rankings on YouTube and Google. February 11. http://searchengineland.com/the-key-to-top-video-rankings-on-youtube-google-35930 (accessed August 28, 2011).

McCaughey, M., and M. D. Ayers, ed. 2003. *Cyberactivism*. New York: Routledge.

McCullogh, M. 2007. New media urbanism: Grounding ambient information technology. *Environment and Planning B, Planning & Design* 34:383–395.

Molnár, V. 2014. Reframing public space through digital mobilization: Flash mobs and contemporary urban youth culture. *Space and Culture* 17 (1): 43–58.

Rheingold, H. 2000. *Virtual Community: Homesteading on the Electronic Frontier*. Cambridge, MA: MIT Press.

Rheingold, H. 2003. *Smart Mobs: The Next Social Revolution*. New York: Basic Books.

Simmel, G. 1949. The sociology of sociability. *American Journal of Sociology 55* (3): 254–261.

Strauss, A., and J. Corbin. 1990. *Basics of Grounded Theory Methods*. Beverly Hills, CA: Sage.

Wasik, B. 2006. March. My crowd: A report from the inventor of the flash mob. *Harper's Magazine*. 56–66.

Wasik, B. 2009. *And Then There is This: How Stories Live and Die in Viral Culture*. New York: Viking.

4

Making Sense of Teen Life: Strategies for Capturing Ethnographic Data in a Networked Era[1]

danah boyd

Keke walked into the room where I was waiting and sat down with a thump, crossing her arms and keeping a physical and psychological distance. I swallowed, knowing that this interview was going to take serious emotional effort on my part. I had spent the last three weeks at her school, observing the social dynamics unfolding in various classes, in the courtyard, and at lunch. I had gone with some of her classmates to the nearby McDonald's and had hung out with some of them at one of the local malls. I had spent hours browsing the MySpace pages of her classmates, trying to get a sense of the norms and gossip at her school. I had also eaten lunch on multiple occasions in the faculty room, listening to the teachers share their headaches and heartaches. Keke's school often overwhelmed me, and I was not always emotionally prepared for what I saw and heard, nor did I always know what to say or do. Only a few days before, I had walked in on two of Keke's classmates having sex in the faculty lounge during class; they had been more annoyed with me for interrupting them than ashamed or embarrassed. I was the one who was ashamed and embarrassed. And, as an ethnographer trained to believe that I should not let my own values shape my feelings, I was ashamed and embarrassed by my shame and embarrassment.

I took a deep breath and started with some small talk, asking Keke why she had agreed to be interviewed for this project. "I need the money," she stated, emotionless. Like many other teens from low-income families that I have interviewed, Keke's only reason for participating was the financial incentive; she was not interested in the research topic and did not see why I—as an adult—cared about what teens were doing with technology. I quickly realized that she was going to answer any question I asked with as few words as possible. So I decided that I needed a different strategy, and I asked her to walk me through the previous day, describing what she did from the moment she woke up through the point at which she went to sleep. As she set about describing her day, I noticed that she was talking about everyone else but herself; she was not personalizing what she did during the day. Whenever she made an "I" statement, it was stated as a neutral fact, but whenever she talked about others, she added adjectives and emotion. As I returned to my core research questions, I shifted from asking her about why she chose to do different things and, instead, asked her to describe what her friends did.

Slowly, Keke started opening up, but she stayed guarded. She was able to talk about others with expressivity, but she kept her own motivations and feelings locked tight. She became animated when she started talking about the drama around her, revealing her love of shopping and boys. I started to sense that something was weighing on her that went beyond the conversation at hand, but I could not put my finger on it. Keke—a 16-year-old black girl living in Los Angeles—dressed well, using clothing to flatter her curves. In listening to her street-slanged speech, I began to see that she was not particularly shy or unemotional by default and that she did not dismiss adults outright. This left me puzzled, unsure of why she seemed distant to me. I realized that I came from a very different cultural backdrop—and that she had every reason to question my sincerity—but that did not seem to be insurmountable in this particular conversation. So I asked about friends and significant others, getting her to detail her social life, gossip between her friends, and the various dramas that were playing out at school. I knew that she was carefully revealing some things while choosing not to reveal others, but I also got the sense that I was not asking the right questions.

I knew that she was getting more comfortable with me when she switched from talking about other people's drug use to telling me a story of getting high herself, so I continued down this line of inquiry, making sure to refrain from signaling any judgment. Her comments about drugs prompted me to ask about parties. Much to my surprise, the stone-cold look from earlier returned to her face. Then she said, "I would rather read a book than go to a party," and laughed. And then she got serious again. "We can't have a party without somebody being a Blood or somebody being a Crip and then they get into it and then there's shooting. Then we can't go to my friend's house because it's on the wrong side of [the street].

You know what I'm saying? It's the Mexican side." As Keke started raging against the street gangs in her community, emotions poured out of her. I sat there, making sure that she knew I was listening to everything she had to say, maintaining eye contact, and trying to convey compassion while silently being devastated by all that she told me. As I was using body language to be supportive, she began to describe the racial dimensions of her world, detailing gang fights and describing where she physically could and could not go in her community. I asked how she felt about it, and the biggest weight she was carrying became visible: "'Cause we black, we automatically gang bangers. Mexican, you automatically gang bangers. I just hate that stereotype—they killed my brother 'cause they thought he was a gang banger. My brother's not. So it was just another life wasted because [of] what you thought, and I just hate that." As she continued describing the violence and racism in her community, she wove in details about how her brother had accidentally crossed the wrong lines and was shot in front of her. Anger and sadness poured out of her, and I sat there taking it all in, feeling her pain, frustration, confusion, and sadness.

When she was done, she looked at me with wide eyes and thanked me for listening. I thanked her for sharing her story. As we closed the interview, I told her that there were other people that she could talk to and that I could get her a list of names if she wanted. She dismissed my offer and told me that talking to adults at school always got people into trouble and that it just was not worth it. Besides, she noted, she had her momma. She smiled at me in a way that conveyed that my listening to her made her feel better. As she walked away, I ducked into the faculty bathroom and cried.

...

My research agenda focuses on how technology fits into the everyday lives of teenagers. My goal is to understand and convey the cultural logic that underpins why teens do what they do. I want to uncover and describe how teens see the world and how this shapes their approach to and engagement with technology. I want to see technology from their perspective in order to get at what they take for granted. In order to do this, I incorporate many different ethnographic methods into my research, including online and offline participant-observation, semistructured ethnographic interviews, content analysis, and a practice that anthropologist

James Clifford referred to as "deep hanging out," where scholars bring theory and reflexivity to bear during any act of interpretation (see Geertz 1998).

Although I use research practices and theoretical frameworks well-established in anthropology and sociology, my line of inquiry primarily concerns how technology reconfigures everyday practices. As with many technology studies scholars, sociotechnical issues drive many of my research questions. Yet this does not mean I only talk with teens about technology. In describing the emotional tenor of my two-hour interview with Keke above, I did not once mention technology even though technology was the anchor for our conversation. In most interviews, technology seeps in without me even having to look for it. With Keke, we talked about girls using AOL's instant messenger because they are "boy crazy," how MySpace reveals cliques that are visible in the schoolyard, and how cell phones are the new Nikes, both in terms of their potential as a status marker and as objects to be stolen. Keke described YouTube "hood fight" videos and talked about how she thought teens were "stupid" to put them up online for the police to see. And we talked about how she was really into Harry Potter fan fiction but did not let anyone around her know about it because it was not "cool." All of these technology-centric elements are important, but they make much more sense when understood in context. Wanting to understand the context in which technology operates is what prompted me to start interviewing teenagers in the first place, over six years ago.

I do use social media in my research. I spend countless hours surfing teens' social network site profiles, reading their tweets, and otherwise observing their online traces. I use many online ethnographic techniques developed by previous Internet studies scholars (see Hine 1998; Markham and Baym 2008; Miller and Slater 2000). However, I also purposefully go out and meet with teens face-to-face. Social media certainly make it much easier to peek into people's lives, but it is also quite easy to misinterpret online traces. This became acutely real to me when I received a phone call from an Ivy League college admissions officer in 2005. The college was interested in the application from a young black man from the South Central neighborhood in Los Angeles—a notoriously gang-ridden community. The teen had written a college essay about leaving gangs behind, but the college had found his MySpace profile, which was filled with gang insignia. The admissions officer asked me a simple question that has stuck with me ever since: "Why would he lie to us in his college essay when we can tell the truth online?" Having spent a lot of time in that part of Los Angeles and analyzing online profiles of teens living there, I offered an alternative explanation. Without knowing the specific boy involved, I surmised that he was probably focused on fitting in, staying safe, or, more directly, surviving in his home environment. Most likely he felt as though he needed to perform gang affiliation online—especially if he was not affiliated—in order to make certain that he was not physically vulnerable. Although I never got to interview that young man—nor learn if he was admitted to the college—I cannot help but wonder how many people wrongly think that they can interpret online content without understanding the context in which it is produced.

My Networked Field Site

Ethnographers disagree about whether or not one can study an online community solely by engaging with the community online. Tom Boellstorff (2008) argues that an online-only ethnography is appropriate in a community like Second Life, where participants primarily interact online, but he is in the minority. Even those who specifically study online communities often find value in engaging with participants face-to-face. For example, gaming scholar T. L. Taylor (2006) purposefully attends face-to-face gatherings of gamers to get a better understanding of their mediated dynamics. Internet-only ethnographic research may have value, but, as other scholars have highlighted, recognizing continuities between online and offline contexts and taking circumstances into consideration are essential when trying to understand mediated practices (Kendall 2002; Bennett 2004; Miller and Slater 2000).

   Although I have done online content analysis for over a decade, I have found that I cannot get a deep understanding of mediated practices without engaging with people face-to-face in at least one of the physical environments they inhabit. Given that most of my work concerns a population whose interactions span multiple modes and media, I find it is important to try to get at their practices from different angles. I do not traipse across the United States because I need more air miles or enjoy staying in motels; I do so because I have found that it is the only way I can get a decent picture of teens' lives. When I meet teens face-to-face, they add depth and context to what I see online. More importantly, they show me where my first impressions were inaccurate or wrong. Thus, I purposefully collect data both online and offline.

Multi-sited fieldwork is quite common in ethnography, including ethnographic studies of mediated interactions (Green 1999; Marcus 1995), but there is no consistent framework for relating the different sites to one another. Some scholars discretely collect and then synthesize online and offline data about individuals (Haythornthwaite and Wellman 2002; Orgad 2008), while others emphasize interactions or communities and follow the relationships between people and activities as they move between online and offline environments (Hodkinson 2002; Kelty 2008; Wilson 2006). Focusing on the importance of following interactions from online to off and vice versa, Leander and McKim (2003: 211) argue that "tracing the flows of objects, texts, and bodies" allows ethnographers to account methodologically for the relationship between online and offline practices. While following people and content as they move between environments is analytically ideal, it is often not practical. And, in my research with teens, I have found it nearly impossible to move seamlessly between different environments in order to get a holistic picture of a particular teen.

In my first two projects on social media, I focused on adult early adopters of social network sites and blogs (Donath and boyd 2004; boyd 2006, 2008). As other scholars had learned (Baym 1993; Rettberg 2008; Taylor 2006), I found it both effective and efficient to identify participants online and reach out to them directly. Although I was not asking research questions that required obtaining a representative sample, having access to a large database of social network site profiles and blogs made finding diverse perspectives simpler than with more traditional recruiting methods. When I approached participants online, the response rate was extraordinarily high, and it was easy to start talking with someone long before I would schedule time to meet face-to-face.

In 2004, I began outlining a research protocol to interrogate teen practices using social media. Like previous scholars (e.g., Richman 2007), I intended to "lurk" online and observe teens' interactions on MySpace, but I also imagined contacting teens directly through MySpace in order to interview them face-to-face. As I set my research plan into motion, "stranger danger" rhetoric concerning MySpace exploded (Marwick

2008). The news media, safety organizations, police officers, and parents began telling teens that they should not talk to strangers online because any stranger might be a child predator. While I may be unassuming in person, it quickly became apparent that I could not approach teenagers online without violating what they were hearing with respect to "creepy" strangers. It also became clear that teens were less likely to respond to my requests than adult bloggers and social network site users had been. Moving from MySpace to interview proved to be a dead end.

To address the methodological challenge of doing multi-sited fieldwork without being able to move seamlessly between field sites, I decided to organize my ethnographic project around a set of discrete field sites, linked by social media. To do so, I built on the work of Jenna Burrell (2009), who argued that one could understand a field site as a "network composed of fixed and moving points including spaces, people, and objects." By integrating different field sites through a common phenomenon, it is then possible to see the phenomenon as a continuous system and capture the coherence and fluidity of the different spaces people occupy, even if they are not explicitly connected. In other words, it is possible to build a networked field site.

My ethnographic study of teens' engagement with social media has four discrete components: 1) immersion in teen pop culture and subculture; 2) participant-observation and content analysis of teens' online traces on social media sites; 3) participant-observation and "deep hanging out" in physical spaces where teens gather; and 4) semistructured face-to-face ethnographic interviews.

In order to understand cultural references that I encounter, I rabidly consume media that is popular with teens. I watch popular TV shows and movies and read books and magazines that I hear about from teens. I visit popular teen-oriented websites, play the most popular games, and try to appreciate the memes that surface. I surf YouTube to listen to bands and musical artists that are popular with teens, and I try to keep up with celebrities that they adore. This does not mean that I, myself, am a big fan of Kim Kardashian or *Jersey Shore* or Jay-Z, but I find that having a baseline knowledge of the cultural references that teens use is essential for building rapport and understanding the context in which they operate. Still, teens regularly use references that completely evade me, and I am constantly reminded of just how old they think I am.

Online, I participate in and gather data from MySpace, Facebook, YouTube, Twitter, Xanga, LiveJournal, Formspring, and a host of smaller social media services. I follow teen-oriented "trending topics" and download countless profiles to analyze. I have watched teen girls "catfight" on uStream and tracked discussions of proms, SAT tests, and political mobilization over immigration issues. I have read teens' messages to Beyoncé and watched their obsession with Justin Bieber and Lady Gaga grow.

Immersing myself in pop culture and observing teens from the sidelines is a crucial part of my fieldwork but only in that it gives me a foundation upon which to engage teens. The most significant part of my research tends to center on my unmediated interactions with teens. Over the six years during which I have worked on this project, I have interviewed, observed, and casually engaged with teens in 21 continental U.S. states and the District of Columbia in a wide array of communities—rich and poor, urban, suburban, and rural, north, south, east, and west. I have attended sports games (including at least six homecoming football games), casually lingered at diners, and loitered in movie theater parking lots; I have hung out in skateboarding parks, cafés, and the International House of Pancakes. I have watched teens socialize with peers at the beach, at all-ages music venues, on buses, in parking lots, and at youth centers. I have visited high schools and after-school programs. Regardless of my personal beliefs, I have respectfully attended a large church in many of the communities that I have visited precisely because religious life plays a key role in the lives of many teens that I meet. I also talk with adults who are involved with teens—parents, teachers, law enforcement officers, social workers, youth ministers, and many others.

While I use varied means of collecting data, conducting ethnographic interviews plays a central role in my research process. In my study of teens' social media practices, I have conducted, recorded, and transcribed interviews with 144 teenagers; my colleague Alice Marwick—who has traveled with me on more recent trips—conducted another 21 interviews with teens using the same interview protocol and a similar approach to interviewing. We have interviewed teens ages 13 to 19 representing a wide array of racial, ethnic, religious, and socioeconomic backgrounds. Some of the teens that we met came from two-parent households; others lived with a single parent or moved between homes; still others lived with relatives, were in foster care, lived in a group home, or were homeless. We have interviewed high school dropouts, homeschooled teens, teens from prestigious magnet or private schools, and teens who attended public schools. We have interviewed straight and gay teens, conservative and liberal teens, sporty teens, self-identified geeks, teens who are passionate about school, teens who are illiterate, teens on the homecoming court, and teens who have been bullied.

Identifying Teens to Interview

Given the importance of interviewing to my fieldwork—and given the previously discussed issues involved in identifying teens online—one of my biggest challenges is finding diverse teens to interview. In order to interview teens, I first identify various local "communities"[2] where I believe I might be able to interview teens. I consciously account for the qualities of that community and the breadth of my local connections. I go out of my way to find diverse communities, but I am also aware of how important it is to have a local informant who can help me navigate the community. Thus, I visit communities where I know someone who can help me identify a cross-section of teens. Over the years, I have worked with educators, librarians, parents, after-school programs, and youth centers. I once used a recruitment firm to identify teens but found that such firms do not have as much breadth as local community members and, more importantly, that teens recruited for marketing research have an amazing penchant for speaking in sound bites in a way that feels outright eerie and utterly unlike the majority of teens that I meet. Given the biases of recruiting firms, I prefer to work with local informants who have direct access to teens because of what they do either professionally or personally. My local informants are typically friends-of-friends, people I have met at conferences, or people that I have met through my blog. I typically identify three to four potential field sites based on connections for every community that I end up visiting.

Every community has its own flavor, biases, and limitations. Thus, in choosing communities to visit, I try to identify communities that are as different from the others that I have visited as possible. I have visited low-income communities and wealthy communities, communities where most residents are immigrants, urban and small-town communities,

communities shaped by single industries, and communities that reflect varied religious, political, and racial differences.

Once I have identified a community, I start talking to local informants to see if they can help me identify a range of different teens. I try to find local informants who believe in my project and want to help me. I send them a detailed description of what I am looking for, emphasizing that my goal is to interview diverse but "typical" teens who reflect that particular community. I specifically ask them not to identify teens whose parents work in technology or who are academics. I also explain that I am not looking for teens who are especially passionate about technology or those who are particularly exceptional along any traditional axis. It is common for local informants to want to bring out teens that are local stars in academics, sports, music, debate, etc., so I explain that this is not what I want. And then I rely on them to use their best judgment, knowing full well that I will always miss certain aspects of each community.

When I work with local informants, I know that their view of their community will affect which teens they identify for me to interview. I try to account for how their biases might affect whom I am meeting. The most common issue I encounter is that many local informants are determined to make the community look good by only introducing me to teens who are extraordinary. At other times, I sometimes encounter more systemic biases. In one community, the local informant refused to introduce me to any teens of color, even though only 47 percent of the teens in the local school were white. When I pushed her into explaining why, she told me that she did not think I would be safe in those neighborhoods. Like all ethnographers, I struggle with what it means to be an outsider (Geertz 1973; Harrison 2008).

In anthropology, there is a long-standing debate about what it means to generalize from ethnographic data. Some ethnographers argue that generalization simply cannot be achieved through ethnographic analysis, and they reject generalization as a goal (Denzin 1983). Others—sometimes referred to as "post-positivists"—are committed to external validity and believe it is important for ethnographers to be conscious of sampling in order to achieve generalizability (Schofield 2002; Hammersley 1992). Although I can certainly see both sides of this debate, I tend to believe that it is possible to understand a broader population's cultural logic by working conscientiously to hear diverse perspectives.

Furthermore, although I recognize cross-disciplinary work is heretical in some scholarly communities, I am committed to working with quantitative scholars who are trying to understand broader trends. Thus, I go out of my way to map out general practices in order to help quantitative scholars build rigorous instruments to interrogate specific practices. Given this, I work diligently to sample different communities and different types of teens until I feel as though I have reached a saturation point (Glaser & Strauss 1967).

In order to be able to make broader claims, I try to understand how the teens that I am meeting fit into the broader picture. In each community, I obtain census data to understand the demographic makeup. Upon arrival, I use Google Maps to drive to different parts of the town in order to get a feel for the area. I visit the local mall and movie theater to see who is around, and I try to attend a school sports event to see which teens show up. I surf Facebook and MySpace to find visible accounts associated with that community. And when I start interviewing teens, I use a technique from Penelope Eckert (1989) and ask teens to map out their school's lunchroom dynamics in order to see which types of teens I am meeting and not meeting. These maps—and the cliques that teens identify—tend to provide valuable insight into the local community. When I know that I am getting a very limited range of teens, I sometimes ask teens to help me meet teens from other groups at school, or I try to find additional informants who might be able to help me reach different groups of teens.

Once the local informant has helped me identify teens, I send along a packet of information, including a description of the project, a questionnaire, and a consent/waiver form. Depending on what is appropriate in a particular community, I may send these packets via email, through postal mail, or ask the local informant to hand the packet physically to the teen or their guardian. In some cases, the local informant gives me contact information for the teen or the parent; in other cases, the local informant arranges the interview. I give teens the option of meeting me at their homes—provided that a parent or guardian is present—or at a public place of their choosing. I have interviewed teens in schools, libraries, youth centers, fast food establishments, and cafés. I have met them at their parents' place of work and at their grandparents' homes. Once, I even met a teen at a bar; his mother was an alcoholic, so the bartender had been looking after him since he was a boy.

Given human subjects requirements, I ask teens who are under the age of 18 to get the permission of a parent or guardian to participate. When teens meet me in public places, they are required to bring their signed consent form with them. In a few cases, the local informant has signed in lieu of the legal guardian. Once, I allowed a 17-year-old homeless teen to sign a separate form indicating that he was in the process of being emancipated. I believe that I have both an ethical and legal responsibility to obtain parental permission, but I have also made a conscious decision to respect teens' agency. While I respect the intentions behind parental consent, I am not convinced that this one-size-fits-all model always makes sense. As previous scholars have noted, relying on parental consent causes unique challenges when children are abused, homeless, or otherwise outside of traditional models of home and family (Vissing 2007). Thus, I tend to focus on what seems most appropriate given the circumstances.

Confronting Ethical Concerns

When I meet up with teens for an interview, I start by outlining what they can expect from our discussion. I explain that everything they tell me is confidential and will not be shared with their parents. There is one exception to this, but I have chosen not to state it clearly during the opening preamble. When underage teens speak of being abused, I am ethically—and, in some cases, legally—required to report this to local authorities. I struggle with this requirement, in part because I spent eight years volunteering for V-Day, an organization that worked to end violence against women and girls. At V-Day, I met numerous abused teens and was involved in a series of interventions. While I am deeply committed to helping teens get out of violent situations, I am also aware that the arrival of social services into the lives of high-school–aged teens is not always helpful. Although I would prefer being able to be open with teens, I have strategically decided to implement a "don't ask, don't tell" policy and try to avoid any conversation that might lead me to learn about abuse when minors are involved. Still, in two cases, I did learn of parental abuse involving minors, but both were already in the process of managing it; one teen was in a group home as a result, and the other was living with a different parent. Additionally, I have talked with teens who are over the age of 18 about abuse issues. Two 18-year-olds and one 19-year-old have given me detailed descriptions of the abuse they face at home and their attempts to manage it. When issues of abuse—or other at-risk issues—emerge, I talk with teens about what resources are available to them. On more than one occasion, I have given help line or local contact numbers to teens whom I thought could use support.

In explaining the confidentiality process, I also tell teens that I will never use their real names or any information that might identify them directly. After an interview, I use a baby name website to choose a pseudonym and then use this for my notes on that teen (i.e., I chose the name "Keke" to represent the teen discussed above even though that is not her given name). I intentionally forget teens' real names and replace them mentally with the pseudonyms I have chosen. Whenever a teen asks, I tell them what pseudonym I used for them. When I interview teens in a city, I use the city name as the reference, but whenever I interview teens outside of a major urban region, I identify them by their state. I change the names of their friends and school and purposely avoid using any specific references that might identify a teen.

I also purposefully obscure data that I collect as part of my online observations and content analysis. I work to scrub identifying information from all digital material. When I use screen shots of profiles in talks or in papers, they are typically heavily modified (using Photoshop) to erase identifying information. I either blur photos or use substitute photos from friends, my childhood, or young adults who have content available through Creative Commons. When I quote text from profiles, I often alter the quotes to maintain the meaning but to make the quote itself unsearchable. Even when online information is "public," I feel as though I have an ethical responsibility not to reveal the identities of the teens that I interview or observe. Just as previous researchers have used photographs but obscured names or images (Goldstein 2003; Bourgois & Schonberg 2009), I use digital content to convey impressions without directing attention to specific people.

After explaining how confidentiality works to teens, I next explain how the interview will proceed and clarify that teens may opt not to answer any question that I ask or may quit the interview at any time. I intentionally give them the incentive—typically cash—up front so that they do not feel pressured to stay to receive the incentive. I also explain that they may choose to ignore any question I ask and that I would rather they said "Not gonna answer that" than lie to my face. This usually makes them giggle. I ask them if they have any questions about the protocols. The most common question that I get at this stage is: "What will this be used for?" I explain that my work is academic in nature and that I publish my work in scholarly journals and give public presentations. I explain that my work is sometimes used to shape public policy or to affect how technology is developed.

When I have addressed all questions that teens have, I then proceed to the interview itself. My interviews with teens have lasted between one and four hours, with the vast majority of them taking between 90 minutes and two hours. I audio record the interviews for transcription. While I have a notepad in front of me, I rarely take many notes because I am conscious to keep eye contact the entire time. If anything, I write small notes to myself to make sure that I come back to a topic as we veer off in various directions. I enter into the ethnographic interview with a semistructured interview protocol, but my priority is to make certain that I understand teens' lives, so I rarely stay on script.

The Set and Setting of an Interview

Interviewing is first and foremost about set and setting. It requires identifying places where conversing feels natural while also working to create situations in which teens feel comfortable sharing their story. It is about choosing a space where a conversation can take place and then creating the situation in which the teen is most likely to talk. No setting is perfect, and it is important to be able to adjust. For example, I prefer that parents do not overhear the interview, but when I am interviewing in people's homes, I must be prepared that they might even though I arrange the situation to minimize that. When I am asking teens questions about family life, I actively watch for any signal that they might be uncomfortable and abort if I think a parent is listening in. In adjusting the interview in response to how a teen reacts to my questions, I create a setting in which teens are able to open up.

The interviews that I conduct with teens are semistructured and ethnographic in nature. While I enter an interview with an interview protocol, my priority is to get a sense of that teen's life, values, and perspective. Ethnographic interviewing is not just about following a protocol to make certain that each scripted question is answered; rather, the interview is driven by my interest in trying to understand who this particular teen is and what she or he thinks about the world. It requires reading the situation, interpreting the metacommunication, and reacting to what the teen is saying and implying (Briggs 1986). Throughout the interview, I work simultaneously to make an informant comfortable and to create openings for them to share their stories (Weiss 1994). The question that I ask the most often is "Why?" While I enter into an interview in order to understand how technology inflects a teen's daily life, I rarely ask any of the questions on my interview protocol; they are more useful as a mental guide to shape what topics I want to make sure that I cover. This is what makes my interviews semistructured. They are ethnographic because I am trying to understand how people understand their worlds, rather than simply trying to elicit answers to specific questions. Furthermore, they are ethnographic because I also draw on participant observations from my time in their community and situate what I learn in a theoretical tradition (Spradley 1979).

I believe that people—including teenagers—make reasonable decisions in response to their environment. Given their situation, values, and knowledge, they engage with technology in ways that make complete sense to them. My goal is to get at their personal logic in order to understand why what they are doing makes sense to them. I then try to situate what I learn in a broader body of data and theory. It is easy to look at Facebook profiles and judge people's decisions; it is a lot harder to understand and respect why someone makes a particular decision and how this decision fits into the cultural setting in which she or he operates. Situating teens' practices is not easy; I regularly have to face my own biases, interpretive limitations, and judgmental tendencies.

Consider what happened when I interviewed Daniela, a 16-year-old Latina girl who had numerous risqué photos on her MySpace profile. When she first showed me her profile, I had to swallow a gasp. While I do not consider myself particularly prudish, I was not prepared to have a minor show me nude photos of herself. Trying not to be judgmental, I asked her cautiously about her choice of photos. She told me that she thought that they made her look "hot." I asked her how she felt about others seeing them, and she told me that she hoped that she was going to get picked up by a modeling agency. Because of this, she accepted all friend requests and regularly befriended people on MySpace who she thought might work in the modeling industry. She pointed to other celebrities—like Tila Tequila—to highlight how Internet fame was possible. I did not tell her that Tequila got her "break" when a Playboy scout approached her in a mall. Instead, I asked her if she was concerned that she might lose opportunities because of these photos; she scrunched her face with confusion over my question. I tried to clarify, highlighting that college admissions officers often look at applicants' profiles. As soon as it was out of my mouth, I knew that I was using a bad example. She responded with a snort, explaining that she would never get into college anyhow, so why worry about it.

From Daniela's point of view, her body was an asset and her only chance to "get out." Given my personal and professional training, it was hard for me not to see Daniela's photos as illegal child pornography. Still, who was I to question her dream of fame and fortune and glamour? Who was I to assume that the middle-class ideal of college was an appropriate path? I listened to her talk about her home life and her struggles with school, her fascination with reality TV and her obsession with "self-made" celebrities. She had examples of success stories, and she was determined to be one of them. She thought my anxieties were unfounded. Out of a sense of ethical responsibility, I decided to let her know that some might argue that the images she made available could be construed as child pornography and that this might get her into unexpected trouble. She rejected my message with an eye roll, and I felt like a prude after all.

In talking with Daniela about her nude images, I was faced with my own subject-position as an adult who represented middle-class adult values and expectations. Not only did I feel uncomfortable just accepting her images at face value, but I was also revealing that I was judgmental through the questions I asked. In the process, I failed to acknowledge her belief that fame was more accessible for her than college. I reproduced a middle-class narrative, effectively obscuring her reality as an undocumented teen who lived through the collapse of the DREAM Act and the increased scrutiny of young immigrants. Not only did Daniela not have the grades to get into most colleges, she was also ineligible for most college financial aid programs. When blurting out the question about college, I revealed my own culturally constructed values in a way that showed my biases.

Anthropologists have long argued that ethnographers must be reflexive in their practice, consciously aware of how their own biases in the research process affect what they can see (Clifford & Marcus 1986; Strathern 2004; Haraway 1991). Despite that awareness, this process is often fraught and difficult to manage (Watson 1987; Behar & Gordon 1996). For me, reflexivity is both an ideal for which I strive and a process that shapes how I think about research. I work hard to manage my own interpretive biases and address the effect I have on the research setting, but that does not mean I am—or should be—a neutral or objective researcher. I am, always, an outsider (Harrison 2008; Fine & Sandstrom 1988). My own subject-position is fundamentally a part of the process, and I try to account for this in my analysis. It is impossible to be completely nonjudgmental when doing research, and, in my conversations with teens, I constantly ask myself what I am inadvertently conveying to them. I try to make sure that the questions that I ask do not have assumptions baked into them, but they inevitably do, and I struggle to account for my biases both during the interview (so that I can adjust the conversation) and afterwards (as I code my transcripts and reflect on what I have learned).

What researchers wear also affects how they are perceived—and, thus, introduces significant biases and signals (Pascoe 2007). Although I am typically a fairly flamboyant dresser, I try for a simpler look when I am interviewing teens. Early on, I grew my hair long and removed all of my visible piercings; as I grow older, I just try to dress in jeans and T-shirts. I do not use much makeup or do my hair. I never pass as another teenager, but I try to signal that I am not a parent figure or teacher through my mannerisms and dress. My interviews are most effective when teens see me as someone who shares their values, so I try hard to minimize signals that might be off-putting, even though I know that there are certain things that I cannot hide—I am white, female, in my 30s (which makes me old in the eyes of my respondents), and from the North. I am well-educated and living an upper-middle-class life, although I easily slip into a speaking pattern that reflects that I did not grow up in a privileged community. That said, I purposely try not to reveal my sexuality, religion, or politics.

My queer identity and familiarity and comfort with different religious traditions, political persuasions, and working-class language and cultural norms can be quite beneficial in certain circumstances. Teens who identify with me for one reason or another appear to be much more likely to open up to me, while teens who see me as a complete outsider tend to be wary of my presence, and I must work harder to earn their respect. Given this, I do not tend to correct teens when they perceive me to be more like them than I might be. For example, in Atlanta in May 2009, when the issue of Barack Obama's election came up, white teens typically assumed that I was Republican—presumably because, as one teen explicitly told me, I was white. Black teens assumed I was a Democrat, either because, as one teen told me, I did not dress like the white people they knew, or, as another one explained, because I was from "up North." I did not try to counter their perceptions unless they asked, but I did ask them why they perceived me in particular ways.

Balancing insider-outsider status is an ongoing challenge of doing research, but when I succeed, teens stop focusing on my outsider status, even if they do not see me as an insider. When I meet a teen, I try to find common ground as quickly as possible and verbally signal allegiance. When I interview teens, they fill out a simple questionnaire about their media habits, interests, demographics, and tastes before our conversation; I scan this to find connections. I also typically open up the interview by asking them about what they are most passionate about or interested in and hope that I will be able to ask intelligent questions about whatever topic emerges. I use references to current events or pop culture as opening topics if I think that the teen I am interviewing might have an opinion on who won the Teen Choice Awards or what happened during the NBA finals.

Creating an environment in which teens feel comfortable opening up about their lives is the hardest part of interviewing teens (Raby 2007). Once teens are comfortable, they are typically happy to tell their story. The most challenging interviews are inevitably those where the teen I am talking to is not comfortable with me. When I am lucky, I find an in, but this is not always the case. For example, I met a 16-year-old boy who fabricated stories for over an hour, perhaps unaware that I both recognized the TV shows that contained the storylines he was feeding me and also that I asked him the same question multiple times to assess whether or not he was being consistent.

While there are teens who will never open up, most teens are quite willing to engage once they believe that they can trust me. Trust is a crucial part of the ethnographic process (Geertz 1973). Teens need to trust me to be willing to talk with me about their lives, and I need to trust them to be honest. I purposefully introduce particular lines of inquiry to assess their comfort with me. For example, I often use drugs and alcohol as a gauge. Early on, I will ask how common drugs and/or alcohol are at their school abstractly. At another point in the interview, when talking about the different cliques at school, I will ask which groups use substances. Depending on the teen, I will ask about drugs and alcohol in relation to parents, parties, and things that get teens into trouble generally. Typically, teens begin by talking in the third person, but as they grow more comfortable, they begin using first person plural ("we") language and, eventually, talk about their own attitudes toward drugs and alcohol. Even when teens are not personally using drugs or alcohol, they always have an opinion on these topics; getting their honest opinion is more important to me than learning whether or not they use substances.

I use many simple stylistic techniques to elicit certain kinds of responses (Weiss 1994). Catching teens off-guard through a surprising question is often the best way to get an emotional reaction instead of a thought-out one; I use this technique when I want to see the immediate reaction. Conversely, when I want to see teens process something slowly, I will actively use silence. If I ask a question and a teen answers, the expectation is that I will then ask another question. If, instead, I stay silent and maintain my gaze, the teen will often repeat their answer with more clarity, providing a more precise explanation to the initial question. I use rapid-fire, yes-no questions when I want to draw in a teen's attention and questions that elicit long responses when I want to have a moment to sit back and watch the teen's body language. When I interview teens, I am not only looking for their answers but also for their reactions, their metaphors, and their cultural references (Briggs 1986). I want to understand how they explain themselves just as much as what they say. Thus, I use a variety of different techniques to elicit different kinds of responses, all the while being conscious of making sure the teen I am interviewing continues to feel comfortable talking with me.

While some teens approach an interview with suspicion and distrust, many are ecstatic to have someone interested in their lives. These interviews bring new challenges. The moment that 14-year-old Hunter began speaking, I knew that focus was going to be a significant challenge in our conversation. While Hunter had older siblings, they were out of the house, so he lived alone with his mother, who worked long hours. I only had to mention the topic of attention for Hunter to describe his struggles with ADHD before bouncing off to talk about how difficult it is not having health insurance since his mother is in the country illegally. Before I could even ask another question, Hunter went off on a tangent about immigration and identity politics, telling me about reading "Ghettonation" and struggling with being the "whitest black guy you'll ever meet" and only wanting to be friends with smart people and deciding that "Outsourced" was a good TV show, because his Indian friends thought it was funny. While everything that came out of Hunter's mouth was fascinating—and it was very clear that he was a precocious teen starved for attention and support in his low-income community—ethnographic interviews are not simply unstructured conversations.

When teens are especially chatty, I sometimes have to interrupt them and structure the interview more intentionally. For example, with teens who have serious attention issues, I find that it is often valuable to switch topics regularly so that they follow my lead rather than going on their own tangents. When teens start going too far off-topic, I purposefully break the gaze and pretend to look at my list of questions; they typically trail off. Occasionally, I have to state explicitly that we need to stay on topic. But such an oppressive statement can destroy the trust that I have built; thus, I only do this when absolutely necessary to get control over the interview.

Interviewing teenagers is exhausting. When I leave an interview, I am completely depleted after having put all of my energy into being fully attentive to the teen. But my job is not done. After an interview, I turn on the recorder and do a brain dump on tape, highlighting what stood out and giving myself notes for what to look for in the transcript. This typically takes an additional 20 or so minutes after an interview. These oral notes serve as the basis for my field notes. Only then do I collapse. I have found that I can meaningfully do two interviews per day and, when absolutely necessary, can stomach three. But four is impossible—I cannot get anything meaningful from doing an interview when completely brain-dead. When I need to release my exhaustion or address the emotional pain that I feel after an interview, I drive my car out of earshot of other people and let out a primal scream. I have found that screaming, crying, and jumping around do wonders for helping me work through what I feel after an interview.

Living and Breathing Teen Culture

Getting into the field requires more than just setting up interviews. Even before arriving at a particular field site, I start reading the local paper and surfing websites about the community and schools. In doing so, I develop my ability to understand local references so that, say, when a teen talks about "the Tigers," I know they are talking about their archrival. When I am decompressing from a day of interviewing, I visit local establishments and talk to adults about the community. For example, while in Iowa, I spent every night at a bar that was clearly popular with locals. The bartender told me countless stories about the different community leaders and the local politics as I downed glass after glass of club soda and tipped him profusely. Upon leaving that town in Iowa, I got pulled over by a police officer for speeding. I decided to use that encounter as an opportunity, and, for three hours, the cop shared his perspective on life in Iowa (and why California, where I was residing, was the devil's land).

Immersing myself in pop culture, social media, and local communities is all a crucial part of collecting ethnographic data. Nevertheless, while I gain a lot from living and breathing teen culture, interviewing teens directly still plays the most important role in my fieldwork. The data that I collect from interviewing teens—grounded by observational data and situated in cultural theory—helps me understand when and why teens engage with technology and other cultural artifacts, although my processes for analyzing these data are outside of the scope of this chapter.

Teen life is increasingly intertwined with technology, but the traces that teens leave through technology are not rich enough to convey their practices. Much to the surprise of many adults, teens actually care about privacy (boyd and Hargittai 2010) and take measures to make accessible content meaningless to outside viewers (boyd and Marwick 2011). Getting at what teens do and why they do it requires triangulation and perseverance. It requires being embedded in teen culture and talking with teens face-to-face. Social media may increase the visibility of certain teen practices, but it does not capture the full story. More often than not, getting at the nuances of teen life in a networked era requires going back to foundational research methods.

Notes

1. This chapter benefited immensely from Mary Gray and Jordan Kraemer's brilliant suggestions. I am also deeply grateful to Christian Sandvig and Eszter Hargittai for their critical feedback. Finally, I would like to thank Mimi Ito, Jenna Burrell, Cori Hayden, Barrie Thorne, and Peter Lyman for their methodological guidance.

2. "Community" is a contested word, both online and off (Joseph 2002). Lacking a more adequate term, I'm using community to refer to a group of people and a space bounded by physical geography or personal relationships, a particular school or an organization.

References

Baym, N. K. 1993. Interpreting soap operas and creating community: Inside a computer-mediated fan culture. *Journal of Folklore Research 30* (2/3): 143–177.

Behar, R., and D. A. Gordon, ed. 1996. *Women Writing Culture*. Berkeley: University of California Press.

Bennett, A. 2004. Virtual subculture? Youth, identity and the Internet. In *After Subculture*, ed. A. Bennett and K. Kahn-Harris, 162–172. New York: Palgrave Macmillan.

Boellstorff, T. 2008. *Coming of Age in Second Life: An Anthropologist Explores the Virtually Human*. Princeton, NJ: Princeton University Press.

Bourgois, P., and J. Schonberg. 2009. *Righteous Dopefiend*. Berkeley: University of California Press.

boyd, d. 2006. A blogger's blog: Exploring the definition of a medium. Reconstruction, 6 (4).

boyd, d. 2008. None of this is real. In *Structures of Participation in Digital Culture,* ed. J. Karaganis, 132–157. New York: Social Science Research Council.

boyd, d., and E. Hargittai. 2010. Facebook and privacy settings: Who cares? *First Monday 15* (8).

boyd, d., and A. Marwick. 2011. Social privacy in networked publics: Teens' attitudes, practices, and strategies. Presented at Oxford Internet Institute Decade in Time Symposium, September 22.

Briggs, C. L. 1986. *Learning How to Ask*. Cambridge: Cambridge University Press.

Burrell, J. 2009. The field site as a network: A strategy for locating ethnographic research. *Field Methods 21* (2): 181–199.

Clifford, J., and G. E. Marcus, eds. 1986. *Writing Culture: The Poetics and Politics of Ethnography*. Berkeley, CA: UCLA Press.

Denzin, N. K. 1983. Interpretive interactionism. In *Beyond Method: Strategies for Social Research*, ed. G. Morgan, 129–146. Beverly Hills, CA: Sage.

Donath, J. and d. boyd. 2004. Public displays of connection. *BT Technology Journal 22* (4): 71–82.

Eckert, P. 1989. *Jocks and Burnouts: Social Categories and Identity in the High School*. New York: Teachers College Press.

Fine, G. A., and K. L. Sandstrom. 1988. *Knowing Children: Participant-Observation with Minors*. London: Sage.

Geertz, C. 1973. *Interpretation of Cultures*. New York: Basic Books.

Geertz, C. 1998. Deep hanging out. *New York Review of Books 45* (16): 69–72.

Glaser, B. G., and A. L. Strauss. 1967. *The Discovery of Grounded Theory: Strategies for Qualitative Research*. Chicago: Aldine.

Goldstein, D. M. 2003. *Laughter Out of Place: Race, Class, Violence, and Sexuality in a Rio Shantytown*. Berkeley: University of California Press.

Green, N. 1999. Disrupting the field: Virtual reality technologies and "multisited" ethnographic methods. *American Behavioral Scientist 43* (3): 409–421.

Hammersley, M. 1992. *What's Wrong with Ethnography? Methodological Explorations*. London: Routledge.

Haraway, D. J. 1991. *Simians, Cyborgs, and Women: The Reinvention of Nature*, 183–201. New York: Routledge.

Harrison, F. V. 2008. *Outsider Within: Reworking Anthropology in the Global Age*. Urbana: University of Illinois Press.

Haythornthwaite, C., and B. Wellman. 2002. The Internet in everyday life: An introduction. In *The Internet in Everyday Life*, ed. B. Wellman and C. Haythornthwaite, 3–41. London, UK: Blackwell.

Hine, C. 1998. *Virtual Ethnography*. London: Sage.

Hodkinson, P. 2002. *Goth: Identity, Style and Subculture*. Oxford, UK: Berg.

Joseph, M. 2002. *Against the Romance of Community*. Minneapolis: University of Minnesota Press.

Kelty, C. M. 2008. *Two Bits: The Cultural Significance of Free Software*. Durham, NC: Duke University Press.

Kendall, L. 2002. *Hanging Out in the Virtual Pub: Masculinities and Relationships Online*. Berkeley, CA: University of California Press.

Leander, K. M., and K. K. McKim. 2003. Tracing the everyday "sitings" of adolescents on the Internet: A strategic adaptation of ethnography across online and offline spaces. *Education Communication and Information 3* (2): 211–240.

Marcus, G. E. 1995. Ethnography in/of the world system: The emergence of multisited ethnography. *Annual Review of Anthropology 24*: 95–117.

Markham, A. N., and N. K. Baym. 2008. *Internet Inquiry: Conversations about Method*. London, UK: Sage.

Marwick, A. 2008. To catch a predator? The MySpace moral panic. *First Monday 13* (6), 3. http://www.uic.edu/htbin.cgiwrap/bin/ojs/index.php/fm/article/view/2152/1966). Retrieved December 3, 2008.

Miller, D., and D. Slater. 2000. *The Internet: An Ethnographic Approach*. London: Berg.

Orgad, S. 2008. How can researchers make sense of the issues involved in collecting and interpreting online and offline data? In *Internet Inquiry: Conversations about Method*, ed. A. N. Markham and N. K. Baym, 32–53. Los Angeles: Sage.

Pascoe, C. J. 2007. "What if a guy hits on you?" Intersections of gender, sexuality, and age in fieldwork with adolescents. In *Representing Youth*, ed. Amy L. Best. New York: New York University Press.

Raby, R. 2007. Across a great gulf? Conducting research with adolescents. In *Representing Youth*, ed. Amy L. Best. New York: New York University Press.

Rettberg, J. W. 2008. *Blogging*. Cambridge, UK: Polity Press.

Richman, A. 2007. The outsider lurking online. In *Representing Youth*, ed. Amy L. Best. New York: New York University Press.

Schofield, J. W. 2002. Increasing the generalizability of qualitative research. In *The Qualitative Researcher's Companion*, ed. A. M. Huberman and M. B. Miles, 171–203. London: Sage.

Spradley, J. 1979. *The Ethnographic Interview*. New York: Harcourt, Brace, Jovanovich.

Strathern, M. 2004. *Partial Connections*. Walnut Creek, CA: AltaMira Press.

Taylor, T. L. 2006. *Play Between Worlds: Exploring Online Game Culture*. Cambridge, MA: MIT Press.

Vissing, Y. 2007. A roof over their head: Applied research issues and dilemmas in the investigation of homeless children and youth. In *Representing Youth*, ed. Amy L. Best. New York: New York University Press.

Watson, G. 1987. Make me reflexive—but not yet: Strategies for managing essential reflexivity in ethnographic discourse. *Journal of Anthropological Research* 43:29–41.

Weiss, R. S. 1994. *Learning from Strangers: The Art and Method of Qualitative Interview Studies*. New York: Free Press.

Wilson, B. 2006. Ethnography, the Internet, and youth culture: Strategies for examining social resistance and "online-offline" relationships. *Canadian Journal of Education 29* (1): 307–328.

5

The Ethnographic Study of Visual Culture in the Age of Digitization

Paul M. Leonardi

Ethnography—from Greek ἔθνος, group of people, and γράφω, to write

Writing about a group of people is hard work. Even if the researcher vowed to take an objective stance and simply describe what people did, how they did it, and why they did it, he or she would eventually run into problems of representation. Whose perspective do you take? What activities are important enough to include in the ethnographic record? Who gets to decide what counts as an important activity? In grappling with these questions—either implicitly or explicitly—the ethnographer does more than produce an objective text about a group of people; he or she produces an account of culture that is, itself, culture-laden. Because no ethnographic account is ever completely straightforward, Van Maanen (1988) eloquently describes how readers of an ethnographic text learn as much about the culture in which the ethnographer is embedded through the choices he or she makes in the presentation and description of data as they do about the culture of the informants about whom the author writes.

This chapter is a cultural tale about how ethnographers ply their trade in writing about groups of people whose work constitutes a "visual culture" in an age where visual representations are rendered digitally. A visual culture is one in which people's work and social interactions are intimately connected to the drawings, sketches, animations, and other images they use daily. Put another way, in a visual culture, people traffic in representations; they use visual representations to persuade, to convey meaning, and, simply, to accomplish their work tasks. Members of a visual culture develop a shared visual literacy that dictates what visual representations are appropriate in their work, how and when those representations should be used, and how they should be interpreted. As Latour (1986: 9–10) suggests, "A new visual culture redefines both what it is to see and what there is to see."

I have spent the last several years as an ethnographer of the visual culture of engineering. Hence, my examples in this chapter will focus on engineering work, though I suspect that the arguments I make will be applicable to ethnographers who find themselves dealing with any occupation whose members' work is enabled and constrained by their use of visual representations. Over the last two decades, numerous authors have described engineering as an increasingly prime example of a visual culture (Bucciarelli 1994, 2002; Collins 2003; Downey 1998; Ewenstein and Whyte 2009; Fleischer and Liker 1992; Henderson 1999; Sims 1999; Vaughan 1996; Vinck 2003). Engineers do not simply work with drawings, plans, and sketches; rather, they think with and think through them, they communicate with other engineers by modifying them, and they develop engineering knowledge by studying and experimenting with them. Interaction with representations of physical systems so permeates the work of most contemporary engineers that Henderson (1999: 27–28) writes, "The visual culture of engineers is not made up of school-learned drafting conventions but rather the everyday practices of sketching, drawing, and drafting that construct their visual culture—a visual culture that in turn constructs what and how design engineers see."

Today, it is unlikely that a researcher would enter an engineering organization and see blueprints or sketches strewn across tables and desks. In fact, on my first visit to an engineering organization as a field researcher, I was amazed by the lack of paper in the office. What I saw, instead, was the back of a lot of heads. Engineers were seated in front of their computers staring at digitized drawings, sketches, and animations on the screen. Occasionally, I saw two or more engineers huddled around one computer, all looking at the same image on one person's screen. The visual representations of physical objects (like an engine) or physical processes (like a car crash) with which contemporary engineers work are almost exclusively digital. To be sure, many scholars have documented how engineers frequently work with digitized drawings as opposed to paper and pencil drawings (Adler 1990; Bechky 2003; Liker, Haddad, and Karlin 1999; Malhotra et al. 2001), and much recent research has documented engineers' turn toward the use of computer-based simulations (most often in three dimensions) to make recommendations for the performance of physical systems (Boland, Lyytinen, and Yoo 2007; Carlile 2004; Dodgson, Gann, and Salter 2007; Leonardi and Bailey 2008). Authors like Turkle (2009),Loukissas (2009), and Bailey, Leonardi, and Barley (2012) argue that the shift toward digitization in engineering design and analysis portends deep changes in not only how engineers work, but what they know and how they know it. In short, understanding how engineers and other technical workers make the shift to a world of digital, visual representations may be key to explaining society's transition from a mechanical to a computational infrastructure.

For ethnographers of visual culture, digitization poses new challenges. This chapter is focused on discussing how field researchers can deal with some of the issues of studying visual culture in the age of digitization. My goal is to examine how an ethnographer might enter a physical space like an office or a testing facility and observe, document, and analyze people's interactions with digital artifacts in those settings. I am not, in this chapter, concerned with ethnographies of digital spaces, like social network sites, games like World of Warcraft, or virtual worlds like Second Life. For discussions of how ethnographers deal with the particularities of data collection in these digital spaces, I recommend that the interested reader consult books by Boellstorff (2010), Nardi (2010), and Pearce (2009).

I divide this chapter into three parts. The first part focuses on issues of access to the site. How does one gain approval from a university's institutional review board and negotiate entrée to a site where individuals work intensively with digital artifacts? The second part focuses on observation and analysis. How does a researcher record people's interactions with visual representations with which they work on their computers? And how can these representations be used in data analysis? Finally, the third section explores the difficult job of writing and publishing one's findings based on such data.

Rather than discuss several different research projects, I will constrain my focus to only one and interrogate it deeply. The experience on which I draw in this chapter comes from my research into the development, implementation, and use of a new computer-simulation technology for crashworthiness engineering work at Autoworks (a pseudonym), a major automaker located in the United States. Crashworthiness (a vehicle's ability to absorb energy through structural deformation) is assessed by

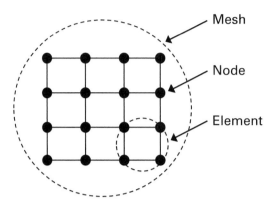

Figure 5.1
Relationship between nodes, elements, and mesh in finite element analysis.

engineers who conduct physical crash tests and computer simulations. Because the cost of administering and recording the data for physical crash tests (building a prototype vehicle, loading it with instrumentation, crashing it into an object, and interpreting the findings) takes so long, Autoworks encourages its engineers to use finite element simulation models to predict a vehicle's crashworthiness and provide recommendations for how a vehicle structure can be changed to increase performance in an impact. Finite element analysis is a computational technique that divides the actual geometry of a part into a bounded (hence finite) collection of discrete elements. The elements are joined together by shared nodes. Nodes are the locations where values of unknowns (usually displacements) are approximated. This collection of nodes and elements is commonly called a "mesh" (see figure 5.1).

The vast majority of an engineer's time is spent in iterative cycles of building finite element simulation models, analyzing their performance, and making suggestions for changes in design. To reduce the time and effort it took engineers to set up and analyze simulation models, engineers in Autoworks' research and development (R&D) labs developed a new software tool called CrashLab. CrashLab is used for preprocessing (setting up mesh models in ways that can be analyzed by a solver to produce desired results[1]) the finite element models that safety and crashworthiness engineers use to make predictions about how a vehicle will respond in a crash. The idea for CrashLab emerged out of Autoworks' R&D

organization in 1995. After nearly 10 years of developmental work, CrashLab was deployed into the user community in September 2005. I followed the effects that CrashLab had on engineers' work from its time of deployment through 2007. The main research question of the study was as follows: how do organizations and technologies co-evolve through activities of development, implementation, and use?

Data on CrashLab and the work system in which it was embedded were obtained through the use of ethnographic techniques. I spent nine full months over a two-year period (2004–2006) conducting interviews and observations with people who were involved in all aspects of Crash-Lab's lifecycle. I began by identifying key informants I knew were involved in CrashLab's development, and through these interviews acquired the names of others who were also involved. Fortunately, Autoworks maintained a very detailed and accurate database of employee contact information and I was able to use this database to track down informants even if they had moved into new positions within the company. I conducted interviews with members of five different organizations within Autoworks. Additionally, I conducted interviews with informants in three technology supplier organizations who helped, at various points in time, to build CrashLab. I also conducted several interviews with other individuals who were involved with CrashLab but who were not members of any of these organizations, such as Autoworks senior management, consultants from other supplier firms, and professors at nearby universities. In total, I conducted 58 interviews with people involved in changing CrashLab's features.

I also collected data on the work of crashworthiness engineers before CrashLab was implemented, the activities of developers, trainers, and managers during implementation, and the work of engineers after Crash-Lab was implemented. During each of these activities I utilized four primary data sources: Observations made of informants at work, artifacts that informants produced or used in their work (e.g., screenshots of computer simulations, test request forms, best-practice guidelines), interviews conducted with informants about their work, and logs kept by informants tracking their use of CrashLab. These data collection methods resulted in 134 observations (each of which was three hours or more in duration) with crashworthiness engineers, 51 interviews with engineers who used CrashLab, 17 additional interviews of people such as managers and implementers who were also in some way involved with CrashLab, and more than 500 digital artifacts used by engineers. My analyses of these data have resulted in several publications (Leonardi 2009, 2010a, 2010b, 2011a, 2011b).

Access

In any workplace ethnography, the researcher's access to the phenomena he or she wishes to study is regulated by at least three gatekeepers: The university's Institutional Review Board (IRB), the management or leadership of the organization under study, and the individuals who actually conduct the work. Reaching an agreement for access to the research site through each of these three gatekeepers requires a distinct approach. Although one might think that the IRB is the place to begin negotiating access, I would argue that it is really in the researcher's best interest to start with the organization's management. Without the consent of management, all the IRB approval in the world will do little good. Thus, there is little point to devote one's efforts to the IRB process unless the researcher knows that he or she will be able to "get in" the door at the organization. For this reason, I begin by discussing the negotiation of access with the organization of interest.

The Organization

Autoworks is a large company. It has more than 300,000 employees spread across engineering, financial, and manufacturing centers around the globe. Thinking about gaining access to a company of this size can be quite daunting. Of course, the ideal strategy would be to solicit help from the CEO and have him or her open doors for you all the way down to the people you would like to observe. Like most researchers, I do not hobnob with too many CEOs, especially those who run multibillion-dollar companies, so this approach was not feasible. One strategy I have often used to great success is to begin by finding somebody in the organization's R&D labs. Why the R&D labs? Well, in most firms, members of R&D typically share what Dougherty (1992) calls a "thought world" with the researcher. Unlike individuals in sales, marketing, advertising, product development, finance, and so on, individuals who work in corporate research are devoted to advancing science. They hope, of course, that their research will culminate in useful and profitable products for the company. But this goal notwithstanding, they understand what it is that you are after because they are often in the same shoes. Finding a member of R&D who understands the principles of academic research and who is excited about the topic you are interested in exploring is a solid way to get your foot in the door at the organization.

Many corporate R&D labs have internship and fellowship programs available for outside researchers. These programs are centrally administered and provide outside researchers with two very important items (I will come back to these later): ID badges and email addresses. From their perspective, internship and fellowship programs are great ways of tapping talent at relatively low cost. From the researcher's perspective, affiliation with one of these programs provides institutional legitimacy (or insider-ness) that is hard to achieve by any other means.

My route into Autoworks came through the company's R&D labs, with which my university had an ongoing relationship. After some investigation around campus, I found a mechanical engineering professor (not at all my discipline) who had close relationships with people in Autoworks' R&D labs. I met with this professor and outlined my research objectives. It was clear that he had no clue what I was talking about or what it meant to conduct an ethnography. He listened politely and, by the end of our hour-long conversation, he seemed to understand, generally, what I wanted to study. He told me that the topic sounded interesting, but that he would not make the contact for me within R&D because he had made a connection for another student whom he did not know well, the student performed very poorly, and his relationship with key players in Autoworks' R&D was damaged as a result.

I understood his concerns and took it upon myself to show him that I was trustworthy. To do that, I procured letters from two organizations at which I had conducted ethnographic research in the past. Both letters spoke to the fact that I was a responsible researcher, and each letter writer mentioned that they thought more highly of the university and its capabilities once I had finished my research project. I sent these letters to the mechanical engineering professor, and, apparently, they were enough to persuade him to take a gamble on me. Two days after I sent the letters to him, he copied me on an email in which he introduced me to his contact at Autoworks. With that initial contact in hand, I navigated to a researcher who was a director of R&D's "work systems group"—a group that was responsible for improving engineering process at Autoworks, as opposed to developing new technologies for cars and trucks (e.g., GPS devices or airbags). Through a series of phone calls and formal applications with the director of the work systems group, I eventually wound up as an R&D "intern" for a six-month stint. The agreement I made to secure this internship was that I could study the topics in which I was interested, but I had to provide monthly reports to R&D and to the product development groups I studied that summarized my findings and made recommendations for how those groups could improve their work processes. I reasoned that these deliverables were a fair trade for access to an interesting research setting.

The central problem with entrée to the organization through R&D, however, is that because they are engaged in research and often do not contribute directly to the firm's profits, the research labs are often low-status players in the corporate environment (Thomas 1994; Workman 1995). For this reason, at most firms, R&D cannot simply say, "We're studying this process. We'll start observing you next week." Instead, R&D has to ask permission to conduct a study and find a "project champion" (this is what Autoworks called it) within a product development division who will help negotiate access to the people with whom you really want to spend time.

The reason why I was so keen to conduct this study at Autoworks was that I had seen a presentation at my university in which an R&D engineer discussed a new simulation technology under development at the company and expected to be released to the crashworthiness engineering community soon. Both the technology and the timeframe of its release sounded ideal. The technology was supposed to "revolutionize" crashworthiness engineering work by automating simulation analyses, and it was in its final months of development and soon to be deployed. Thus, if I could follow this technology, I would be able to witness not only part of its development, but its implementation and use, too. Upon arriving at Autoworks, I did some initial leg work to make sure the technology was going to be implemented when it was supposed to be and that crashworthiness engineering was the right organization to observe. After verifying that the technology, its time frame, and its user community would be ideal for the study, I sought out a "project champion"—someone who could see the benefit of my study and would ensure I was able to carry it out.

The project champion I identified was the director of Autoworks' Safety and Crashworthiness division. To convince this director to let me study his engineers, I had to give a series of presentations in which I discussed my research question and the methods I would use, and, most importantly, described what benefit all of this research would be to the division. The trickiest item was the explanation of data collection. I explained to the directors that I would sit behind engineers as they worked. I explained that I would, with their permission, audio record their dialogue with each other and things they said out loud. I described how I would follow the engineer I was observing to meetings and to tests at the proving grounds. No one objected to any of these methods. But when I said I would be asking engineers for screenshots of the computer-models with which they worked and copies of PowerPoint presentations they prepared to summarize their recommendations, the directors became very uneasy. Questions surfaced about whether or not I would leak confidential information to competitors. (I thought about joking that the sales data suggested no one would be interested in stealing their designs, but I thought this joke would be unwise.) Instead, I discussed how I would only ask for copies of digital artifacts that were of interest for the project, and I would make sure that those artifacts had images or descriptions that were generic enough so that outsiders could not identify the vehicle they referenced. That calmed nerves some, but not a lot. The saving grace came when I explained to them that I was being employed by Autoworks as an official "intern" and as part of the internship process I had to sign nondisclosure agreements for protected company information. I also assured them that my internship "boss" (the director of the R&D work systems group) had the right to review any paper that I published from the data I collected at Autoworks. I am confident that it was because I was a (temporary) "inside man" that the directors finally agreed to allow me to collect digital artifacts from the engineers I studied.

The Institutional Review Board

After lining up access at the field site, the researcher must next secure approval for the study through his or her university's institutional review board. IRB applications can be, at times, quite onerous. I have found that once I have negotiated access to the site I wish to study and have received a letter from the site endorsing the study, the IRB process is much more manageable. Sometimes, an observational study like the one I conducted at Autoworks can even qualify for an exempt review if that support letter from the organization is presented as part of the application. An exempt review (as opposed to an expedited review) means that only one member from the IRB has to review the application; the application does not have to undergo deliberation at the monthly board meeting. The upshot is that exempt reviews result in faster decisions and typically require less revision than an expedited or full review. Research projects qualify for exempt review if they undertake observation in "public settings" and the names of the informants are not recorded anywhere in the observer's notes, in legends or keys made of those notes, or on an informed consent form. The letter from the organization helps to establish the research site as a "public setting," because the researcher is now invited into a community and can observe people at work, just as one's coworkers can. Another advantage of an exempt status through IRB is that the researcher must only secure "verbal consent" from the informants, as opposed to formal "written consent," which must be documented on an informed consent form. The verbal consent is an enormous advantage for a workplace field study. On more than one occasion, I have found myself confronted with an informant who refused to read or sign a written consent form, but was happy to be observed. To avoid this situation, it is much easier to simply read the informant a quick statement, ask for their verbal consent, and move on.

I can only imagine the alarm bells that would sound if I wrote on my application to the university's IRB that I would be collecting screenshots and PowerPoint presentations from my informants. How would I explain to them the delicate negotiations that occurred with the director of the Safety and Crashworthiness division? Would it suffice to say that I signed a nondisclosure agreement as part of my "internship" papers? I do not know with certainty the answers to these questions, but I suspect that I would not like those answers if I heard them. When it comes time in the IRB application to write about the collection of digital artifacts, I usually indicate my plan for the collection of these data sources by writing something like: "I plan to collect work artifacts used by informants if they wish to share them. I will only collect artifacts that do not identify the informant in any way. These artifacts will be stored either in a locked cabinet in the researcher's office or on a password protected, non-networked hard drive that is kept in the researcher's locked office." Such phrasing is truthful, but a bit vague. I have never received a question from an IRB (on the Autoworks study or any other) using this language.

The Worker

With IRB access secured, travel plans made, and the houseplants watered, the researcher can finally go "into the field" to conduct the long-anticipated research. The problem, at this point, is that although management may endorse your study and even announce to workers that they should participate in it (as they did at Autoworks), workers still must be convinced that you are not a threat to their productivity. This is a valid concern. Informants typically have a lot to do. If they spend time during their day talking with researchers, they might not complete all of their assigned tasks. Not completing tasks on schedule could force them to stay late at work to catch up, which disrupts personal time, or it could get them in trouble with the boss. Typically, these fears on the part of the worker can be easily overcome in the first few minutes of observation. The more difficult challenge is convincing the worker that you are really interested in learning *how* he or she works and that you are not interested in how they could work *better*. I often experienced this latter concern at Autoworks, and it slowed my initial research progress.

For many organizations that were born during the second industrial revolution, time and motion studies are still a fresh memory. Time and motion studies are the most popular byproduct of America's first major business fad: scientific management.[2] This new orientation toward work was promoted by efficiency experts of the day, most notably Fredrick Taylor (1911/1998) and Frank Gilbreth (1911/1993). In the mid-to-late 1800s, U.S. industrial enterprise was heavily dependent upon the knowledge and skills of craft workers (Thompson 1967). Craft workers spent years learning a particular trade and taught that trade to apprentices and others who were willing and able to learn. As Gilbreth (1911/1993: 94) observed, in the mode of craft production, "all excellent methods or means were held as 'trade secrets' sometimes lost to the world for generations until rediscovered." From an organizational management perspective, the idea that one person would hold both the knowledge and skill to complete a particular task proved problematic, because productivity depended entirely on that worker and few others like him or her. With increase in mass production in the United States, craftwork was increasingly proving not only impractical, but also burdensome to management, who, without knowledge of the craft themselves, were beholden to the worker's time constraints and wage demands.

With the development of scientific management, Taylor aimed to solve these problems. He suggested that by extracting the knowledge required for a specific task from a worker, a management scientist could examine, evaluate, modify, improve, and teach it to countless others. Not only did Taylor claim that an individual who had the time to evaluate a task could improve it more effectively than someone performing the task, he also asserted that:

In almost all of the mechanic arts the science which underlies each act of each workman is so great and amounts to so much that the workman who is best suited to actually doing the work is incapable of fully understanding this science, without the guidance and help of those who are working with him or over him. (Taylor 1911/1998: 9)

To extract knowledge from the worker and evaluate the performance of that work, Taylor and Gilbreth, among others, pioneered a method that would become known as the "time and motion study." The method was quite simple but powerful in its effects. The observer, typically someone unfamiliar with the work of the laborer, would directly observe the laborer in action, recording his every movement and timing how long he took to perform those movements. Learning the details of a job and discerning the possibilities for improving it involved investing an enormous amount of time. The observer (or scientific manager) had to watch the laborer perform an activity enough times to know that, as Taylor suggested, the laborer was not simply "putting on a front" for the observer. Moreover, the observer had to watch multiple laborers in order to determine which actions constituted "best practices." Once the data collection phase was complete, the observer retreated from the shop floor or construction site to his office to analyze the findings. Thus, as Gilbreth (1911/1993) suggested, the methodology of a time and motion study should include both direct observation and analysis that compares practices across a variety of workers to make recommendations for optimal performance of work. With such an analysis complete, the scientific manager would not only have abstracted from the worker the knowledge necessary to perform a task, but could also modify the practice to improve performance and efficiency and teach it to new workers.

During my first few days at Autoworks, before informants understood why I was observing their work, they considered my interests suspicious. In fact, many engineers thought I was in their midst sent by management to perform a time and motion study. One of my first interactions with an informant (I) illustrated these concerns and the misconceptions informants had about why someone would want to watch them work:

I: *Is this a time and motion study?*

Me: *No, it's not a time and motion study.*

I: *So you're not like Fredrick Taylor or something?*

Me: *No, I'm just here to learn about your work.*

I: *I'm sorry.*

Me: *Why is that?*

I: *Because you're going to be bored.*

Me: *Well I don't know anything about crashworthiness work, so it will all be exciting for me.*

I: *Even if I'm just optimizing element sizes?*

Me: *See, that sounds exciting already.*

I: *What if I just check my email?*

Me: *Well, will you let me read it with you?*

I: *Sure.*

Me: *Then that will be exciting, too.*

I: *Will you follow me to the bathroom?*

Me: *Okay, the excitement's gone now.*

I: *[laughing] So, you don't have a stop watch, right?*

Me: *[laughing] Do you want to check my bag?*

I: *No, I'm just kidding. So you said this was, what did you call it?*

Me: *An ethnography.*

I: *Oh, like an anthropologist.*

Clearly, the concept of ethnography was more foreign to engineers at Autoworks than that of a time and motion study. Informants were certainly justified in their confusion, since, from the point of view of the person who is being observed, the ethnography does look remarkably like a time and motion study. Within the anthropological tradition, the basis for any ethnography is fieldwork. Pioneers of the method, such as Malinowski (1922) and Mead (1928), suggested that to understand the nature of a social system, researchers had to immerse themselves in the daily actions of those they were studying. Malinowski went to the archipelagos of New Guinea and Mead to Samoa to spend a considerable amount of time living and working with the individuals they were studying. Thus, like that of the scientific manager, the ethnographer's method involves observing (Spradley 1980), documenting (Van Maanen 1988), and analyzing (Lofland and Lofland 1995) the routine actions of those under study. While most pundits argue that the most important tool in the ethnographer's toolkit is his notebook, in which he writes field notes to record his observations, many researchers are now also finding value in collecting data in other ways, such as through the acquisition of digital artifacts.

I have found that the best way to conquer these misconceptions, or the ignorance, surrounding the goals of an ethnographic study is to do a really good job with the first person you observe. Make them feel comfortable around you. Do not ask too many questions that distract them from their work. And, most importantly, listen. People love to talk about their work, and they rarely have an audience content to listen to them do so. During my first observations at a site like Autoworks, listening well proved tremendously advantageous. Even though I was tempted to ask questions in my first observations because there were things I did not understand, I refrained. I listened when the informant talked and probed only in the areas in which he most clearly wanted to discuss. I have found that by following this practice, informants warm up to the researcher quite quickly. They tell their coworkers "this observation thing is not so bad," and others become interested in being observed. If using this strategy, the researcher should plan that the first few observations will be directed at generating goodwill and buy-in from informants, and not necessarily collecting the highest-quality data.

Observation and Analysis

Why spend so much time observing?

Observation of people conducting routine activities lies at the core of the ethnographic method (Barley 1990a; Fine 1993; Geertz 1973; Lofland and Lofland 1995; Spradley 1980). Organizational ethnographers typically make two assumptions about people's engagement with their work that undergirds support of observation. The first assumption is that although interviews are useful for uncovering attitudes and beliefs about work and for eliciting histories of and people's interpretations of events, direct observation is necessary to capture a holistic understanding of the work culture in which people are embedded. Research has repeatedly shown that people have a difficult time articulating what work they do and how they do it (Collins 1974; Dreyfus and Dreyfus 1986; Orr 1996). Therefore, people's actual conduct of work is the most revealing source of data an ethnographer can collect about the contours of a social system. Individuals' actions produce and perpetuate a social system, but they are also influenced by it. Therefore, observing the actions people take to complete their work, when they take those actions, and how those actions are performed not only provides a descriptive understanding of "how" people work, but it can also help explain "why" they work in certain ways.

The second assumption is that an informant who is being observed in an organizational context performs certain actions because he or she believes such actions are necessary to fulfill his or her work role. In this sense, people's actions do not lie. Although an informant may inadvertently or even purposefully alter his or her actions when under the watch of the ethnographer, people are notoriously bad at maintaining a facade for long. They are bad at it because trying to perform actions in ways that violate a normal routine often proves to be too much of a cognitive load for people to handle (Louis and Sutton 1991) and because, at some point, they have to get their work done and therefore cannot afford to dissimulate their practice for long (Roy 1959). The upshot is that even though they know they are being watched, people act the way they have to in order to get their jobs done. Howard Becker (1996: 62) provides a compelling example:

When we watch someone as they work in their usual work setting ... we cannot insulate them from the consequences of their actions. On the contrary, they have to take the rap for what they do, just as they ordinarily do in everyday life. An example: when I was observing college undergraduates, I sometimes went to classes with them. On one occasion, an instructor announced a surprise quiz for which the student I was accompanying that day, a goof-off, was totally unprepared. Sitting nearby, I could easily see him leaning over and copying answers from someone he hoped knew more than he did. He was embarrassed by my seeing him, but the embarrassment didn't stop him copying, because the consequences of failing the test (this was at a time when flunking out of school could lead to being drafted, and maybe being killed in combat) were a lot worse than my potentially lowered opinion of him. He apologized and made excuses later, but he did it.

In fact, most ethnographers seem to agree that, when in their work settings, even the informants who prove most theatrical after meeting the researcher slip back into their normal set of actions after about 30 minutes of observation. Thus, long, repeated stints of observation can reliably capture the "normal" and "routine" actions informants engage in to accomplish their work.

I typically capture the interactions that occur in each observation in a number of ways. I sit behind the informants at their desks while they work, and I follow them when they go to meetings and talk informally with colleagues. I accompany informants, like the engineers at Autoworks, to places like the corporate proving grounds to watch physical crash tests, and I also go along with them to vehicle tear-downs, where they are able to inspect the state of the parts after a physical test. During all of these activities I take notes on my small laptop computer, indicating the types of activities the informants are conducting, why are conducting them, and with whom or what they are interacting. Additionally, I record talk occurring during all observations on a digital audio recorder. Using audio recordings allowed me to document the conversations informants have and to capture their personal thoughts about different matters, which I encourage them to speak out loud as they work. I also let the audio recorder run when engineers are working silently at their computers. All of the audio recordings are later transcribed verbatim. I integrate these audio recordings of dialogue with the field notes. By using the digital time stamp on the audio recorder in conjunction with the observation records, I am able to document how long informants work on particular tasks. The combined observation records (field notes with corresponding dialogue) for one observation are normally between 20 and 30 pages of single-spaced text. I have found that attending to all the details of an engineer's work typically makes it difficult to observe longer than three or four hours a day.

Why collect digital artifacts?

For ethnographic data collection of a visual culture, it is also important to obtain the copies of the digital artifacts with which informants work. Why not just describe the documents in the field notes? The example below helps to illustrate why securing the actual digital representations is so important.

I had spent two months at Autoworks trying to understand, from the engineers' perspective, why they *needed* and *wanted* a new technology like CrashLab. At the beginning of my third month, I began to see a pattern in my observations that no one had articulated explicitly in any of the interviews I conducted. At Autoworks, design engineers (DEs) were responsible for generating the architectural drawings for a few parts for which they were fully responsible, but crashworthiness engineers functioned in an integration capacity. When it came time for an engineer to test a vehicle's crashworthiness via simulation, he or she accessed the corporate parts database, found the computer-aided drafting (CAD) files for all of the parts that needed to be included in the model, and then assembled all of the parts into a model representing the complete vehicle.

DEs drafted and updated parts at many different junctures in the engineering process. A DE responsible for part A might change the shape of his or her part, while another DE, responsible for part B, might not. If the changes in the shape of part A made the part larger, it might then infringe on the space in which part B was located. If this happened, the DE responsible for part B would also have to redesign his or her part to accommodate the changes in part A. In a perfect world, a change in part A's design would instantly trigger a series of changes to all of the other affected parts. However, many times DEs did not communicate with each other about changes in their parts, and they were often even unaware that changing a part would affect the design of another. As a result, when crashworthiness engineers went to download parts from the shared database, not all parts were in the same stage of development. As one engineer observed:

A lot of times I get the parts ready to assemble, and I find out that they don't fit. Like two parts are occupying the same vehicle coordinates. That can't happen.

Different matter can't occupy the same space. You know? So obviously something is wrong. One DE updated one part and, who knows why, but the other DEs didn't update their parts to match. So you have maybe two or three parts all intersecting and overlapping by maybe 10 or 20 millimeters. That's a problem that happens a lot.

In the math-based environment of simulation, two parts can occupy the same space in a coordinate system, but in a physical environment that is not feasible. If this occurred, a crashworthiness engineer would discover, to his or her dismay, that the parts overlapped one other.

Many of the models that crashworthiness engineers assembled using CAD files from the shared database contained overlapping—or "penetrating"—parts, which significantly affected the solver's ability to predict the results of a particular test. If a penetration was substantial, the solver would return an error message indicating that it could not solve the model until the overlapping parts were fixed. If a penetration was minor (just a few millimeters), the solver most likely would be unable to detect it, and the software would solve the model anyway. In that case, the simulation would produce results that could not be achieved in a real-world test scenario, because in the physical world, as the crashworthiness engineer I quote above observed, two parts cannot occupy the same space. To assure a high degree of correlation between simulation and test, it was essential for engineers to fix any major penetrations in their models that would affect their results. Identifying and resolving overlapping parts required, like so many other engineering practices, a series of trade-offs. Fixing every penetration in a model could take an engineer upward of a week— if he or she could even identify them all.

But penetrations did not always occur because of the lack of communication among DEs. Once a version of a particular part was drafted in CAD, the DE would place the electronic file on the shared server for the crashworthiness engineer to download. Engineers opened the CAD files and exported the line data (which represents the geometry of the part) into a finite element preprocessing tool. With these tools, engineers could discretize CAD geometry into finite elements, producing a workable mesh for analysis. Due to preprocessors' discretization limits in computational power and constraints on the shapes elements could take, it was often difficult for an engineer to create a mesh that followed the geometry of a part with complete accuracy.[3] Instead, most meshes looked similar to the

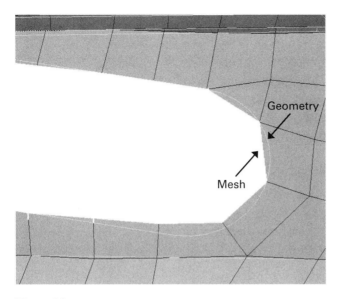

Figure 5.2
Discrepancy between mesh and geometry (potential cause of part penetration).

mesh of the flange presented in figure 5.2. In this particular example, the geometry of the flange (indicated by a thin, light-colored line) specifies a hole in the center of the part. When generating the shapes of the elements, the preprocessor is not capable of exactly following the curvature of the hole, so the mesh extends past the geometry into what should be open space. When examining one part on its own, separate from the others in the system, the discrepancy between geometry and mesh that resulted from the discretization of a CAD file into a finite element file did not present much of a problem. However, when it came time to assemble a complete vehicle model, the hole in the flange had to be filled by another part. Since the mesh extended past the geometry of the flange, there was likely a penetration with whatever part was placed into the hole. Depending on the location, such a penetration could significantly alter the results of the analysis, making correlation between simulation and test (in which the flange and the part going through its hole could not physically occupy the same space as it could in a math model) difficult to achieve.

What I discovered during my observations was that DEs and crashworthiness engineers often got into fights with each other over part penetrations. Crashworthiness engineers would blame DEs for not enacting some version-control mechanisms for their parts, and DEs would blame crashworthiness engineers for doing a sloppy job converting CAD drawings to finite element meshes. From my observations, I knew that this "blame game" caused many problems at occupational boundaries. For example, engineers from one occupation would blame engineers from another for delaying the launch of a vehicle or for causing the vehicle to fail critical government tests. What was unclear, however, was whether or not the blame that each group foisted upon the other was indeed warranted. Explaining how penetrations arose and whether people were justified in assigning blame would, eventually, turn out to be very important in predicting whether engineers would use the new CrashLab technology. Collecting digital artifacts like the one in figure 5.2 proved necessary, later during analysis, to make an empirical statement about the proportionality of blame to causes of part penetrations. By having copies of the parts in my database, I was able to locate instances in the field notes where blame occurred, and then index instances of blame to particular screenshots of parts. I could then analyze those parts, like the flange in figure 5.2, to determine whether the penetration occurred because of mesh translation or poor version control. Without these images, this analysis would not have been possible, and I would not have been able to explain a crucial factor for why CrashLab was accepted by some groups and rejected by others.

To index field notes to digital artifacts requires a great deal of discipline in the writing up of field notes. The method I have found most successful is illustrated in figures 5.3a, b, and c. Figure 5.3a is an excerpt from the observation record of two engineers at work: Damen and Balaji. This excerpt shows text taken from field notes interspersed with lines of dialogue transcribed from digital audio recordings. The field notes were taken in real time on my laptop as informants worked, and the dialogue was captured with a digital audio recorder. At the end of the day, I transcribed the audio and inserted it into the appropriate location in the field notes. Each time an informant uses an artifact, a note is made in the observation record indexing that particular artifact. Figure 5.3b is a reproduction of a printed file from a Microsoft Excel spreadsheet, and figure 5.3c is a screenshot of a part the engineers were working with.

To move easily between the observation record and the digital artifact, I place all of the artifacts into a database (which I usually get a research

12:25

Damon picks up a piece of paper off the table to the left of his monitor. The paper has a table on it. There are four columns and over ten rows. There is handwriting along the right side of the table. [See Att. # 5]

Me: What's on that piece of paper?
D: It's a matrix of the iterations. I'm just making sure I have all the changes necessary for a specific run.
Me: Are these runs you still have to do, or ones you have done already?
D: I've done [he counts with his finger] five. Today Bilaji did the bottom four and there are five in the middle I'm preparing. It just happened that these three are very easy to do once you get the first one done. The second one's kind of stand alone. The next four depend on the first two, so they kind of come in bunches.

Damon turns back to his computer. He moves through several menus at the bottom of the Hypermesh screen. He brings up a new image. The images of the CBS bar, with two inserts attached to the brackets Damon has been welding on. [See Att. #6]

12:30 pm

Damon calls over to Balaji who is working at his computer in the adjoining cube.

D: Hey Bilaji, these two are almost done. Do want to give me a control file or do you want me to create it.
B: Take it from the V-store.
D: Just grab one?
B: Yes.
D: Once I do it can I put it back in?

Damon and Bilaji swivel in their chairs to face each other. Bilaji picks up a piece of paper off his desk. It appears to be the same paper Damon has. They both hold their papers low over their laps and look down at them. Although they face each other, they do not look up. Bilaji glances up at Damon occasionally, but Damon remains looking down.

B: Just put it from where the rest are.
D: That way they'll be in the same spot.
B: Yes.
D: In 4a, what's the difference between that and 2b?
B: 2b is going to be [missing] brace.
D: Yes.
B: Yeah. Don't worry about 4a. Did you finish 4a?
D: No, because –
B: Don't worry about 4a. You can call this point 7. See, that's the one I yesterday deleted the footprint.
D: How about I called it 4a then so there's no 2b.
B: Yeah.
D: So 4a is 0 point 7. [Writes on the piece of paper]
B: Correct. Now you see the bottom two ones?
D: The bottom two? Yes.
B: I submitted those yesterday where I modified that.
D: Do you want it modified? 4a?
B: Probably not. I think we get enough information about this.
D: Because all you did was to cut a flange.
B: Yeah, I cut the footprint really close to the rail. I deleted those elements too.
D: It's up to you.
B: I think we'll get enough information from the rest. Make it point 7 and see if it [missing].
D: Ok. Hey, all the jobs we submitted yesterday went in. None of them crashed.
B: No, that's good.
D: Yeah.

Figure 5.3a
Excerpt from completed observation record.

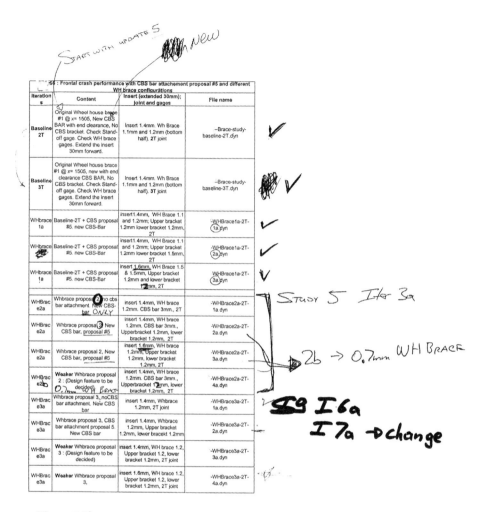

Figure 5.3b
Photo copy of attachment 5.

assistant from computer science to create). I then place hyperlinks in the observation record that will transport the researcher to the artifact in the "artifact database." In this way, I am able to keep close tabs on both the action and the artifacts that help comprise the action.[4] By arranging observation records and artifacts in this way, the analysis of the image presented in figure 5.2 is made possible.

By taking such care to integrate field notes, recorded dialogue, and digital artifacts into a single observation record, the researcher is poised

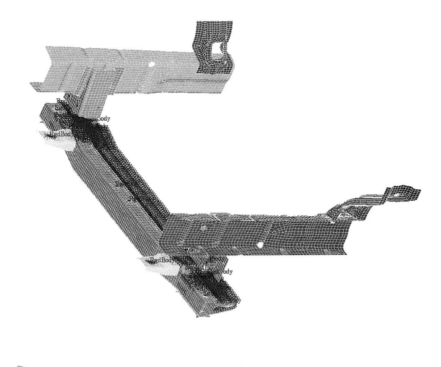

Figure 5.3c
Screenshot of attachment 5.

for a more fine-grained and trenchant analysis of ethnographic data than a simple interpretive coding allows (see, for discussion, Lincoln and Guba 1985; Taylor and Trujillo 2001). Such "analness," as my students sometimes call it, allows the researcher to engage in an "action approach" to data analysis. Such an approach takes as its primary unit of analysis the actions informants take as they conduct their work.

Actions are small but concrete types of behavior. Reading an error message from a computer screen is an action; calling someone on the phone is an action; placing an accelerometer on a model is an action; and submitting a math model to a solver is an action. Actions can be observed directly and recorded by taking notes. Once they are in written form, they can be read, their text can be pointed to, and they can be given a code. Concrete actions can be grouped together into events—the collection of multiple, smaller actions (Becker et al. 1961: 26–28). Thus, the actions of picking up a piece of paper and calling someone on the phone can be grouped into a trying-to-discover-why-a-model-bombed-out event, just as the actions of strategically placing an accelerometer and submitting a model to a solver can be grouped into a preprocessing-a-model event. These events can then be subjected to the kinds of techniques of analysis (e.g., Strauss and Corbin 1998) that allow the researcher to understand why they occur, what their consequences are, and how they connect to other events.

What is the point of such a detailed coding of actions? Triangulation. Becker (1958: 656) suggests that if observations are coded at the level of actions, they can be standardized in a form "capable of being transformed into legitimate statistical data." Counting the number of actions taken by informants in the course of their work can be a simple way to triangulate the findings made through the qualitative interpretations of the data. For example, Barley (1990a) suggests that as he began to sort his data in a qualitative manner, he noticed a subtle shift in the interactions among his informants. The analysis seemed to suggest that the new computerized imaging modalities he watched informants use were shifting the power relations among actors in the social order of the two hospitals he observed. By counting identifiable actions from his notes (e.g., "usurping the controls" or "giving someone directions"), Barley was able to verify quantitatively the insights generated by his qualitative sorting of the data (Barley 1986, 1990b).

Although an "action approach" to data analysis can allow the analyst to sum qualitative data in quantitative form, which can help confirm or deny the theories that emerge from analysis, it can also help reveal more subtle and consistent patterns in the data. By coding specific actions from the data, an analyst can construct data matrices that can be statistically analyzed. For example, using simple tests such as an analysis of variance, or ANOVA, can help determine whether or not actions occurred more frequently during one period than during another, or if they were conducted more consistently by one group than another. Thus, by coding actions, the ethnographer can triangulate the descriptive and inductive findings of qualitatively coded data with simple quantitative analyses of mean frequencies, which might help uncover patterns in the data that would otherwise be overlooked due to its sheer volume.

To analyze the data I collected on crashworthiness engineers' work and the activities of those who implemented CrashLab, I followed the steps outlined above. I began by coding all field notes in the qualitative software analysis program Atlas.ti for the specific actions informants conducted in their work. I coded more than 100,000 lines of text. My codes revealed over 500 different kinds of actions. I then sorted and grouped the actions together into larger events of which they were constitutive, revising categories when I uncovered more data that suggested revision was necessary and after discussing my emerging categories with my informants (Miles and Huberman 1984). I did these discussions informally at the end of observations and, more formally, during the monthly presentations I was required to make under the auspices of my "internship." Once this basic coding and sorting process was complete, I followed the more advanced, theoretically grounded steps outlined by Strauss and Corbin (1998). I then followed Glaser's (1978: 120–126) method of theoretical sorting to determine which events were most important in explaining how CrashLab merged with the social systems of crashworthiness engineers at Autoworks. After identifying a number of ideas and theories about relationships in the data, I took counts of those activities and/or events that seemed most important. I used several statistical techniques to compare the occurrence of these actions and events across time and across groups.

How to collect digital artifacts

All of the above discussion presupposes that the researcher will be able to acquire the digital artifacts with which informants work. How is this done? The answer to this question has two parts, what I call the pitch and the carry.

In the first part, the researcher has to make a pitch to the informant about why he or she needs the artifact. I have found this is often hard to do if the researcher does not explain at the observation outset that he or she will be asking for artifacts. I typically begin my observation with a given informant by letting them know I am trying to understand *how* they do their work. I remind them that they carry out much of their work by using digital representations and other digital artifacts and so, at times, I may want to have copies so I can have a full understanding of the complexities of their job. At this point, informants fall into two typical categories of response. The first category represents the acceptors. After this pitch they usually say "okay" and then start work. The second category represents the critics. After the initial pitch, the critics are concerned that giving you copies of their digital artifacts will somehow get them into trouble. This is where the ID badge and the email address that I spoke of above come in so handy. When a critic responds with his or her concern, I point to my ID badge and remind them that although I work for the university, this study is supported by the company's management and they are paying me as an employee (both true statements). I then tell them that all of the artifacts they provide me are protected under a confidentiality agreement (a true statement) and that they can give me the documents by emailing them to me at my company-sponsored email address.

The email address is one more stamp of the researcher's legitimacy and provides the illusion that all of the data that they send will remain at the company (not exactly true). Typically, these actions put even the critics at ease. I find it best not to clear up the ambiguity in their interpretation that the artifacts they give will stay behind the company firewall. My negotiation with the company's management is explicit that I can take artifacts with me. I have found, over the years, that it is easier and more beneficial not to volunteer too much information about all of this for fear of alarming the critics. If (and this has happened) the organization will not provide me with a corporate email account, I will ask the direct manager if he/she will create a temporary folder in his or her email client to store artifacts that people will send. I then have the critic send the artifact via email to their manager (they have no problem doing this) with my name in the subject line, the manager files it away, and later I arrange with the manager to take those artifacts off his or her hands.

As should be clear from above, I find that sending digital artifacts via email is the easiest way to carry them with you. But it does require some logistical maneuvering to get all of the artifacts that someone works with. My normal strategy is to ask informants upon our first meeting to create a temporary folder on their computer desktops. I typically ask them to name it something like "Files for Paul." Throughout the observation sessions, whenever I ask for a screenshot or copies of a presentation, I ask them to save a copy to this folder. Most engineers know how to make screenshots because they use these shots often for reports. But some informants do not know how to make screenshots, and I need to teach them how to do so. At the end of the observation session, I ask informants to attach as many artifacts as will fit into an email and send them to me in as many emails as are needed. Doing things in this way is less of a burden to the informant and increases one's likelihood of carrying away the digital artifacts one deems necessary to fully understanding the work.

Writing it Up

Writing it up is the most difficult part. How do you summarize months of observation and mountains of data into a short article? This is the dilemma that many ethnographers face. To deal with it, many ethnographers publish books where there is more room to present data and tell a wider story. But many social scientists do not find themselves in "book fields." Instead, they are expected to publish the results of their ethnographic study in journal articles where they are normally limited to 20–30 pages of double-spaced text (don't forget the one-inch margins!). On top of these normal constraints, ethnographers of visual cultures, like engineering, are faced with yet another obstacle: what to do with all of these digital artifacts?

When I first began writing up my findings for publication in journal outlets, I made a mistake that is common to all ethnographers. I assumed that because I learned it in the field, the reader needed to know it too. The result of this mistake was that I found myself including more excerpts from my field records and more screenshots of digital artifacts than were necessary to convey the key points I was exploring in my article. Very quickly, journal editors pushed back. They said things like, "Why do you need all these images?" "We can't publish all of these figures." "Do you really need the screenshot to tell your story?" In reflecting on these comments, I discovered that I often mistook my needs for analysis with my needs for data exposition in the article. In other words, having a digital artifact like the one presented in figure 5.2 was essential to my ability to do a good analysis of the data. But I did not need to show the image to tell the story.

To give a concrete example, my article entitled "Innovation Blindness" (Leonardi 2011a) chronicled the development of CrashLab at Autoworks. The thesis was that various groups often fight over ideas for new technologies because they do not recognize that they each believe the technology should solve a different organizational problem. When the groups get together, they often bring prototypes of potential technological solutions to their specific organizational problems as a means of focusing conversation. But these prototypes focus conversation around features of the technology and obscure the fact that those features were created with the hopes of solving a particular problem that may be different from the concerns held by other constituents. The result is that the development of the technology is mired in disagreement. To help illustrate this process— and to explain why it took 10 years and several million dollars to develop CrashLab—I included in the submission three images of various proto- types that engineers brought to their meetings. Here is what two of the reviewers had to say:

Reviewer 1: I understand your point about the differences in features. But why do we need these images? I don't think they really add anything. They just show three prototypes that all have different features. I don't think there is really any value-add with these images.

Reviewer 2: The images are cool, and they really help to illustrate your point. But I doubt the journal will let you publish them. I would find some way to take them out and replace them with a table or something. I know it's less engaging to the reader, but I just can't see the journal putting these in for space reasons. Also, did you even get permission to publish these? Would "Autoworks" be upset if they saw these images?

The senior editor concurred with the reviewers and asked me to remove the images. I ended up publishing a simple table that compared the vari- ous features of the different prototypes and putting an asterisk next to the features from those prototypes that eventually made it into the final ver- sion of CrashLab. What is interesting about these reviewer comments is that they show people's reticence and discomfort with the publication of images. Looking back, I can see that a table worked well enough to con- vey the message I was trying to send. It is interesting, though, that the concerns about publishing images were not confined to whether they added value or not, but, as reviewer 2 suggested, it is unclear to most how to handle images. Will the journal have space? How do you indicate that you received permission to publish them?

I provide this example to underscore the point that although a researcher may have worked hard to gather digital artifacts during his or her fieldwork, spent egregious amounts of time writing up the observa- tion record in a way that indexes those images, and slaved through a detailed analysis of the data that included an informant's use of the images, one should not be under the illusion that these images will appear in print. The digital artifacts an ethnographer collects provide essential information about a visual culture. This information is of primary value for analysis rather than exposition of data. I believe this is an important point to remember.

Confidentiality Matters

There are times when the presentation of some visual image is both warranted and acceptable by editors. When presenting images, the researcher has to be careful to maintain the anonymity of the research site. Many times, names of files that are particular to the company appear in screenshots, or the numbers in a table or the data points in a graph are confidential information. At Autoworks, I ran into the issue that the company's legal team was very concerned whenever I would present a graph that summarized the results of a simulation analysis. They were concerned because sometimes, as engineers worked through various design iterations, they generated solutions that would provide outstanding performance—for example, a five-star frontal crash test rating from the National Highway Traffic Safety Administration. But because of the politics of the design process, the overall structure of the vehicle might evolve to favor fuel economy rather than occupant safety. For this reason, the legal team was very concerned that if I showed actual data that a safer vehicle was possible than the one that was eventually built, Autoworks would be open to a lawsuit.

To deal with this issue, I had to make some alterations to the story and the data to maintain the anonymity of the research site and those involved when writing about CrashLab. This entailed changing names, dates, relationships between people and departments, and, in some cases, even descriptive statistics about the company or about the technology or vehicle-development process. As Kunda (1992) suggests, I maintained relations between numbers to illustrate analytic points. To be completely explicit, I fabricated all of the vehicle impact-performance data that I have ever presented in charts and figures in articles or chapters. I always provide a note indicating that the data are fabricated in the publication. I have maintained the original shape of the curves or the magnitude of the results in such cases, but the data are not by any means the real data with which informants were working. Thus, to include digital artifacts and present the data within a limited number of pages while still achieving a readable and understandable narrative, researchers will have to, as I did, take a bit of liberty with the presentation of events in order to construct for the reader what Fine (1993: 273) calls the "illusion of verisimilitude." This means that the researcher will have to relate some events out of sequence, positioning them in the story as though they occurred at roughly the same time. Additionally, he or she will have to make deliberate choices about which parts of the story to tell and which parts to leave out. So, although the researcher attempts to provide rich data, there is always more to the story than meets the eye (Golden-Biddle and Locke 1997).

Conclusion

I believe the ethnographic method can provide important insights into worlds we know little about, while at the same time helping us abstract findings from those worlds in ways that help explain others. These insights can only be derived from intently watching people—studying them in the course of their everyday work. In a visual culture like engineering, watching people at their jobs also means dealing with the reality that they work constantly with digital artifacts. As I have tried to convey in this chapter, these images thoroughly shape the way people think, see, reason, and interact in the workplace. I have tried to provide some lessons I have learned through trial and error while conducting ethnographic studies in visual cultures.

   Although I have spent a good deal of time explaining how to deal with the realities of collecting and analyzing digital data in a physical space, I would encourage ethnographers of visual culture to remember that without careful watching and recording of what informants do, even the richest research site will bear little intellectual fruit. Watching is tedious, but enlightening. Informants regularly joked with me that I had watched them for so long that I could do their jobs. Indeed, I did feel a bit like the Cantaleño apprentice loom operators in Manning Nash's (1958) vivid portrait of the industrialization of a Guatemalan village, who learned how to work the looms by sitting quietly behind the experienced operators for months at a time without ever touching the machine. I will always be amused by my informants' disbelief that I could actually enjoy what I was watching. As two informants joked with me one day:

I1:   *How can you sit there and watch us so long? I mean it's like you must be bored out of your mind. It's like on TV, what kind of shows do you see? There's hospital shows, lawyer shows, and detective shows. You never see any engineering shows. How come? Because it's boring, man! I wouldn't watch an engineering show.*

I2:   *Hell no! Can you imagine it? "Vijaykumar P.E. The world's most dangerous performance engineer."[5] He doesn't drive a cool car, but he designs one.*

I1:   *Yeah, you probably write, "This guy maximizes a window, minimizes a window, wiggles the mouse, and maximizes the first window again." You must be falling asleep. What can you learn from that?*

I2:   *Maybe you should forget this whole ethnography thing and just do a time and motion study on us. Then you would only be bored for like a week and you could go home and lay on the beach in the sun.*

They were right. It would have been much easier to collect data if I were conducting a time and motion study. But the visual culture of engineering is so rich with the potential for understanding fundamental sociological questions that watching, learning, and struggling with digital data makes even the prospect of a sunny day at the beach a little less exciting.

Notes

1. A solver is a program run on a supercomputer that applies equilibrium equations to each element in a finite element model and constructs a system of simultaneous equations that is solved for unknown values to produce measures of a vehicle's performance given the parameters specified in the setup of a simulation.

2. For a discussion, see Barley and Kunda (1992) and Shenhav (1995).

3. Finite element preprocessors have several automated routines to control the shape of elements. Element shape is an important concern for the accuracy of a model because elements are used to ensure quality.

4. Diane Bailey at the University of Texas at Austin School of Information invented this system. I am indebted to her for teaching it to me.

5. Vijaykumar is the informant's last name (pseudonym of course). He is mocking the popular 1980s TV show *Magnum PI*.

References

Adler, P. S. 1990. Managing high tech processes: The challenge of CAD/CAM. In *Managing Complexity in High Technology Organizations,* ed. M. von Glinow and S. Mohrman. New York: Oxford University Press.

Bailey, D. E., P. M. Leonardi, and S. R. Barley. 2012. The lure of the virtual. *Organization Science 23* (5): 1485–1504.

Barley, S. R. 1986. Technology as an occasion for structuring: Evidence from observations of CT scanners and the social order of radiology departments. *Administrative Science Quarterly 31* (1): 78–108.

Barley, S. R. 1990a. Images of imaging: Notes on doing longitudinal field work. *Organization Science 1* (3): 220–247.

Barley, S. R. 1990b. The alignment of technology and structure through roles and networks. *Administrative Science Quarterly 35* (1): 61–103.

Barley, S. R., and G. Kunda. 1992. Design and devotion: Surges of rational and normative ideologies of control in managerial discourse. *Administrative Science Quarterly 37* (3): 363–399.

Bechky, B. 2003. Sharing meaning across occupational communities: The transformation of understanding on the production floor. *Organization Science 17*: 99–120.

Becker, H. S. 1958. Problems of inference and proof in participant observation. *American Sociological Review 23* (6): 652–660.

Becker, H. S. 1996. The epistemology of qualitative research. In *Essays on Ethnography and Human Development,* ed. R. Jessor, A. Colby, and R. Schweder, 53–71. Chicago: University of Chicago Press.

Becker, H. S., B. Geer, E. C. Hughes, and A. L. Strauss. 1961. *Boys in White: Student Culture in Medical School.* Chicago: University of Chicago Press.

Boellstorff, T. 2010. *Coming of Age in Second Life: An Anthropologist Explores the Virtually Human.* Princeton, NJ: Princeton University Press.

Boland, R. J., K. Lyytinen, and Y. Yoo. 2007. Wakes of innovation in project networks: The case of digital 3-D representations in architecture, engineering, and construction. *Organization Science 18* (4): 631–647.

Bucciarelli, L. L. 1994. *Designing Engineers.* Cambridge, MA: MIT Press.

Bucciarelli, L. L. 2002. Between thought and object in engineering design. *Design Studies 23* (3): 219–231.

Carlile, P. R. 2004. Transferring, translating, and transforming: An integrative framework for managing knowledge across boundaries. *Organization Science 15*: 555–568.

Collins, H. M. 1974. The tea set: Tacit knowledge and scientific networks. *Science Studies 4*: 165–186.

Collins, S. T. 2003. Using ethnography to identify cultural domains within a systems engineering organization. *Bulletin of Science, Technology & Society 23* (4): 246–255.

Dodgson, M., D. M. Gann, and A. Salter. 2007. "In case of fire, please use the elevator": Simulation technology and organization in fire engineering. *Organization Science 18* (5): 849–864.

Dougherty, D. J. 1992. Interpretive barriers to successful product innovation in large firms. *Organization Science 3* (2): 179–202.

Downey, G. L. 1998. *The Machine in Me: An Anthropologist Sits Among Computer Engineers*. New York: Routledge.

Dreyfus, H. L., and S. E. Dreyfus. 1986. *Mind over Machine: The Power of Human Expertise and Intuition in the Era of the Computer*. New York: Free Press.

Ewenstein, B., and J. Whyte. 2009. Knowledge practices in design: The role of visual representations as 'epistemic objects'. *Organization Studies 30* (1): 7–30.

Fine, G. A. 1993. Ten lies of ethnography: Moral dilemmas of field research. *Journal of Contemporary Ethnography 22* (3): 267–294.

Fleischer, M., and J. K. Liker. 1992. The hidden professionals: Product designers and their impact on design quality. *IEEE Transactions on Engineering Management 39*: 254–264.

Geertz, C. 1973. *The Interpretation of Cultures*. New York: Basic Books.

Gilbreth, F. B. 1993. *Motion Study: A Method for Increasing the Efficiency of the Workman*. London: Routledge/Thoemmes Press. (1911).

Glaser, B. 1978. *Theoretical Sensitivity*. Mill Valley, CA: The Sociological Press.

Golden-Biddle, K., and K. D. Locke. 1997. *Composing Qualitative Research*. Thousand Oaks, CA: Sage.

Henderson, K. 1999. *On Line and on Paper: Visual Representations, Visual Culture, and Computer Graphics in Design Engineering*. Cambridge, MA: MIT Press.

Kunda, G. 1992. *Engineering Culture: Control and Commitment in a High-Tech Corporation*. Philadelphia: Temple University Press.

Latour, B. 1986. Visualization and cognition: Thinking with eyes and hands. *Knowledge in Society 6*: 1–40.

Leonardi, P. M. 2009. Why do people reject new technologies and stymie organizational changes of which they are in favor? Exploring misalignments between social interactions and materiality. *Human Communication Research 35* (3): 975–984.

Leonardi, P. M. 2010a. Digital materiality? How artifacts without matter, matter. *First Monday 15* (6). http://www.uic.edu/htbin/cgiwrap/bin/ojs/index.php/fm/article/viewArticle/3036/2567.

Leonardi, P. M. 2010b. From road to lab to math: The co-evolution of technological, regulatory, and organizational innovations in automotive crash testing. *Social Studies of Science 40* (2): 243–274.

Leonardi, P. M. 2011a. Innovation blindness: Culture, frames, and cross-boundary problem construction in the development of new technology concepts. *Organization Science 22* (2): 347–369.

Leonardi, P. M. 2011b. When flexible routines meet flexible technologies: Affordance, constraint, and the imbrication of human and material agencies. *Management Information Systems Quarterly 35* (1): 147–167.

Leonardi, P. M., and D. E. Bailey. 2008. Transformational technologies and the creation of new work practices: Making implicit knowledge explicit in task-based offshoring. *Management Information Systems Quarterly 32* (2): 411–436.

Liker, J. K., C. J. Haddad, and J. Karlin. 1999. Perspectives on technology and work organization. *Annual Review of Sociology 25*: 575–596.

Lincoln, Y. S., and E. G. Guba. 1985. *Naturalistic Inquiry*. Beverly Hills, CA: Sage.

Lofland, J., and L. H. Lofland. 1995. *Analyzing Social Settings: A guide to Qualitative Observation and Analysis*. 3rd ed. Belmont, CA: Wadsworth.

Louis, M. R., and R. I. Sutton. 1991. Switching cognitive gears: From habits of mind to active thinking. *Human Relations 44*: 55–76.

Loukissas, Y. A. 2009. Keepers of the geometry. In *Simulation and its Discontents*, ed. S. Turkle, 153–170. Cambridge, MA: MIT Press.

Malhotra, A., A. Majchrzak, R. Carman, and V. Lott. 2001. Radical innovation without collocation: A case study at Boeing-Rocketdyne. *Management Information Systems Quarterly 25* (2): 229–249.

Malinowski, B. 1922. *Argonauts of the Western Pacific*. New York: E.P. Dutton.

Mead, M. 1928. *Coming of Age in Samoa*. New York: Harper Collins.

Miles, M. B., and A. M. Huberman. 1984. *Qualitative data analysis: A source book of new methods*. Beverly Hills, CA: Sage.

Nardi, B. A. 2010. *My life as A Night Elf Priest: An Anthropological Account of World of Warcraft*. Ann Arbor, MI: University of Michigan.

Nash, M. 1958. *Machine Age Maya: The Industrialization of a Guatemalan Community*. Chicago: The University of Chicago Press.

Orr, J. E. 1996. *Talking about Machines: An Ethnography of a Modern Job*. Ithaca, NY: ILR Press.

Pearce, C. 2009. *Communities of Play: Emergent Cultures in Multiplayer Games and Virtual Worlds*. Cambridge, MA: MIT Press.

Roy, D. F. 1959. Banana time: Job satisfaction and informal interaction. *Human Organization 18*: 158–168.

Shenhav, Y. 1995. From chaos to systems: The engineering foundations of organization theory, 1879–1932. *Administrative Science Quarterly 40*: 557–585.

Sims, B. 1999. Concrete practices: Testing in an earthquake-engineering laboratory. *Social Studies of Science 29* (4): 483–518.

Spradley, J. P. 1980. *Participant Observation*. Fort Worth, TX: Holt, Rinehart and Winston.

Strauss, A., and J. Corbin. 1998. *Basics of Qualitative Research: Techniques and Procedures for Developing Grounded Theory*. 2nd ed. Thousand Oaks, CA: Sage.

Taylor, B. C., and N. Trujillo. 2001. Qualitative research methods. In *The New Handbook of Organizational Communication: Advances in Theory, Research, and Methods*, ed. F. M. Jablin and L. L. Putnam, 161–194. Thousand Oaks, CA: Sage.

Taylor, F. W. 1998. *The Principles of Scientific Management*. New York: Dover. (1911).

Thomas, R. J. 1994. *What Machines Can't Do: Politics and Technology in the Industrial Enterprise*. Berkeley: University of California Press.

Thompson, E. P. 1967. Time, work-discipline, and industrial capitalism. *Past & Present 38*: 56–97.

Turkle, S. 2009. *Simulation and its Discontents*. Cambridge, MA: MIT Press.

Van Maanen, J. 1988. *Tales of the Field: On Writing Ethnography*. Chicago: University of Chicago Press.

Vaughan, D. 1996. *The Challenger Launch Decision: Risky Technology, Culture, and Deviance at NASA*. Chicago: University of Chicago Press.

Vinck, D., ed. 2003. *Everyday Engineering: An Ethnography of Design and Innovation*. Cambridge, MA: MIT Press.

Workman, J. P. 1995. Engineering's interactions with marketing groups in an engineering-driven organization. *IEEE Transactions on Engineering Management 42* (2): 129–139.

6

Social Software as Social Science

Eric Gilbert and Karrie Karahalios

For my dissertation, I built a Twitter application.[1] To understand why, imagine the following. Somebody you bumped into once at a conference starts calling you constantly. You do not have caller ID, so you either pick up the phone blindly or just let it ring, potentially missing calls you care about. You have to listen to what they say before the phone is available for the next call. You would probably be furious with the person. But, we permit a very similar thing from Twitter. Everyone gets unlimited access to your attention. Anyone can tweet as much as they like and crowd out everyone else. The application I built tries to make educated guesses about your social life, letting you render your Twitter stream *socially* instead of temporally. Using it, you can choose to pay the most attention to the people with whom you are closest, for example.

With modern social media like Facebook, Twitter, and email, relationships are the stuff that makes the system *social*. Thus it struck me as odd that social media is not rendered *socially*. For example, we have colleagues with whom we correspond intensely, but not deeply; we have childhood friends we consider close, even if we fell out of touch. Or, take this example: some human resources departments (Tahmincioglu 2008) have taken to cold-calling an applicant's Facebook friends instead of asking for references! One HR manager said that by using social media, "You've opened up your Rolodex for the whole world to see." Of course, sometimes they call someone hoping for a reference, "only to find that you were just drinking buddies." Today's social media completely intermingle our diversity of ties.

While social media sites may disregard this diversity, sociology has studied it for decades, calling it *tie strength*. I wanted to build an application (or "app") that people found useful, but behind-the-scenes, I was effectively modeling tie strength. My little Twitter app would speak to decades of research in sociology. I put an app on the Web for everyone to use, much like a startup would, yet I would also have a place at the scholarly table discussing what constitutes tie strength.

The large-scale social life we see on the Internet is a magnificent opportunity for social science. Others have argued that the data we leave behind on massive sites like Facebook can tell us new things about social behavior (Lazer et al. 2009). Here, however, I make a different argument. *You can also do social science research by building social software.* Sure, Facebook data are great—if you can get them. But even if you find yourself among the lucky few who can, Facebook data have limitations. Consider the following research question: How would social behavior change if we changed the meaning of a Facebook "friendship," perhaps requiring you to use friendships in order to keep them? In other words, friendships could decay and disappear after a certain amount of disuse. You cannot answer this question with Facebook data. You might answer it, however, if you owned the Facebook code. You could change the interface and the experience to examine any question you wanted.

This chapter is about my personal experiences building social software to do social science research. It explores the tensions between doing research and what effectively looks like running a startup. And, it did often look like running a startup. I took a victory lap around the lab whenever somebody blogged about my app. I also panicked and hot-swapped code to fix critical bugs. This is a very new method, pioneered by only a few researchers, including myself and (most notably) the GroupLens lab at Minnesota (grouplens.org). Admittedly, we are still working out the kinks.

Like any method, building software to do research has benefits and drawbacks. You can generate "big data," or at least much more than you could hope for from a lab experiment. People probably behave more naturally because you gave them a compelling reason to come to your site. In other words, they did not come to do an experiment for the good of science. In the long term, you might actually demonstrate the importance of social science to a major segment of the economy. On the other hand, building an open app on the Web means that you cannot control the demographics of your sample, nor can you make a realistic argument that it comes close to being representative.

I begin the chapter by presenting what I built and why, simply because it is hard to dissect a case study before presenting the case itself. I think it also shows what we can learn by building tools that allow for data collection, rather than analyzing data we obtain elsewhere. Then, I explore the tensions arising from having "users" in one perspective and "participants" in another. I conclude the chapter by reflecting on the implications of this method for sampling and simple pragmatic matters, like paying for all those servers to handle the Internet crashing down on you.

Tie Strength

To set the stage, it is necessary to talk briefly about tie strength. This is the social-science backdrop for my application. Tie strength is a diffuse concept: it refers to a sense of closeness with another person. When that feeling is strong, we call it a *strong tie;* when it is weak, we call it a *weak tie.* Who are you close to? Who are your acquaintances? Mark Granovetter (1973), who introduced the concept, had this to say about its definition: "Most of us can agree, on a rough intuitive basis, whether a given tie is strong, weak, or absent" (1361).

And based on this rough intuition, there have been studies showing why tie strength matters. For example, the right mix of strong and weak ties produces better deals for companies (Uzzi 1999), and strong ties can influence mental health (Schaefer, Coyne, and Lazarus 1981) and obesity (Christakis & Fowler 2007), among other things. In his book, *Getting a Job*, Granovetter (1974) analyzed the importance of weak ties in finding employment. While strong ties roughly know the same people, weak ties may be more dispersed and may collectively know a more diverse set of potential employers and connections to employers offering more helpful information in such a situation than strong ties might.

While most studies initially define tie strength as a feeling toward another person, researchers usually operationalize it as a single, countable measure. Since these studies want to learn about everyday life, we see interview questions to measure tie strength such as "How many times have you talked in the last month?" and "How often do you chat about political and social issues?" For these studies, in these contexts, this makes sense.

In contrast, for the work described in this chapter, I returned to the original intent of tie strength: how close we feel to the people in our lives. We have a remarkable amount of data; in social media, as opposed to real life, every interaction that takes place on a particular platform can be recorded. In earlier work that set up the application I describe here, I showed that a quantitative model could map traces from social network site interactions to tie strength (Gilbert and Karahalios 2009). For example, I found in this work that the number of "intimacy words" you exchange with someone is a strong signal of tie strength. In the app I describe next, I put this model into practice online.

We Meddle

Using the Twitter application programming interface (API)[2] and my quantitative model described earlier, I built the app *We Meddle* (wemeddle. com; figure 6.1). WeMeddle creates community lists of the people you follow (see figure 6.2) and automatically infers tie strength between you and all the Twitter users you follow (i.e., how close your relationship is to each other person). This client interface would let you see your Twitter stream in a way that was not possible in any other Twitter client: you could skew your stream by emphasizing tweets from either your strong ties or your weak ties, at the expense of the other. Drawing on literature

we meddle˙

We build Twitter lists and streams.

Yes, we meddle. Like a sweet, nosy grandma.

We learn from your past to render Twitter anew.

Sign in with Twitter

You'll come back after you log in.

demo video   contact

Figure 6.1
We Meddle's homepage (http://wemeddle.com).

Figure 6.2
We Meddle's lists interface, grouping my Twitter contacts using social tie strength and community.

about what kinds of benefits different ties provide (Constant et al. 1996; Granovetter 1973; Schaefer et al. 1981; Wellman and Wortley 1990), the client would also let you do things like "only show me weak ties who posted a link" and "emphasize strong ties who said something positive" (see figure 6.3). For example, if most of your strong ties on Twitter are from the same community, you may already be familiar with what they tweet. A tweet from a weak tie may expose you to something new.

While I was designing and implementing this client interface, Twitter released a new feature built directly into its infrastructure called Lists (Stone 2009). Twitter Lists let users group accounts together under one name. It seems that Twitter intended Lists as a way for users to curate their own Twitter feed. For example, you could make a list called "economics" and put economists in it. Then, as an added benefit, the rest of Twitter could find your list and use it to discover economists on Twitter. From discussions on the Web and chats with other users I knew, it seemed clear to me that no one would use Lists to make their own, personally

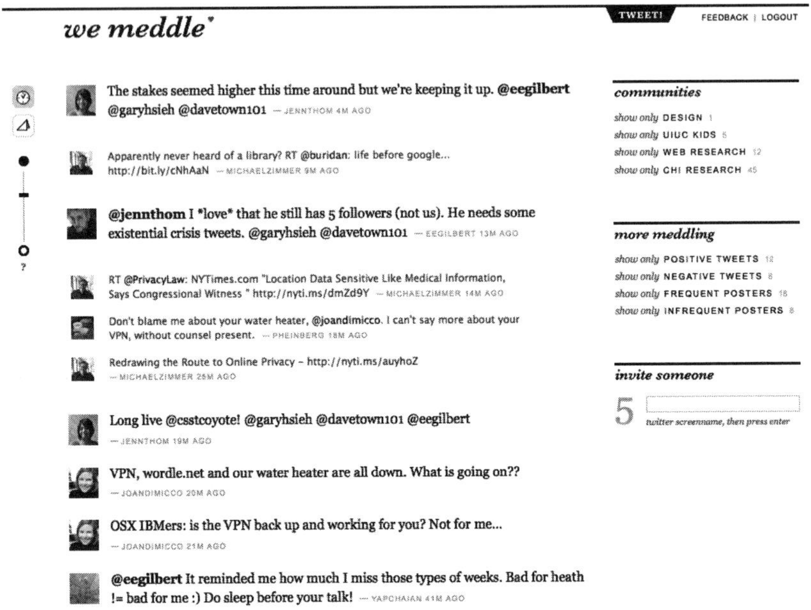

Figure 6.3
We Meddle's Twitter client interface.

meaningful groups. It just was not worth the effort to make lists you did not intend to share and publicize.

While I found Twitter Lists interesting, I was already designing and coding a client interface for the purpose of reading and writing tweets. That is all I envisioned We Meddle would be when I started out. The client was an exciting, cutting-edge design idea (at least to us), but it was an idea that would require buy-in from users: they would have to abandon their existing practices, their existing Twitter clients (e.g., TweetDeck, Twitter's own Web client, etc.), and switch to We Meddle. I knew that kind of commitment would limit who tried We Meddle. So I hurriedly produced an application that used my existing tie strength code to make Twitter Lists instead, putting the more general Twitter client on hold. My Lists tool would automatically make personally meaningful tie strength lists with the option to tell the system what it got wrong. My intuition was that it would be much easier to subtract a few mislabeled accounts than to add each one manually, and people could use tie strength without buying into the idea completely.

This Lists tool became a key component of We Meddle. We Meddle now consisted of two parts: a lists interface and the original client interface. The lists interface (figure 6.2) automatically generated lists of people you could export into Twitter from We Meddle. This saved users lots of work, because they didn't have to assemble lists by hand. Once they had a list, they could see only tweets by people on that list, limiting all of their incoming tweets to just a subset. In addition, the client interface (figure 6.3) let users alter a Twitter stream based on the tie strength of the twitterer, the sentiment of tweets, the frequency of tweets, and the presence of links. This became an advanced way to use We Meddle.

The following is what a user would see on We Meddle. After logging into We Meddle for the first time (figure 6.1), you would see the lists interface (figure 6.2). By clicking a link in the top-right corner of the page, you could go to the client (figure 6.3). We Meddle's lists interface would autogenerate lists of the people you follow: your Inner Circle (i.e., strong ties), your Outer Circle (i.e., weak ties), and lists corresponding to social groups in Twitter's social network (Newman 2006). In figure 6.2, you see my strong ties at the time, my weak ties, and two communities roughly corresponding to "human-computer interaction (HCI) researchers" and "Internet researchers."

After We Meddle computed its suggested lists and displayed them to you, you could drop someone by clicking on them. When you were happy with the list, you could save the list in Twitter. (We Meddle would send the list back through the Twitter API, where it would be stored.) Storing the list in Twitter meant that you could access it from any Twitter client, using it in ways a particular client would afford. For instance, the popular Seesmic Web client[3] let users view each list in its own column, meaning that you could slice the conventional Twitter stream into multiple views. You could go to Seesmic and see your strong-tie list in one column, your weak-tie list flowing in another and a particular social community (e.g., "HCI researchers") flowing in yet another.

We Meddle's Client

The We Meddle Twitter client, like other Twitter clients, showed users the stream of tweets created by the Twitter accounts the user followed. However, the We Meddle client made one very crucial break from this design pattern: different people got different amounts of screen space. The client's main slider control (figure 6.3, left), gave users the ability to emphasize strong ties at the expense of weaker ones, or the other way around. As a user would slide the control, We Meddle adjusted the profile picture size, typeface, font size, and opacity. Pushing the slider all the way to the top totally removes weak ties from the interface, and vice versa. Placing the slider in the middle replicates Twitter.com, where everybody appears the same. (As you change the controls, the interface updates in real time. I managed this by using jQuery[4] and custom JavaScript.) In figure 6.3, I used the slider to skew the stream toward my strong ties at the expense of my weaker ones. Strong ties appear larger, in a more salient font, and with more saturation. In other words, they demand more visual attention.

All told, it took me about three solid months of development to build We Meddle. In January 2010, I rolled We Meddle Lists out to the Web. The client was not ready for another 45 days. Thinking that no one would ever work with my code again, I cut corners. I did not include comments in any of it. My software engineering professors would faint to hear this, but I absolutely recommend cutting corners to anyone building software for research. Concentrate on what matters: the research, not the code. It just has to run *now*.

At the time of this writing (2011), over 3,000 people from 52 countries had used the site. About 20,000 people visited the main URL, http://wemeddle.com. It is probably fair to say that most dissertations get seen by very few people. It felt wonderful to see my work out in the open, used by thousands of people.

The Tension Between "User" and "Participant"

Software companies have users that they work *for*, while researchers have participants that they work *on* (or ideally, with). Over and over while building We Meddle, I encountered the same tension: the tension between building something people want and designing a halfway-decent academic research project. In retrospect, I probably should have anticipated the tension's importance before it smacked me in the face during design. In other words, what person would spend their free time doing what academic experiments usually ask people to do? Filling out surveys and responding to basic visual stimuli are not what most people consider fun, and that is why the people who participate in research are paid. The gap between a useful tool and a useful research project is huge. And yet, I naively wanted to bridge it. I wanted my app to be something people wanted to use while simultaneously generating good data. Over and over, this ended up driving the design of my dissertation.

The most apparent instance of this tension is in the primacy of the lists interface over the client interface. As I said earlier, when my advisor Karrie Karahalios and I first discussed We Meddle, the client interface was our reason for doing it. Social streams flood you with information. Only time serves to organize it. We both felt that if you had a reasonably sized stream and a day job, then you needed help. So I started sketching out what would become the client interface. But I did not simply want to write what the HCI literature would call a "systems paper." I wanted to say something new about tie strength in computer-mediated communication. The We Meddle client interface did not contain an obvious way to get data about that. If We Meddle made decisions based on tie strength, how would people know that? How would We Meddle know that it had guessed correctly or not? Even if We Meddle provided a mechanism, would people actually use it? The point of the client is to render a Twitter stream more efficiently and more effectively than the traditional way. If that is the point, then why spend extra time providing feedback for We Meddle's guesses? We did finally decide on a mechanism—a hidden "correct We Meddle" option that reveals itself on mouse-over. We did not count on people using it, however.

After Twitter released its Lists infrastructure, I pitched the idea of making "tie strength lists" to Karrie. She was skeptical. After a while, I convinced her that while making tie strength lists was more boring than the client interface, it would generate much better social data. The natural process of making lists would direct We Meddle users through a process of dropping incorrect We Meddle guesses, something resembling a traditional experimental task. We would get valuable data on what constitutes tie strength in computer-mediated communication, while our users would get their lists. This is why the lists interface is the first thing people see after logging into We Meddle. Users can only get to the client interface by clicking a very small link at the top of the page. I even wrote the text of the link to discourage users from jumping to the client before finishing their lists: "When you're done with lists, try the new We Meddle client."

Because of the time I spent developing it, it hurt to bury the client interface like this. I really liked the client interface, and I used it myself to read Twitter. Putting it another click away ensured that my user numbers for it would take a substantial hit.

The tension comes through more subtly across the design of the lists interface. For example, users cannot add people to the lists We Meddle generates, something we purposely designed into the system. If people can add anyone they want, how can we be sure that Inner Circle still means strong ties? Perhaps the user started from We Meddle's suggestions but branched off to create a list with a different meaning. Limiting users to deletions became a key decision for the research project. It allowed us to argue that the Inner Circle and Outer Circle retain their meanings over time. When a user removes an account from the Inner or Outer Circle, we learn where the model makes mistakes. The clicks are crucial data: during the natural process of using We Meddle, users leave a trail from which we can study tie strength. Of course, users can add people to their Inner and Outer Circle lists outside We Meddle. They can go anywhere that has a list interface and put whomever they want in them. But we did not want to be the people who allowed them to do this, and we planned to discuss this case in follow-up interviews. I set up a "Get Satisfaction"[5] forum where people could leave feedback about We Meddle. Addition to lists was the most requested feature (see figure 6.4). A startup would have added the feature immediately or, more likely, never would have launched without it.

Elsewhere, I sacrificed the other way: usability at the expense of precision. In figure 6.2, note that the page has four different lists. During early prototype sessions, I sent the design out to my committee members. One replied that I should consider moving the community lists (not the focus of my dissertation) to a second page, thereby clearly privileging the tie

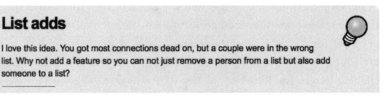

Figure 6.4
A user requests list additions, our most requested feature.

strength lists. I decided, however, to flood the interface with faces simply to make it more attractive, to give the appearance there is more going on. The more faces, the better, so I kept all the lists together on one page. In retrospect, I am happy with this decision, although it was a hard call at the time.

Tradeoffs like these happened all the time. Should I put this link in the center or at the bottom? Centering it will ensure that people see it and click it faster. Should I explain this part of the interface in detail so users do not get frustrated, or should I avoid explanation for fear of influencing their choices? The design process is subtle, and I was bad at documenting it. As far as the little design choices go, I can only warn that hundreds of little tradeoffs lurk behind every button and link.

Finding Users

I had finally built We Meddle, and now I wanted people to use it. What was the best way to make that happen? I did not have a strategy to gain users. I did the most direct (and naïve) thing: I told people about it. I announced We Meddle on Twitter and on Facebook. I posted the site to the various mailing lists where I lurk. My advisor posted We Meddle announcements on MIT's mailing lists (where she attended graduate school) in an effort to seed it outside my home institution. I relied on other people spreading it from there. Finding your first 10–100 users is often very hard, and those first few did trickle in slowly. But as an academic project, without venture capital investors to please, I could be patient. (Plus, the early, slow trickle of users allowed me to fix all the bugs in We Meddle's early code.)

Of course, this is a convenience sample, dramatically skewed toward the kind of people who not only use Twitter, but also like to play around with new, experimental tools. What kind of person had a chance to see We Meddle? Many people tweeted about We Meddle, thereby pushing it into their friends' Twitter streams. This "path of least resistance" was a diffusion pattern that has its own implications. That is a major downside for anyone whose work depends on very broad claims. You have to limit your claims to this population, over which you have little control. I am sure it distorts some of our findings, and this is one of the kinks I referred to at the beginning of the chapter. In the end, however, I checked to confirm that my We Meddle data matched what I found in my earlier work (Gilbert and Karahalhios 2009), which had not used a convenience sample. The convenience sample is a downside, but you cannot overlook this method's major upside. I got a sample of over 200,000 online relationships that was used to validate my tie-strength model. Whereas in traditional lab studies we may struggle to bring in 40 people, who each receive approximately $20 for participation, this larger sample cost $0 in terms of respondent compensation.

Another problem with this approach became clear only later, after my dissertation, when I submitted my first paper on We Meddle to a peer-reviewed venue. Online, I mostly hang out with other academics in my field. My Twitter network, like my Facebook network, is full of academic peers. Sure, I have friends from former lives, and family too, but my professional network forms the core of my online presence. I suspect it is the same for most academics. Consequently, just about everyone who qualified to review my paper had seen We Meddle and many had tried it. The anonymity I expected in a computer science peer-review process was completely gone. People often make the case that no true anonymity exists in peer review anyway. Indeed, in some social science and engineering fields, double-blind peer review is not the norm. Nonetheless, my case was extreme. Everyone who qualified to review my paper already knew who wrote it and probably had a personal experience with the software—they had tested it on their own personal networks. Editors had a difficult time finding impartial reviewers for my work.

Operational Issues

A few weeks after We Meddle's release, I was working late at night on the software. I already had three or four servers under my control at the time, and I often recycled them for whatever task I needed done, like analyzing data, storing code, crawling large data sets, and so on. We Meddle ran on one of these servers. Roughly 1,000 people had come to the site, leading to about 100 logins. These users reported some bugs, and I fixed them. Now, We Meddle hummed along pretty nicely. Late this night, I used SSH to log into the We Meddle server remotely—I think I wanted to sync some new code against my version control system. After a few seconds, I still did not have a connection, so I switched over to my browser and read

Hacker News. I returned a minute or so later—still no connection. Normally an SSH connection takes a few seconds at most. SSH told me that the We Meddle server had a network connection (i.e., no one had tripped on the Ethernet cable) and an SSH server was running, but I could not log in. Two minutes now. I decided to do a search for "we meddle" on Twitter. A few minutes earlier, someone with a huge following in South Korea (over 50,000 followers) had discovered We Meddle and tweeted about it. I ran the Korean tweet through Google Translate to get the gist of it, and the guy had liked it a lot. New We Meddle tweets from his followers popped up in the search results every few seconds.

I tabbed back to my terminal window to see if I had a connection to the server yet. Finally, I did. A few commands later, I could see hundreds of people trying to do first-time We Meddle logins simultaneously. If We Meddle were just a normal Web server, this would have been no problem. Serving a static html page takes a fraction of a second, and then the connection closes. We Meddle, however, does a lot of work for a new user. For each one, We Meddle makes thousands of Twitter requests to get the data it needs. Multiplying this process by a few hundred, I saw the problem: with 100,000 open network requests, We Meddle had reached the server's network limit. Sure enough, new tweets popping up in the Twitter search results complained about We Meddle being down.

This happens so often on the Web that it has a name: the Slashdot Effect. A sudden spike in traffic due to a popular site's referral can bring a small site to its knees. We Meddle had already been on its knees; now, it was on its face. Karrie and I had considered this problem ahead of time, but decided that if we encountered it, we could count ourselves lucky. The solution is usually simple: buy more hardware. I knew we could easily buy the hardware and bandwidth from a cloud computing provider, like Amazon Web Services.[6] Any startup would have done it ahead of launching. The startup mythology says that it is suicide to lose your first users because of an unresponsive server. However, I had a problem most startup founders do not have: I was a poor graduate student. I had a 9-month-old baby and a wife working full-time to support us. My back-of-the-envelope calculations suggested that buying enough capacity to handle the South Korea spike would have cost more than our rent and grocery bill combined. I could have run up my credit cards, with no hope of repaying them anytime soon, but I wanted to stay married. I was lucky enough to be funded on a fellowship, but that also meant no grant money to spend on cloud computing. Most graduate students I know are in similar situations.

By now, the university network administrators had noticed the unreasonable amount of traffic going in and out of the We Meddle server. Their monitoring software had started limiting the number of packets We Meddle could transfer, probably fearing some virus had compromised a machine on their network. Later on, I also realized that Twitter itself did not like how much data We Meddle wanted to transfer. I had to apply for a special exemption, which took Twitter weeks to approve. I wish I had budgeted for this time.

I snuck out of my home office quietly and headed to the lab. I needed to find every machine on which I had an account. If I strung enough machines together, I hoped I could handle the traffic spike before it went away. At the lab, I took stock: one iMac, two Linux machines and two FreeBSD machines, all hooked up to the high-speed Department of Computer Science network. I logged into one of the FreeBSD machines and quickly wrote some code to handle new We Meddle users. I replicated this process on the other machines, spending more time than I wanted on the iMac because it does not normally do this sort of thing. Finally, I pieced together some very simple dispatch code on the main We Meddle server. Whenever a new request arrived, the code checked the current time. If the time in milliseconds is divisible by 6, I dispatched to the iMac; if the remainder is 1 modulo 6, I sent the traffic to one of the Linux machines, and so on. I even directed some of the We Meddle traffic back to an old fileserver I had on my home Comcast network.

The code rewrite had taken me a few hours, and, unfortunately, I missed the majority of my traffic spike. (And, of course, I broke We Meddle a few times as I deployed code directly to the live site, without testing it first.) I still saw higher than average traffic from South Korea for the next day or two, but high traffic would not test my new infrastructure until later. Looking back now, I am proud of my kludgey little infrastructure. It reminds me of what I've read about the Web's early days. But it is clearly out of date by today's standards. I certainly lost users because I opted for something minimal and homegrown. No startup would have done what I did. However, I was also able to afford rent that month.

Conclusion

My research is rooted in two fields: sociology and HCI. My biggest frustration with sociological studies of the Web is the focus on what is, rather than on what could be. The social Web, like all technological artifacts, got designed. It does not have to be the way it is, and this is what I love most about HCI and design. HCI and design view technology as malleable. As I see it, there is room to marry these two philosophies. I think We Meddle exemplified this hybrid approach. I was able to say something new and interesting about tie strength—that it behaves the same way across two social media sites, Twitter and Facebook—and it absolutely made my day when We Meddle solved somebody's real-world problem. For example, one We Meddle user tweeted that the site makes sure "important friends won't be buried in an ocean of other tweets."

This was a new approach, and as with all new approaches, it had its kinks. I wrote here about the ones I found most vexing: the tension between building and experimenting, sampling, finding users, and scaling. Scaling may seem totally mundane—not worth writing about—but I spent the most hours struggling with that aspect of the project. Unlike the Web of 1995, today people have high expectations for design and scalability. You cannot hope to participate if you stand out like a sore thumb. I hope that in exposing my difficulties with balancing the building and experimenting, as well as with finding users, I can save people time and headaches. Moreover, I hope that this essay reveals some interesting new problems of method—problems I want resolved.

Notes

1. The "I" in this chapter refers to the first author whose dissertation project is described here. The second author was first author's advisor.

2. See http://dev.twitter.com—APIs allow developers to retrieve data from sites they do not own, like Twitter.

3. Seesmic has now been acquired by Hootsuite. See http://hootsuite.com.

4. See http://jquery.com.

5. See http://web.archive.org/web/20100522011130/http://getsatisfaction.com/.

6. See http://aws.amazon.com.

References

Christakis, N. A., and J. H. Fowler. 2007. The spread of obesity in a large social network over 32 years. *New England Journal of Medicine 357* (4): 370–379.

Constant, D., L. Sproull, and S. Kiesler. 1996. The kindness of strangers: The usefulness of electronic weak ties for technical advice. *Organization Science 7* (2): 119–135.

Gilbert, E., and K. Karahalios. 2009. Predicting tie strength with social media. In *Proceedings of the SIGCHI Conference on Human Factors in Computing Systems,* 211–220.

Granovetter, M. S. 1973. The strength of weak ties. *American Journal of Sociology 78* (6): 1360–1380.

Granovetter, M. 1974. *Getting a Job: A Study of Contacts and Careers.* Chicago: University Of Chicago Press.

Lazer, D., A. Pentland, L. Adamic, S. Aral, A.-L. Barabási, D. Brewer, N. Christakis, 2009. Computational social science. *Science 323* (5915): 721–723.

Newman, M. E. J. 2006. Modularity and community structure in networks. *Proceedings of the National Academy of Sciences of the United States of America 103* (23): 8577–8582.

Schaefer, C., J. C. Coyne, and R. S. Lazarus. 1981. The health-related functions of social support. *Journal of Behavioral Medicine 4* (4): 381–406.

Stone, B. 2009. There's a list for that. https://blog.twitter.com/2009/theres-list. Accessed March 31, 2012.

Tahmincioglu, E. 2008. Facebook friends as job references? http://www.nbcnews.com/id/26223330. Accessed October 14, 2011.

Uzzi, B. 1999. Embeddedness in the making of financial capital: How social relations and networks benefit firms seeking financing. *American Sociological Review 64* (4): 481–505.

Wellman, B., and S. Wortley. 1990. Different strokes from different folks: Community ties and social support. *American Journal of Sociology 96* (3): 558–588.

7

Hired Hands and Dubious Guesses: Adventures in Crowdsourced Data Collection

Aaron Shaw

"What if we used Mechanical Turk to do it?" It was one of those hare-brained, off-hand suggestions that bubbled up frequently enough in our brainstorming sessions that I no longer remember exactly who said it. There were three of us around the conference table that day, our diagrams and notes on the floor-to-ceiling dry-erase boards, our laptops, papers, and cell phones spread across the table. As soon as the sentence came out, smiles spread across each of our faces. The faculty principal investigator on the project started to chuckle out loud. The laughter spread, and in a few seconds we were mapping out the hypothetical steps and implications of the idea. We left the room still talking, the conversation light with excitement and anticipation.

Something about the idea of crowdsourcing our data collection seemed completely appropriate. We had struggled for weeks to arrive at a compelling research design and found ourselves confronting a very concrete data collection problem: how to do an extensive content analysis of several hundred websites at once. The questions we wanted to ask about each site were fairly simple, but far too numerous to make it practical to answer them all without the help of a very large team of research assistants. Knowing that we didn't really have the organizational or financial resources to undertake that effort, we had started to consider scaling back the study and other alternatives. Then came the Mechanical Turk idea: we thought we would distribute the work as a massive set of microtasks through an online labor market. As it turned out, we had no idea what that would entail.

Mechanical Turk is a Web service operated by Amazon.com and the most widely known commercial platform for distributed work online, which is also known as crowdsourcing, or human computation. A decent definition of crowdsourcing is *the disaggregation and distribution of large tasks across a large group of people over the Internet.*[1] To illustrate what this actually means, imagine that you have 100 million photos that you need to make sure do not include any child pornography, hate speech, copyright violations, or something similar.[2] The automated methods of filtering images for this kind of stuff turn out to be imperfect in a bunch of ways, so you cannot trust them 100% of the time. As a result, you need to verify that these automated methods work by at least reviewing a sample of the images by hand. Crowdsourcing the solution to this problem would entail that you use some system (probably also online) to enable as many people as possible to review as few or as many photos at a time as they want (probably in exchange for very tiny amounts of money for every photo reviewed).[3] Other examples of crowdsourcing and human computation involve very different kinds of problems and people, as well as more or less complicated procedures.

Over the past five years or so, crowdsourcing of many different kinds has become a growing area of investment and innovation in Silicon Valley as well as in several research communities. At the same time, crowdsourcing remains a relatively foreign concept among social scientists. The purpose of this chapter is to both introduce the idea of using crowdsourcing for social science research and to address some of the challenges I have encountered in trying to actually do so. Despite the fact that writing something like this makes it seem like I am setting myself up as an expert on the subject, I have really been more of a spectator sitting somewhere off to the side of the avant garde of the crowdsourcing industry and the research communities involved in advancing the development of new techniques and tools for managing "collective intelligence." In the process, I have developed multiple research projects that utilize crowdsourcing both as a field site where I have recruited research subjects as well as a source for distributed research assistance. In the material that follows, I discuss practical issues involved in this work that extend beyond such a novel, unusual field of study.

The biggest concerns with crowdsourcing any aspect of a research project boil down to the fact that the practice of crowdsourcing tends to be (1) organized like poorly compensated online piecework, and (2) very boring. In addition, customizing many of the interfaces through which online crowdsourcing takes place can require significant computer programming knowledge, and some of us who choose to use them enlist the help of a software engineer at some point. As a result, you, the researcher, wind up confronting digital-age variants of organizational problems that have plagued large-scale divisions of scientific, industrial, and bureaucratic labor for several centuries. How do you hire and manage employees to contribute to a project without sacrificing quality? How do you collaborate with colleagues who have completely different training and vocabulary from your own? How do you learn to use new tools without wasting resources? None of my graduate theory and methods seminars prepared me adequately to confront these challenges, despite the fact that I now believe they have been commonplace in academic research for a long time.

In a classic 1966 essay, Julius Roth described the problems with using what he called "hired hands" to conduct research work.[4] His analysis speaks to a general problem of any research project employing multiple people and technologies to perform data collection or analysis: "When the tasks of a research project are split up into small pieces to be assigned to hired hands, none of these data-collectors and processors will ever understand all the complexities and subtleties of the research issues in the same way as the person who conceived of the study. ... Since the [research] director often cannot be sure what conceptions of the issues the hired hands have as a result of his explanations and 'training,' he must make *dubious guesses* about the meaning of much of the data they return to him. ... As he gains in quantity of data, he loses in validity and meaningfulness" (Roth 1966: 193, emphasis added).

Roth could just as easily be speaking of a more typical study with one or two paid research assistants as a crowdsourcing study employing thousands on Mechanical Turk or some other Web-based platform. Irrespective of the type or scale of work you do, the critique (as well as his humorous ethnographic examples of hired hands undermining researchers' objectives) should strike terror into your heart if you had assumed that farming out your scholarship to people or machines was going to be a straightforward affair.

At the same time, I disagree with part of Roth's premise, as well as his conclusion. Problems of data quality and uncertainty apply even when research assistants do not perform your data collection for you. The difficulties of calibrating and coordinating diverse sets of people, sociotechnical systems, and techniques affect even those projects where there is only one researcher involved. Data collection methods and artifacts may or may not, in Langdon Winner's (1986) famous phrase, "have politics," but they are also far from neutral instruments that exist only to serve the scholarly will in a direct or unmediated way. It takes a lot of practical learning and work to apply any method effectively, and the process usually entails numerous failures and mistakes. Furthermore, the quality of data does not necessarily increase in inverse proportion to its quantity. The failures, mistakes, and "dubious guesses" that so often look like bad research work often feed into the construction of a more nuanced, intelligent understanding of a particular process, method, or person.

A narrower form of my argument may be more straightforward: *creating and managing an effective division of intellectual labor lies at the heart of any ambitious research project.* By "research project" and "intellectual labor" here I really mean the whole gamut—all the stuff that researchers, research assistants, colleagues, and supervisors do in addition to the methods and the tools involved in data collection and analysis. For a variety of reasons I explain below, crowdsourcing has illustrated the value of this broad perspective to me many times over. As social scientists, many of us may cling to the myth of the heroic scholar, laboring away in monastic, dusty solitude and publishing brilliant (sole-authored!) articles or books. However, the reality of scholarly labor is almost always more interesting and complicated, involving teams of assistants, administrative staff, librarians, statisticians, or—increasingly for those of us doing work involving digital media—software, engineers, websites, and Internet users about whom we may know shockingly little. The names or accomplishments of these individuals or tools may appear in footnotes and acknowledgments, but the labor of their contributions often remains invisible, with the heavy brush strokes of collaboration, paid work, and research administration obscured behind a polite veneer of attribution.

Scrutinizing the division of academic labor from this point of view can get a little uncomfortable. What began in my research group meeting that day as a starry-eyed foray into crowdsourcing research has forced me to recognize some of my shortcomings as a scholar as well as the extent to which I have capitalized on the contributions of others to my work in a way that feels unfair and even a little exploitative. At the same time, I still hope that these realizations may make me a better researcher in the end. Crowdsourcing has shown me that in the course of a collective endeavor, almost everyone and everything involved will, at some point, make "contributions" that are either unproductive or an active hindrance to the progress of the project. The interesting questions arise when you try to figure out how to learn from all these failures and "dubious guesses."

Crowdsourcing and the Division of Scientific Labor

As I suggested above, the need to divide an overwhelming amount of academic labor drove my collaborators and I to use crowdsourcing for our data collection. In this regard, our motives resemble the reasons human computation and crowdsourcing were developed in the first place. Historical examples of the division of academic labor overlap with the earliest cases of human computation, which in turn gave rise to contemporary crowdsourcing techniques.[5] In 1759, a team of three French astronomers used calculus to work out an accurate estimate for the date on which Halley's Comet would pass closest to Sun. In doing so, the three, Alexis Clairaut, Joseph Lalande, and Nicole-Reine Lepaute, had to perform literally thousands of arithmetic calculations *by hand*, a task that they completed in part by dividing the labor and devising systematic procedures to check for errors. The techniques they developed became the foundation for subsequent practices of scientific calculation and computation, which grew in scope and ambition as calculus and statistics became prominent fields of research and innovation. Following the two world wars, during which human computers even calculated the ballistics tables used in the field to aim various weapons, human computation waned in prominence as mainframe computing became feasible and outpaced the processing power of people alone.[6]

Ironically, the diffusion of digital computing networks that followed the mainframe era has also brought with it a renaissance of human computing, more commonly referred to now as crowdsourcing. As was the case with human computation, much of the innovation in crowdsourcing has happened through scientific research. The 2001 NASA clickworkers project, in which visitors to a NASA website could volunteer to label craters in photos of the surface of Mars, represents the foundational example of contemporary academic crowdsourcing (Benkler, 2006: 136–138;

Kanefsky, Barlow, and Gulick, 2001).[7] Since then, a number of scientific projects have adopted similar techniques to engage amateur citizen scientists in data collection and classification.[8] In addition, a growing number of commercial crowdsourcing platforms have made paid, distributed work more accessible. Using these platforms, computer scientists and computational linguists have begun to apply more refined filtering techniques to some of the data collected by crowds in order to improve the precision of results (e.g., Quinn and Bederson, 2011; Sheng, Provost, and Ipeirotis, 2008; Snow et al. 2008). The result has been a concomitant growth in research on the dynamics and applications of crowdsourcing, including a growing body of work that uses crowdsourcing for social scientific inquiry and to address topics of relevance to social scientists (Horton, Rand, and Zeckhauser 2011).

There are now several websites that make it feasible to recruit a crowd of your own (in exchange for payment or not) and, indeed, several companies have received venture funding for business models based on commercial crowdsourcing of various kinds. In terms of research, the diffusion of these tools and techniques has made it so that you no longer need to be an engineer or a physicist at NASA to experiment with crowdsourcing. Indeed, a few dollars and an hour or so of tinkering can get you access to a crowd of your own through Web services like Amazon's Mechanical Turk, CrowdFlower, or Clickworker (a private company founded in Germany that shares the name of the original NASA project).[9] Likewise, the widespread availability of tools for building Web applications make it so that a few hours of programming from a skilled developer are all that stand between you and your own custom-built crowdsourcing platform … in theory.

User Error

Thinking back to the conversation in the conference room, I can see that my colleagues and I had bought into a number of prevailing theories about crowdsourcing, most of which were wrong. To start with, consider the basic insight behind using crowds for any kind of work: that it can be faster and more effective to recruit a large group of nonspecialist people to perform a research task in a distributed fashion over the Internet than to employ either a small number of highly trained research assistants or computer algorithms. I do not consider this statement untrue, but it leaves out so many important details as to be totally useless when you actually try to crowdsource something. I learned just how useless as soon as I began trying to execute our research ideas on Mechanical Turk.

Once we had secured human subjects approval for our project, I started running pilot jobs on Mechanical Turk. Immediately, I found numerous ways to mess them up. My problems started with simple interface design mistakes, such as asking the workers to enter a date in response to a question, but not requiring that their answer be in a particular format. The resulting data was a mess of words, numbers, and variations of month-day-year formats I had never seen. It also took me a while to internalize some of the terminology Amazon uses to distinguish between the individual microtasks that make up a larger job (they call these "human intelligence tasks," or "HITs," and the larger job itself (these used to be known as tasks, but are now called groups). As a result, I ordered several jobs at once in which each of 10 questions were answered 100 times by a single Mturk worker, instead of 100 workers answering 10 questions one time each (feel free to read that over if you need to, or just trust me when I say it's a totally bone-headed move). Luckily, within a few minutes, one of the workers emailed through the Mturk interface to alert me to the situation and I stopped the job after only 200 or so of the HITs had been completed. Such mistakes were (and still are!) embarrassing as well as costly. I had not accounted for my own ignorance in the original research budget, and after accumulating a handful of similar screw-ups, I had to go to the project principal investigator and explain all the idiotic ways in which I had managed to waste our money in order to ask for some additional funds. Even though Mturk tasks cost about a penny each, when you purchase several dozen or hundreds of them at a time, and the workers respond to your tasks within seconds, the pennies add up fast.

All of these failures forced me to confront the fact that even a crowd will not do your work for you automatically. Crowdsourcing is only as fast and effective as the person designing and managing the task. The idea that you can conduct large-scale projects more efficiently simply by hiring more people falls apart if you do not know how to take advantage of their attention and intelligence. Indeed, my experience suggests a social science corollary to Brook's Law[10]: adding manpower to a large research project likely makes it slower.

Communication Breakdowns

Eventually, after completing a few successful pilots, I ran a pair of controlled experiments on Mechanical Turk. For both of these studies, I worked in collaboration with multiple researchers across different disciplines and organizations, using Mechanical Turk as a subject pool to recruit participants (Shaw, Horton, and Chen 2011; Antin and Shaw 2011). At the same time, my coauthors and I conducted the experiments using different platforms. The first involved a Web-based application that software developers and researchers in a university setting had designed to handle traditional survey and content analysis tasks. The second study ran on the CrowdFlower platform, originally built for the purpose of commercial, enterprise-scale crowdsourcing jobs. In both cases, there were several unanticipated hang-ups in the process of actually getting to the point where we could run the study. Some of these problems stemmed from using two relatively new pieces of software that still had numerous bugs.[11] Others emerged later, the products of communication breakdowns between myself and the software engineers.

In both experiments, the biggest communication breakdowns concerned the process of assigning participants into groups. It is only a slight exaggeration to say that *random* and *unique* treatment assignment represent the most fundamental prerequisites for a valid, controlled experiment in the modern sense of the term (see Fisher 1935). Basically, this means that each subject in the study gets randomly assigned and exposed to one, and only one, of the experimental conditions. Meeting these criteria help ensure that the study does not violate the stable unit treatment value assumption (a.k.a. "SUTVA").[12] The bottom line here is that if you mess up either the random or the unique assignment of treatment and control conditions, your experiment cannot generate valid inferences about either any of the differences between the effects of the experimental conditions or any effects the treatment might or might not have on the population at large. In other words, you cannot claim that your experimental treatment caused the results that you found. You can only claim to understand what the results of a controlled experiment mean if you handle the treatment assignment in a systematic way. No exceptions.

Not surprisingly, my collaborators and I wanted to ensure that our engineer collaborators really understood what we meant when we asked them whether the software really met the requirements of random and unique treatment assignment. For the most part, we, the social scientists, did not really try to understand exactly how the Web applications did what they did; however, given the stakes of getting treatment assignment right, we felt we needed to be absolutely certain we understood the steps involved. We would not drop the issue until we were 100% certain that everything worked exactly as we expected 100% of the time.

Needless to say, our software engineer colleagues on both projects found this sort of nit-picky insistence tiresome. On the first experiment with the software developed in an academic research center, hashing out the details of the randomization function generated epic email threads, spanning several weeks and incorporating dozens of examples as all of us tried repeatedly to illustrate our ideas in jargon-free terms. It also resulted in a few more failed pilot studies as we tested and retested the software to make sure it behaved as planned. One afternoon, when we were painfully close to running the study, the lead developer and I spent three hours on the phone, walking through every step of the experiment (as I wanted it to run) and every block of the treatment assignment code (as he had written it). This sort of uncompromising attention to detail allowed the study to succeed eventually, but I still came away wondering why it had taken so incredibly long to do so.

On the surface, my experience working with the private startup *looked* totally different. In that case, I had reached an informal agreement with one of the co-founders to help the company implement some survey work on behalf a prospective client. At the time, the company was extremely small (about five employees), and one of the perks of working with them was that they were excited to help me run experiments using their platform.[13] The three members of the engineering team all had experience building commercial Web applications, and the platform already had an extremely robust set of features as well as an elegant user interface. Everything suggested that the process would be much smoother and faster than my experience with the small academic research center's software developers.

Despite the platform's powerful ability to scale and all the amazing features that were already built in, it still took almost three months of back and forth with one particularly friendly engineer for me to actually run a controlled experiment. Once again, I spent a good part of this time struggling to explain exactly what I meant by the concept of treatment assignment. Instead of randomization, though, the hangup was around ensuring that each worker saw *one and only one* of the treatments. As with the my first Mechanical Turk pilots, fuzzy distinctions between units of analysis, tasks, and groups of tasks made it hard for the engineer and I to figure out exactly what the other person was talking about. As with the first study, we worked through the same conversations three or four separate times.

Eventually, my engineer friend told me about an entire open-source scripting language that had been built into the platform at an earlier point in the development, but that was not included in any of the formal documentation. He thought that I might be able to use the language to make the software do what I wanted. After reading the scripting language documentation and fiddling around with a few more pilot studies, it did in fact turn out that this language could manage the sort of randomization I needed without any customizations.

Unique assignment was harder this time because it undermined some of the assumptions the engineers held about how crowdsourcing tasks tended to work and which they had therefore written into the code. Luckily, I was able to convince them, in the context of a separate discussion with clients interested in using the software to run surveys, that the feature would actually be useful for a wide range of applications, and so the lead engineer felt he could justify putting a couple of hours into implementing the new feature late one night.

In hindsight, nothing about either of these experiences—the one with the developers at the academic research center or the one with the engineers at the startup—strikes me as especially surprising. Perhaps the only part of either story that really defies explanation is why I ever thought the process would be faster, simpler, or less challenging than it turned out to be. As a social scientist with relatively minimal programming experience, I had not anticipated the complexity of software development as a process. I had also failed to explain our needs and concerns in a way that made intuitive sense to software developers, who likewise struggled to explain the inner workings of their code in a way that a nondeveloper could easily follow.

Hired Hands Revisited

In the end, both experiments worked out well, and the experience helped me apply crowdsourcing tools for the purpose I originally intended: distributed content analysis. I have now completed multiple pilots and small-scale side projects applying these techniques and am designing several larger studies. When colleagues learn that some of my research involves data collected through Mechanical Turk, they tend to express disbelief that anybody would actually do crowdsourcing work for so little money. They also often voice doubts that the workers on Mturk and other online labor markets answer questions honestly or perform the tasks requested of them in earnest. They never suspect that my early failures with crowdsourced data collection would derive from my own mistakes or my inability to communicate effectively with software engineers. Such responses overlook the practical challenges of learning how to work with unfamiliar digital tools or the process of software development. They also betray an underlying mistrust of "hired hand research" more generally. While this mistrust is warranted in the context of crowdsourced data, I find it overstated and somewhat ironic. Researchers engaged in crowdsourcing data collection and analysis have developed methods that account for the inevitability of low-quality data with robust techniques to maximize the precision of their results. At the same time, researchers performing more traditional forms of content analysis, interviewing, and survey research have few corresponding solutions to correct for the identical problems.

A little background on crowdsourcing workers provides a useful entry point to a broader discussion of reliability and data quality in the context of crowdsourcing. A diverse population of individuals participate in crowdsourcing as workers in online labor markets or as volunteers in noncommercial projects. For example, while Amazon refuses to make representative data about Mechanical Turk workers publicly available, several informal surveys and qualitative studies provide evidence that the population includes a moderate gender balance as well as individuals from a range of socioeconomic, linguistic, and cultural backgrounds (Ipeirotis 2010; Khanna et al. 2010; Ross et al. 2010). In the experiment

I conducted with John Horton and Daniel Chen, we also found evidence of substantial variation in Internet skills among the participants in our study. Some of this diversity makes Mturk a *more* attractive site for comparative research than traditional laboratories or some other, less diverse online environments. For example, Judd Antin and I found evidence of different motivational patterns across Mturk workers in India when compared with those in the United States. While it does not make sense to claim that such findings are representative of broader national trends in either country, the experiment incorporates the variations in the site's user population into the research design, taking advantage of the fact that Mturk makes it relatively affordable to run a cross-national research project.

The diversity of Mturk workers creates some interesting challenges in the day-to-day process of running a study. Earlier, I alluded to the fact that workers can email you about any task that you post to the site. In that case, a worker alerted me to a problem with one of my tasks, saving me some additional frustration and research funds. In the course of piloting and running the rest of that same experiment, I received close to 100 other emails from workers. Most of them were not nearly so helpful, polite, or grammatically coherent. Many reported problems viewing my task (the majority of these were caused by old versions of Internet Explorer failing to render the site correctly) or simply requested that I submit payments for the task more quickly (I tended to process the payments in monthly batches, which was nowhere near fast enough for some participants). I set up auto-responses and stock replies to common inquires in order to alleviate the inbox traffic, but I had effectively become the payroll and technical support department of a very small, transnational research organization overnight. Somehow, I had wound up at both ends of an outsourcing supply chain at the same time.

In terms of assessing the validity and reliability of data, the diversity of skills, languages, and educational backgrounds among Mturk workers has given rise to some creative solutions that improve upon traditional content analysis techniques. Historically, content analysis research has employed a multistage process to ensure that the results are both valid and reliable (see Krippendorff 2004; Neuendorf 2002). The basic idea behind reliability in this context is that you want to be sure that your results are not simply the product of an idiosyncratic interpretation of the world, but rather correspond to a widely intelligible and acceptable inter-pretation. Methodologically, the state of the art way to test this is pretty simple: you have multiple individuals apply the content analysis instru-ment (or codes) to a bunch of the same content (text, images, videos, or whatever) and then run some statistical tests on the results to calculate the rate of agreement between the coders.

Nothing about crowdsourcing changes the underlying objective here: you still want your results to capture real concepts, and you still need to get some sort of confirmation that these concepts hold up at an intersub-jective level. The core difference just lies in the process by which you go about measuring reliability. The problem with the standard approaches to reliability in the context of crowdsourcing is severalfold. Unlike a more typical research project employing undergraduate research assistants, crowdsourcing, by definition, opens up the project to a wider population of people about whom you, the researcher, know pretty much nothing and over whom you have very little influence. In addition, the scale of participation possible with crowdsourcing makes it feasible for you to incorporate results from even more coders about even more questions than a traditional content analysis study. In this sense, Roth's aforemen-tioned concerns about "dubious guesses" take on a new urgency. The messy data generated by a crowd is, by definition, more dubious than most.

Luckily, a lot of smart statisticians and computer scientists have come up with creative responses to processing unreliable data from multiple coders.[14] The key involves approaching the raw, messy data as an optimi-zation problem: for every data point, we want to maximize the likelihood that we select the correct answer on the basis of the coders' responses. We (or, more accurately, our statistical software), can then treat each coder as possessing an underlying probability of providing a correct response to any question, and can estimate this probability for each coder by asking them to answer a few questions to which we know the answer ahead of time. After establishing the workers' rate of accuracy, we collect multiple responses to every question from multiple coders and weight these obser-vations by the coder's accuracy rate to estimate the answer that is most likely to be correct.

The elegance of this approach stems from the use of "bad" information to produce valid, reliable inferences about the best answers to any particular question. In Roth's terms, you take a lot of dubious guesses, try to figure out how dubious they are, and then use that knowledge to estimate the least dubious guess. Instead of fighting or denying the hired hands problem, this technique takes advantage of it in a clever way.

No Silver Bullets

If you step back from the details, these sorts of algorithmic approaches to maximizing data quality contain more general implications for research design and methods. As I said in the introduction, I think all research work entails a process of combining tools and perspectives in an effort to extract accurate and reliable knowledge about a particular topic. The extent to which this process involves hired hands, online participants, collaborators unfamiliar with social scientific methods, or computational techniques varies from project to project. In the present case, all of these factors introduced sources of error, bias, and uncertainty into my work. As with the failed pilots and bad-quality data that came from some of the respondents in my Mturk studies, I think these sorts of challenges constitute an important part of the learning process that eventually allowed me to produce better studies. In retrospect, it does not make sense to me to even pretend that I could have completely eliminated all the mistakes along the way. Instead, the best I could do was to incorporate these mistakes into my knowledge of the process and try to optimize the process within the limits of that knowledge.

If you think of research as a constructive learning process involving multiple people, procedures, and tools, each of which introduces some sort of bias and error along the way, I think the question of hired hands opens up a broader discussion. The big point here is that any kind of wrong information is still informative—whether about the quality of the data, the reliability of the data collection processes, or the nature of the people participating in the research project. As a result, every dubious guess provides an opportunity to learn and to refine and improve the research project and the finished product it generates.

In this sense, I think there comes a time in any research project when each of us, intentionally or not, undermines the validity, reliability, or accuracy of the work. As researchers, we may do this by imposing an overly idealized vision of the research process on the reality of data collection (which tends to be messy, unpredictable, and biased in some way or another). We may also do this by naively expecting our research assistants and collaborators to share our assumptions, objectives, and desires.

For classic "hired hands" like Roth's research assistants or the typical worker on Mechanical Turk, the reasons behind this have to do with the structural constraints imposed by the division of labor and the dynamics of paid work in labor markets. In these markets, the exigencies of wage earning too often result in people doing a task they find uninspiring, boring, or stupid. In the context of Mechanical Turk and other similar online platforms, these dynamics tend to be exacerbated by extraordinarily atomized and antisocial work environments that do little to counterbalance the intrinsic inequalities between workers and employers.

For collaborators like my software engineer friends, the story gets more complicated: the ways in which they undermined the project's progress and objectives did not seem to stem from the desire to shirk responsibility for financial or other reasons. Instead, there was an underlying misunderstanding that simply took a lot of work and communication to correct. Once everybody was on the same page, they quickly and happily helped me execute randomization in both of my studies.

Needless to say, I am still quite far removed from the vision of crowd-sourced data collection that my colleagues and I imagined around that conference table. In fact, several years later, I am just beginning to realize some of the plans we laid out. It turns out that even when you can do research on and about a networked environment where the cost of attracting thousands of people to participate in your study approaches zero, nobody and no technology will ever truly do all the work for you.

Notes

1. As with many neologisms related to the Internet, competing definitions for crowdsourcing exist. Mine is derived from a combination of the original description by Howe (2008), who coined the term, and my own observations.

2. As it happens, this is roughly the number of photos uploaded to Facebook *every single day*. Source: http://en-gb.facebook.com/notes/facebook-engineering/developing-facebooks-new-photo-viewer/499447633919. To give you some tangible idea of how many photos this is, consider that 100 million sheets of regular thickness (0.0004 in. or 0.01 cm) paper would create a stack roughly 30,000 feet (or 10 km) high.

3. This kind of arrangement raises all kinds of questions, like how you know that the photo reviewers are not also the kind of people who like to post porn everywhere they go on the Internet; how you figure out what to do when two reviewers of the same photo disagree about what constitutes porn in the first place; and whether it's ethically a good thing for anybody to be doing mind-numbing work like this in exchange for such small amounts of money; etc. These are hard questions that are fundamental to crowdsourcing as both a social technology and an economic phenomenon. I'll try to address some of them below.

4. Thanks to the editors of this volume for pointing me to Roth's essay.

5. My account here leans heavily on David Alan Grier's *When Computers Were Human* (2005).

6. It is worth noting that from the late nineteenth century until the advent of the mainframe computing era, the majority of *human* computers were women (Grier 2005). This kind of academic grunt work provided one of the few avenues of scientific achievement accessible to (and culturally acceptable for) women at the time. In all likelihood, the relative invisibility of human computers in the history of science and mathematics derives from this *feminization* of computational labor. In addition, the similarly forgotten fact that the earliest computer programmers were women resulted directly from the legacy of women in human computation. Just as the equipment and research budgets for computing got bigger, the number of women involved in the field declined.

7. In that case, three NASA researchers, Bob Kanefsky, Nadine Barlow, and Virginia Gulick, wanted to identify craters in photographs of the surface of Mars taken by the Viking orbiter and decided to see whether volunteers recruited over the Internet could perform the task as well as a physicist with a PhD (Barlow herself). The results of their study (which they conceived as a side project) suggested that with a little bit of filtering, the accuracy of the results provided by the volunteers was about the same as that of the physicist (Kanefsky, Barlow, and Gulick 2001).

8. I should point out that some of the creators of these projects do not call what they do crowdsourcing and argue that there are fundamental differences between crowdsourcing and citizen science. I think this is fine, but since I prefer a broader definition of crowdsourcing (see above), I tend not to observe such fine-grained distinctions.

9. Full disclosure: I have done paid consulting work with CrowdFlower, which is based in San Francisco, CA.

10. Brooks' (1995) law states: "Adding manpower to a late software project only makes it later."

11. A very distinguished computer science professor only recently explained to me that even the greatest software only has *fewer* bugs; it is never bug-free. I didn't fully understand this until I started collaborating with developers in the process of designing, testing, and improving real code.

12. Since I find the term completely obfuscatory and unhelpful, I avoid using it, but I feel sort of obligated to mention it in case you want to look into this kind of

thing further or intimidate your friends with academic jargon. The assumptions underlying SUTVA get pretty abstruse and discussing them would take me deep into the methodological weeds, so I'm going to just refer you to some really clear articles that explain how it works in more detail: see Holland, 1986; Little & Rubin, 2000.

13. In this regard, my experience collaborating on research with a private-sector organization had some interesting parallels with the discussion by Williams and Xiong (2009). Like them, I found it necessary to consciously frame my work to be more interesting to an audience oriented toward the very practical problems of running a small company. At the same time, the reduced scale of the company also made it much easier to approach anybody involved and start a casual conversation about the company's work and my interests.

14. Everything I am about to say comes directly from previous research in maximum likelihood estimation and human computation (Dawid and Skene 1979; Sheng et al. 2008; Snow et al. 2008).

References

Antin, J., and A. Shaw. 2011. Social desirability bias and self-reports of motivation: A cross-cultural study of Amazon Mechanical Turk in the US and India. Presented at the 2011 ACM Conference on Computer-Supported Cooperative Work. Hangzhou, China.

Benkler, Y. 2006. *The Wealth of Networks: How Social Production Transforms Markets and Freedom*. New Haven: Yale University Press.

Brooks, F. P. 1995. *The Mythical Man-Month: Essays on Software Engineering*. Reading, MA: Addison-Wesley.

Dawid, A. P., and A. M. Skene. 1979. Maximum likelihood estimation of observer error-rates using the EM algorithm. *Journal of the Royal Statistical Society: Series C, Applied Statistics 28* (1): 20–28.

Fisher, R. A. 1935. *The Design of Experiments*. Edinburgh, Scotland: Oliver and Boyd.

Grier, D. A. 2005. *When Computers Were Human*. Princeton: Princeton University Press.

Holland, P. W. 1986. Statistics and causal inference. *Journal of the American Statistical Association 81* (396): 945–960.

Horton, J. J., D. Rand, and R. J. Zeckhauser. 2011. The online laboratory: Conducting experiments in a real labor market. *Experimental Economics 14* (3): 399–425.

Howe, J. 2008. *Crowdsourcing: Why the Power of the Crowd Is Driving the Future of Business*. New York: Crown Business.

Ipeirotis, P. 2010. Demographics of Mechanical Turk. New York University working paper.

Kanefsky, B., N. G. Barlow, and V. C. Gulick. 2001. Can distributed volunteers accomplish massive data analysis tasks? *Proceedings of the Lunar and Planetary Institute Science Conference 32*: 1272.

Khanna, S., A. Ratan, J. Davis, and W. Thies. 2010. Evaluating and improving the usability of Mechanical Turk for low-income workers in India. *Proceedings of the First ACM Symposium on Computing for Development 12*: 1–10. London, UK: Association for Computing Machinery.

Krippendorff, K. 2004. *Content Analysis: An Introduction to Its Methodology.* 2nd ed. Thousand Oaks, CA: Sage.

Little, R. J., and D. B. Rubin. 2000. Causal effects in clinical and epidemiological studies via potential outcomes: Concepts and analytical approaches. *Annual Review of Public Health 21*: 121–145.

Neuendorf, K. A. 2002. *The Content Analysis Guidebook.* Atlanta: Sage.

Quinn, A. J., & Bederson, B. B. 2011. Human Computation: A Survey and Taxonomy of a Growing Field. In *Proceedings of the SIGCHI Conference on Human Factors in Computing Systems* (pp. 1403–1412). New York, NY, USA: ACM. http://doi.org/10.1145/1978942.1979148.

Ross, J., L. Irani, M. S. Silberman, A. Zaldivar, and B. Tomlinson. 2010. Who are the crowdworkers? Shifting demographics in Mechanical Turk. *Proceedings of the 28th international conference extended abstracts on human factors in computing systems* 2863–2872. Atlanta, GA.

Roth, J. A. 1966. Hired hand research. *American Sociologist 1* (4): 190–196.

Shaw, A., J. J. Horton, and D. L. Chen. 2011. Designing incentives for inexpert human raters. *Proceedings of the 2011 ACM Conference on Computer-Supported Cooperative Work.* Hangzhou, China.

Sheng, V. S., F. Provost, and P. G. Ipeirotis. 2008. Get another label? Improving data quality and data mining using multiple, noisy labelers. *Proceedings of the Conference on Knowledge Discovery and Data Mining.*

Snow, R., B. O'Connor, D. Jurafsky, and A. Y. Ng. 2008. Cheap and fast—but is it good? Evaluating non-expert annotations for natural language tasks. *Proceedings of the Conference on Empirical Methods in Natural Language Processing.*

Williams, D., and L. Xiong. 2009. Herding cats online: Real studies of virtual communities. In *Research Confidential: Solutions to Problems Most Social Scientists Pretend They Never Have*, ed. E. Hargittai, 122–140. Ann Arbor, MI: University of Michigan Press.

Winner, L. 1986. Do artifacts have politics? in *The Whale and the Reactor: A Search for Limits in an Age of High Technology*, 19–39. Chicago: University of Chicago Press.

8

How Local Is User-Generated Content? A 9,000+-Word Essay on Answering a Five-Word Research Question

… Or, how we learned to stop worrying (or worry less) and love the diverse challenges of our fast-moving, geography-flavored interdisciplinary research area

Brent Hecht and Darren Gergle

At five words plus a hyphen, our research question was deceptively simple: "How 'local' is user-generated content?" We "simply" wanted to know if Wikipedia pages contained homegrown knowledge, if Flickr photographers were contributing photos of their hometown, if Yelp reviews are produced primarily by locals, etc. This project was so straightforward that for once we could easily explain it to our friends and family. However, the story behind this seemingly straightforward pursuit is anything but. We ultimately produced a piece of research (Hecht and Gergle 2010a) that provided valuable insight about an important question, but in doing so we had to overcome major methodological challenges, foreboding data issues, and a hair-raising last minute scooping of a major portion of our study.

With our backgrounds in computer science, geography, and the social sciences, we had become aware that there were divergent opinions in the academic literature and the popular media about the localness of user-generated content such as Wikipedia articles, Flickr photos, and Yelp reviews. The computer vision community,[1] for example, tended to assume that Flickr photos were touristic in nature (Crandall et al. 2009). In other words, there was an implicit assumption underlying work in this area that Flickr photos were primarily produced by travelers. On the other hand,

many in the social sciences and popular media (e.g., Helft 2009) celebrated the triumph of local information that user-generated content sup-
posedly represented. These folks argued that the user-generated content
revolution was a coup for homegrown knowledge. For instance, well-
known academic geographer Michael Goodchild wrote: "The most
important value of [user-generated geographic information] may lie in
what it can tell us about local activities ... that go unnoticed by the world's
media, about life at the local level. It is in that area that [user-generated
geographic information] may offer the most interesting, lasting and compelling value" (Goodchild 2007).

Our backgrounds also informed us that clarity regarding this divergence of viewpoints was increasingly important for three interrelated reasons. First, the availability and prominence of user-generated content has
been growing exponentially. In the "Web 1.0" era (i.e., the forlorn days
before Wikipedia, Facebook, and Twitter) content was relatively static,
posted by a dedicated Web developer, and overseen by those with a vested
interest in the resource. At the time, a Web search for a geographic entity
like "Evanston, Illinois, USA" would predominately turn up locally produced or curated information, such as the official city homepage or the
official homepage of Northwestern University (which is primarily located
in Evanston). Nowadays, while these pages are still among the top hits, so
are "Web 2.0" user-generated content sites like Panoramio photos and
Evanston's Wikipedia page.

Next, we anticipated that understanding the localness of this new type
of information would provide us and other social scientists with the
methodological and theoretical scaffolding for more targeted questions
about user-generated content. For instance, do the perspectives presented
in user-generated content vary based on the locale of the contributors? Do
certain types of regions, and types of people in those regions, have disproportionately powerful voices? Is content about certain areas (e.g., Uganda)
less locally produced than content about other areas (e.g., California)?

Finally, the computer scientist in both of us knew that those in the
social science community would not be the only ones who would benefit
from a better understanding of the geographic origins of user-generated
content: computer scientists and practitioners also stand to gain. This is
because it is increasingly common for new Web search and data mining
systems—e.g., semantic relatedness algorithms like explicit semantic

analysis (Gabrilovich and Markovitch 2007)—to leverage user-generated content repositories as critical sources of "world knowledge" (Hecht and Gergle 2010b). These technologies inherently take on the viewpoints of the underlying user-generated content. Any systemic trends in the populations providing the lion's share of user-generated content can dominate the viewpoints of the resulting "world knowledge," and this can have an immense influence on technologies and algorithms that rely upon that information for various applications. Furthermore, these applications and their representations have the potential to influence the end-user's world view, making it crucial to identify and understand any inherent biases.

The goal of this chapter is twofold. First, we hope to provide the reader with a behind-the-scenes look at both the content and the practice of a challenging and chaotic interdisciplinary research adventure, with an emphasis on how we solved or dealt with the various problems that came our way. Second, we take this opportunity to present relevant "big data" basic geographic methodologies, knowledge of which we have found to be in demand among our colleagues in the social and computer sciences.[2]

Beginning the Project: Narrowing Things Down

While concise, the first problem with our research question was that it was also overly broad. "How local is geographic user-generated content?" needed some narrowing down before it could serve as the basis for a realistic research project. We decided to focus on three specific questions that could provide evidence toward an answer to our broader one:

1. What is the area of the "spatial footprint" of contributors to various user-generated content repositories?

2. How far away do contributors of user-generated content live from the subject of their contribution?

3. How local are user-generated content repositories as a whole?

The first two questions are at the user level. They inquire as to the behavior of the typical contributor of geographic user-generated content. The last question, by way of contrast, operates at the scale of the entire repository of user-generated content. It aims to aid our understanding of the localness of the "world knowledge" being accessed by important data mining and Web search systems as well as consumers of the repository.

To make this more concrete, let us cast these questions in the context of the English-language Wikipedia (one of several user-generated content sites we examined): First, if we mapped all of the articles about geographic entities (e.g., "San Francisco," "Microsoft Redmond Campus," "London Heathrow Airport") that a single user edited, what would the characteristics of this point pattern be on the surface of the Earth? Second, do Wikipedia contributors who edit articles about geographic entities live near or far from the subjects of these articles? And finally, what is the localness of the English Wikipedia as a whole? For this last question, consider the case of power users, who have been shown to play a disproportionately large role in user-generated content communities (Priedhorsky et al. 2007; Whittaker et al. 1998). If power users display significantly different localness behavior, large disparities could result between the localness of content contributed by the typical user (i.e., a non–power user) and that which is ultimately represented in the whole of the repository. By addressing these three questions, we hoped to provide the first real empirical evidence to back up one of the two contrasting viewpoints regarding the "localness" of user-generated content and highlight the potential impact of such behavioral patterns on technologies, applications, and the consumers of user-generated content repositories.

Understanding Our Data

As we have already discussed, we wanted to look at user-generated content. However, our research was not about any old content, but rather content that is *geographic information*.

Broadly speaking, an "atomic" unit of geographic information is a pair that consists of a location and an associated attribute or set of attributes. Mathematicians and computer scientists refer to the *<location, attributes>* set as a "tuple" (Goodchild, Yuan, and Cova 2007). The location is some spatial footprint on (or near) the surface of the planet Earth. The attributes are any information that "go along with" the spatial footprint. For instance, a canonical example of geographic information is a series of latitude and longitude coordinates (the locations), each with a rainfall total for the past 24 hours (the attribute). Similarly, the maps of voting patterns in the United States commonly generated around an election period are geographic information. The spatial footprints are the electoral districts (e.g., states and counties), and the attributes are the percentages of the electorate that voted for each candidate.

In the context of user-generated content, the location information typically considered consists of latitude and longitude coordinates, but the attribute is entirely dependent on the domain. For instance, a Flickr photo can represent geographic information if the photo is tagged with a latitude and longitude coordinate of where the photo was taken. In this case, the photo itself represents the attribute, and the lat/lon tag encodes the location information. In other words, Flickr geographic information is a series of <*location* = lat/lon coordinate, *attribute* = photo> tuples. Similarly, a Yelp restaurant review can be considered geographic information in the form of <*location* = lat/lon coordinate of restaurant, *attribute* = restaurant review>. As shorthand for "user-generated content with a geographic component such that the content can be interpreted as geographic information," we have introduced the term *geographic user-generated content.*[3]

That is the traditional definition of geographic information and how user-generated content fits into it. However, like a romance in *Fiddler on the Roof*, our project required a slight twist on tradition. We were not simply interested in a single location per unit of geographic information, but instead needed *two* locations: (1) the location of the content described, and (2) the location of the contributor of the content. In other words, we wanted to turn <*location, attribute*> into <*location1, location2, attribute*> or, more specifically, <*location of subject of contribution, location of contributor, piece of user-generated content*>. Traditional geographic methods are not targeted at this particular situation, causing a great deal of anxiety both when we realized we needed to add a twist to a canonical definition and when it came time to formulate analyses to address our research question. Since the publication of our paper, this type of geographic information has been given a name by a well-known geographer (Goodchild 2010)—"bipolar geographic information." This has provided us with a degree of belated comfort. However, at the time we embarked on our project, we had no such validation for what we perceived as a somewhat shaky divergence from geographic formalisms. Because this idea of "bipolar" geographic information is so new and the terminology is not yet standardized, we will refer to "bipolar geographic user-generated content" simply as geographic

Table 8.1

The basic schema for our data collection, populated with example data

Location of subject of contribution	Location of contributor	UGC attribute
(lon = −141.93, lat = 64.068)	(lon = 148.067, lat = −5.633)	Flickr photo
(lon = −87.620, lat = 41.896)	(lon = 74.277, lat = −40.276)	Contribution to a Wikipedia page
(lon = 11.458, lat = 46.542)	(lon = −74.659, lat = 40.349)	Flickr photo
…	…	…

Note that we are specific about which number is the longitude and which is the latitude. People typically say "lat/lon," but encoding points this way is equivalent to writing coordinates in the form (y,x), violating math conventions that have been drilled into us since childhood. This confusion has resulted in a surprising number of silly but costly-to-fix bugs in our code, so we have learned that the few extra characters it takes to declare which is which are well worth their bits/space on the page. UGC: user-generated content.

user-generated content. For the purposes of this chapter, we are always talking about the bipolar variety.

In the end, we hoped to gather data in the form shown in table 8.1. Of course, because we were interested in performing a large-scale data analysis, we needed to extend this table to millions of rows.

The Data Collection Process

A number of websites contain large quantities of geographic user-generated content, but we limited our study to the collaborative encyclopedia Wikipedia and the photo-sharing site Flickr. We chose these services for two reasons. The first is that both repositories make it possible (but far from easy) to ascertain that second class of location information we needed, the *location of contributor*. At the time, they also represented two of the largest and most commonly used user-generated content repositories, with millions of articles on Wikipedia and billions of photos on Flickr. Finally, Wikipedia, with its collaboratively written encyclopedia entries, and Flickr, with its individually uploaded photos, comprise two qualitatively different forms of data that span the user-generated content space.

In the spirit of full "research confidential" disclosure, there was another much more practical reason why we chose to include Wikipedia: we had already written an extensive software library for Wikipedia analysis. This library is called WikAPIdia[4] and we had used it in previous geographic Wikipedia research projects (Hecht and Gergle 2009, 2010b; Hecht and Moxley 2009). The name "WikAPIdia" is a computer science pun and—we are sorry to inform you—will be fully understandable by the end of this section. WikAPIdia provides a set of programming instructions that are helpful for automatically parsing, processing, accessing, and performing algorithms on Wikipedia data. We designed WikAPIdia for large-scale *multilingual* Wikipedia analysis, and it supports 25 separate language editions of Wikipedia. As such, we knew we could use WikAPIdia to examine not just English-speaking user-generated content contributor culture, but that it would function across numerous additional language editions as well. Of course, we were also excited to have to program entirely new analysis software for only one repository of geographic user-generated content. While WikAPIdia had to be modified and extended for this project, we could leverage all of the low-level text-wrangling and bit-pushing work we completed earlier.

Our basic data collection approach was to write separate computer code for each repository, which automatically gathered geographic user-generated content, processed it, and stored it in a large MySQL database. From that structured relational database, we pulled out data in the form of enormous CSV[5] files that we statistically analyzed using MATLAB. With the exception of the final bits of MATLAB code, we wrote all software in Java, a choice we made due to the fact that WikAPIdia is a Java package.

The following subsections describe how we created large data sets of geographic user-generated content from each repository, and the "big data research" lessons learned in doing so. Remember, for each entry in the data set, we needed both *location of subject of contributor* and *location of contribution*.

Data collection: Wikipedia

Collecting the location of the subject of contribution in Wikipedia can be done relatively easily, since Wikipedia community members have tagged with latitude and longitude coordinates hundreds of thousands of articles about topics that have unique spatial footprints (e.g., "Albany, California," "Macalester College," "Michigan," "Carnegie Mellon University"). Large data sets of these latitude and longitude coordinates, along with their associated articles, are downloadable (e.g., DBPedia's "Geo-Coordinates"[6]). In order to get as complete a multilingual data set as possible, we made one assumption that allowed us to propagate information across various Wikipedia language editions: if an article was tagged in one language (most commonly English), the tag could be reasonably passed on to articles about the same place in other languages. The reason this is necessary is that geotagging of articles is much more prominent in English than in other language editions. Fortunately, this language propagation was a piece of cake thanks to WikAPIdia's multilingual features.

Determining the location of Wikipedia contributors, however, was anything but a piece of cake. In the end, we found some semblance of a solution, but the issues we encountered are the cause of a great deal of the project's limitations as well as limitation-induced graduate student anxiety.

Wikipedia records and publishes the IP address (Internet Protocol address) of people who contribute anonymously to Wikipedia; in other words, people who do not necessarily set up registered accounts with the encyclopedia. This strikes most folks as ironic—in a sense you are more anonymous if you are a registered Wikipedia editor than if you are an anonymous editor, because in the former case your IP address does not get recorded—but that is the way it is. Research suggests that around one-fifth of Wikipedia contributions come from these anonymous contributors (Priedhorsky et al. 2007). Having an IP address is an important piece of information when coupled with the fact that IP addresses have rough locations associated with them. This permits several providers the opportunity to offer a service called "IP geolocation," which returns an approximate spatial footprint for an input IP address. In our case, we used IP geolocation to get an estimated position of the computer from which an anonymous edit was made. For the Wikipedia repositories included in our research, this was the source of the geographic data representing the location of the contributor.

However, IP geolocation has some serious limitations. While it is quite accurate at the country scale, examining locations at a more local scale quickly results in increased errors. In other words, while the IP address can tell us that an Internet user is in the United States, it rapidly loses accuracy as we reduce the desired spatial footprint to that of a state, county, city, city block, street, etc.[7] There are many companies that provide IP geolocation services. The one we used—MaxMind Geo IP—we chose for three reasons. First, it has a free version. Second, it has a Java-based application programming interface, or API.[8] APIs are computer code–based interfaces to third-party systems. Most well-known Web institutions have them in some form (e.g., Flickr, Facebook, Wikipedia, Twitter, Google, Bing, etc.). We and many others have found them extremely useful for large-scale online social science research, as well as for making puns out of our own Wikipedia API's name. The third benefit of MaxMind Geo IP for our work was that it publishes a country-by-country accuracy rate[9] so that we could be relatively sure that we were not taking the garbage-in, garbage-out route.[10] All that said, these accuracy levels—70% within 25 miles of true location in Germany, for instance—would make even a pre-May 1, 2000, GPS unit scoff.[11] The best we could do was to describe the accuracy of the process and avoid making claims at scales that were too local for the precision of the methods—always an important rule in geographic research. In fact, this is one reason we grouped (or binned) all data from zero to 50 km (the other reason is described below). After explaining the accuracy limitations, all we could do was leave it in the hands of the reviewers and subsequent readers.

IP geolocation was not the only hitch in our Wikipedia contributor location approach. There was also the challenge of connecting contributors to their contributions. In other words, finding out which IP addresses were the source of which contributions. Wikipedia publishes an entire history of the state of the encyclopedia for each language edition. That is, it allows you to download in a file every version of every article, as well as lots of metadata about each edit, including who made it. However, this download is so large that—in accordance with Murphy's Law of Graduate School—Wikipedia stopped offering it for English right when we needed it.[12] Furthermore, for those language editions for which the "history" download was available, downloading, uncompressing, and processing the data into WikAPIdia was an arduous and time-consuming process. These steps in the research process can be some of the most laborious aspects of large-scale or "big data" research. For instance, when processing these Wikipedia "history" files, we spent several weeks dealing with arcane memory management and parallelization issues (i.e., big-data, small-computer issues) instead of on more directly answering our research questions.

It was these processing challenges that led us to the decision to limit the number of Wikipedia language editions we would analyze. At the time, our WikAPIdia software supported 15 different language editions (it is up to 25 as of this writing), but we knew that even with our optimizations, the cost/benefit tradeoff for doing all 15 languages was not sufficient. As such, we restricted our analysis to Catalan, Swedish, Norwegian, Japanese, and English. Why those languages? Catalan, Swedish and Norwegian were chosen for the practical reason that they are all relatively small (less than 10% of the size of English at the time), and so we knew processing them would be fast. Japanese was included to provide better representation across cultures. With English and Japanese, we had the largest Wikipedia editions for languages primarily associated with both Eastern and Western cultures at the time.

After a great deal of optimization of WikAPIdia and some additional programming to add features to deal with article histories, we had successfully processed the Japanese, Catalan, Norwegian, and Swedish language editions. This meant we could now easily match the latitude and longitude coordinates generated by IP geolocation of contributors to the latitude and longitude coordinates of the articles to which they contributed. However, like the French of the 16th century, we had an English problem. This is typical in our Wikipedia research because it is by far the largest of the language editions and poses significant data-processing challenges.

Obviously, the first challenge was the aforementioned lack of a downloadable and complete history for the English Wikipedia. Since we could not obtain the history through the normal channels, we began looking for alternatives. Fortunately, the nonprofit foundation that runs Wikipedia in Germany has something known as its Tool Server,[13] which the Wikipedia community uses for a variety of purposes ranging from running Wikipedia bots that perform mundane labor on articles to doing data analysis projects like ours. The Tool Server offers access to the databases that lie at the heart of the entire Wikipedia site. In collaboration with another colleague doing Wikipedia research in our lab, we requested[14] and were granted "shell access" to the Tool Server. This means that we could run command-line scripts on the Wikipedia databases, which allowed us to generate our own "history" file for English. We took advantage of the lower-level access provided by the Tool Server to generate a custom "history" file with only the articles in which we were interested: those that discussed geographic entities (i.e., those pages about entities with associated latitudes and longitudes). This greatly reduced the number of article histories we needed to download and, more importantly, increased processing speed for the rest of the English data collection, cleaning, and processing.

This last point is worth reemphasizing. "Big data" researchers sometimes adopt a get-data-first-ask-questions-later tactic, but this has methodological challenges in addition to the usual theoretical concerns surrounding this approach (known by some as the throw-it-against-the-wall-and-see-what-sticks approach). Even with the power of modern computers and "the cloud," one can easily get overwhelmed with the amount of data available for a given problem domain, as would have been the case with our computing setup and a full history of the English Wikipedia. By framing our research questions ahead of time and targeting our data gathering and processing approach to match those questions, we avoided what would have likely been nasty data storage issues and particularly time-consuming (and boring) additional WikAPIdia optimization programming.

Before finishing our discussion of the Tool Server, it is important to note that this was all unproven ground for us. We had no idea if the Tool Server would work, and had trouble getting our initial scripts to run in the environment. These doubts compounded, creating unknown unknowns, but with enough elbow grease and several weeks of late-night programming, we were able to figure things out. We are happy that we were successful, but the "research confidential" backstory is that we were quite nervous about our only option for an essential part of our data collection being filled with so many challenges without existing or even partial solutions.

Data collection: Flickr

Locating Flickr contributors (i.e., determining the *location of contributor*) involved finding users who had populated their current location profile field (figure 8.1) and downloading the information they placed in this

Figure 8.1
A screenshot of a portion of a Flickr user's profile. The field that we mined is the "Currently" field, in which the user is instructed to put the "city you live in now." The country information is prompted separately, but is added to the "Currently" field.

field at a very large scale. There was really no other way to locate contributors other than doing an enormous survey. While a survey approach could have provided us with a better sample in some ways—for example, it would circumvent the selection bias that results from focusing on users that manually fill in their profile information—achieving a response rate and sample sufficient to cover the globe in a fashion comparable to our data would have been practically unmanageable.

The most straightforward approach to downloading the contents of a large number of user profile location fields would be to use the Flickr API. However, we were not interested in the contributor location of all Joe Schmo photographers, but only those who had contributed geotagged photos (i.e., geographic user-generated content). As would have been the case with looking at all English Wikipedia article histories instead of just the geographic ones, downloading information about all photographers would have unnecessarily taxed our data-processing systems (not to mention Flickr's), and, as is described below, taken much, much longer.

Instead, we used a much more efficient "backwards" approach that we have found works well for gathering contributor locations in many contexts, not just for Flickr (see Hecht et al. 2011 for a Twitter example). We first downloaded the metadata about all geotagged photos going back a year from the collection date—information that we would need anyway as it comprises the locations of contributions—and then looked in the metadata to see who had taken them. Only then did we download the contents of the location fields of those users.

We used a Java "wrapper" to the public Flickr API[15] that we wrote ourselves to download this information. However, we could not immediately access all the data we needed. For a variety of technical and financial reasons, most APIs have "rate limits," and the Flickr API is no exception. The consequences of violating these rate limits can be severe. On a practical level, you can get banned and not be allowed to access the site via the API for an extended period of time or permanently. More seriously, violating the terms of use of an API has ethical consequences. In fact, in some venues it can prevent you from publishing from the data you collect.

Conforming to API rate limits often results in downloads that can take quite a while (on the order of days or weeks) along with programming that needs to be more sophisticated than it would be otherwise. As such, it was only after a long time (whether it was several days or a week or two has been lost to memory), that we had downloaded metadata for the 10+ million geotagged photos that had been uploaded by users over a year's time. We then extracted the unique user IDs of all the photographers who had taken these pictures and used the API to download the values of the location fields for their profiles. Once again, we (somewhat) patiently waited for this download to complete. This process of first downloading the geotagged photos and using those to look up the user names of the folks who had contributed them allowed us to eliminate the aforementioned Joe "Doesn't-Contribute-Geotagged-Photos" Schmo from our analyses—and, as noted above, also saved substantial time and effort.

We now had location information for tens of thousands of photographers who took hundreds of thousands of photos. However, while we had the latitude and longitude coordinates of the geotagged photos, the photographer location data were still in the form of current location field entries; that is, plain text. This is analogous to our problem with IP address geographic information in Wikipedia, but instead of IP addresses, we had self-reported text (i.e., we had location information, but not in a format suited to large-scale analysis). More formally, our current location data took the form of toponyms (or names of geographic places). As is noted in our book chapter on doing research on geographic virtual communities (Hecht and Gergle 2011), it is a nontrivial task to convert toponyms into computer-understandable representations such as latitudes and longitudes, just as it is with IP addresses. This is especially true in the case of *vernacular* toponyms such as "San Fran," "The Bible Belt," or "The Windy City" (Jones and Purves 2008), of which Flickr current location fields are chock-full.

We could have run these toponyms through the Google, Yahoo, or Bing geocoders, but we found that they had a variety of show-stopping problems in this vernacular context. Roughly speaking, geocoders turn text location data into more formal representations like latitude and longitude coordinates that are better suited for automated large-scale analyses (just as IP geolocation does with IP addresses), but they struggle with vernacular toponyms. These problems, and the phenomenon of vernacular toponyms in location fields in general, was so fascinating to us that we ended up writing a paper on that specific subject a year later (Hecht et al. 2011). However, in order to get this research done, we could not get sidetracked and had to determine a way to turn these vernacular toponyms into something we could analyze geographically.

Enter the "Wikipedia geocoder," a beautiful marriage of satisficing problem solving and the art of the "twofer." Thanks to our previous efforts with WikAPIdia, we had a large dataset of legal geographic names (i.e., Wikipedia page titles) and corresponding geographic footprints (i.e., the latitude and longitude coordinates tagged to the corresponding pages) at our disposal. We also had millions of synonyms for these geographic names—many of which were highly vernacular—in the form of Wikipedia "redirects." These redirects are what take you to the "San Francisco" page when you type "San Fran" in the Wikipedia search bar. They are also what allowed us to map folks who entered "San Fran" as their current location in Flickr to the latitude and longitude that was attached to the "San Francisco" Wikipedia page. While the "Wikipedia geocoder" did not have as many locations as the Bing, Google, or Yahoo geocoders, it had a much higher precision. In other words, if the Wikipedia geocoder found a lat/lon coordinate for a location field entry, it almost always was correct. Since we had so much data, we were not concerned as much with coverage as we were with precision. In the end, we were able to find latitude and longitude coordinates for over 14,000 Flickr photographers who took over 185,000 geotagged photos during the one-year study period.

The Analysis and Results

Each of our three research questions required individual analyses. For two of these questions, the formulation of the analysis was a piece of cake. The opposite was true for the third. This section is divided up by research question, leaving the thorniest for last.

RESEARCH QUESTION: How far away do contributors of user-generated content live from the subject of their contribution?

To address this question we used a rather simple straight-line metric to calculate the distance between the contributor and the contribution. While there are serious drawbacks to using straight-line distance (which we return to in the limitations section), it is a rather "down to earth" metric that worked reasonably well for this analysis. All we needed to do was calculate the distance between the *location of the contributor* and the *location of the subject of the contribution*. We could then average this distance across all contributions by a single contributor and, presto-MATLAB-o, we would have some analyzable results. We called this statistic the mean contribution distance (MCD), and it has a formula that looks like this:

$$MCD = \sum_{i=1}^{n} \frac{d(C, c_i)}{n},$$

where d is our distance function, C is the contributor location, c is the location of each of the contributor's contributions, and n is the number of contributions by contributor C.

Before discussing the results of this analysis, let us be a little more specific about how we define d. Even though d is "simple" distance, it is important to note that calculating it is not as straightforward as it may seem. Our spatial footprint information—like that possessed by the vast majority of social scientists studying geographic user-generated content—came in the form of latitude and longitude coordinates. We all learned in school (Pythagorean Theorem anyone?) that the distance between two points p_1 and p_2 can be calculated:

$$d(p_1, p_2) = \sqrt{(x_1 - x_2)^2 + (y_1 - y_2)^2}.$$

However, this assumes that the points exist on a flat plane. Spoiler alert: the Earth is not flat, geometrically speaking, that is (Thomas Friedman notwithstanding; Friedman 2005). This annoying fact of nature means that distance calculations must take into account the unique shape of the Earth. We cover this topic in great detail elsewhere (Hecht and Gergle 2011), and make use of our own suggestions in this research. The bottom line is that for global-scale analyses with precision like ours, you cannot simply plug in the latitude and longitude coordinates and assume you are all set. Instead, you need to use something called the *great circle distance*.[16] For a quick reference on great circle distances and other fundamentals of geographic methods, check out the dated-but-still useful website, The Geographer's Craft.[17]

Once our data were whipped into (geometric) shape, we were finally ready to move on to the results. As can be seen in figure 8.2, Flickr tends to be a lot more "local" than any of the Wikipedia language editions. In the words of our paper: "While ~53 percent of Flickr users contribute, on average, content that is 100 km or less from their specified home location, this number drops quite a bit for Wikipedia users. The equivalent number for the English Wikipedia, for example, is ~23 percent, although this number is subject to errors in IP geolocation" (Hecht and Gergle 2010a: 231).

You will note that we set the "local" bar for discussion at a relatively distant 100 km. Ideally, we would have liked to examine our results at a much finer geographic resolution. However, validity issues played the role of party pooper here. Specifically, in addition to our concerns about IP geolocation, the use of latitude and longitude coordinates to encode the spatial footprints of entire cities by Wikipedia and the city-level tendencies of location field disclosure (Hecht et al. 2011) limited the spatial fidelity of our results. In our work, we label these types of issues as instances of the "geoweb scale problem" (Hecht and Moxley 2009). Consider the example of a Flickr user who indicated her location as "Chicago" and took lots of photos on Chicago's far northern Rogers Park neighborhood. Since the user could be anywhere in Chicago—and our

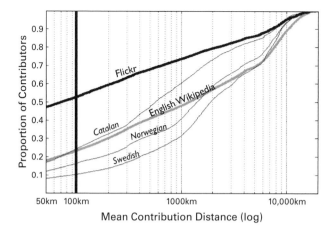

Figure 8.2
Results from our first analysis in the form of the cumulative distribution of the mean contribution distance. On the x-axis is log distance, and on the y-axis is the cumulative proportion of contributors in each repository that had a mean contribution distance at the stated distance. The big bold line at 100 km indicates our binary cut-off for "local" in the study (Hecht and Gergle 2010a).

Wikipedia geocoder will always return the same latitude/longitude coordinate for Chicago—the contributor/contribution distance for these photos would essentially be garbage. While our geocoder may return 20 km—roughly the distance from downtown Chicago to Rogers Park—the distance could easily be 0.1 km or 45 km, approximately the north-south length of Chicago. Extrapolating a bit, this means that we could not report accurately distances that occur at city-scales. To play it safe, especially considering IP geolocation accuracies, we grouped everything under 100 km. In general, issues that relate to geographic accuracy tend to reduce one's ability to make claims at local levels. The bigger the issues, the less locally precise one can be.

Careful readers may note that Japanese Wikipedia is not in this figure—and here is where you get to peek under the hood to see the "failures" that sometimes occur when performing this type of research. During the final step of the analysis of the Japanese Wikipedia, we uncovered an error in our work in MATLAB that truncated the last 10 percent of the data. Unfortunately, we discovered this bug only days before the paper submission deadline, resulting in at least one instance of a curse word being uttered into the abyss of a lab emptied by the extremely late hour.

After lots of hand-wringing and spirited debate, we decided to cut the Japanese analysis from our paper. We had little reason to suspect that the error we had uncovered would change our findings, as we effectively had a random 90% sample of the cumulative distribution. However, in the end, the results were not drastically different from those of the other languages, and we felt the additional asterisks needed to explain what happened would simply raise additional questions and outweigh the value of including the partial analysis.

RESEARCH QUESTION: How local are user-generated content repositories as a whole?   By asking this question, we sought to understand the nature of entire repositories of geographic user-generated content, repositories that are being used as "world knowledge" by important data mining and Web-search systems. We were concerned, for example, that if power users were significantly more or less "local" than the average user, our answer to this question would notably differ from the results presented above. In other words, power users are so influential on these sites that they could completely drown out the localness behavior of the average user. Indeed, the most active 2.5% of users in our Flickr data set contributed 32.8% of Flickr photos, whereas the bottom 90% contributed only 40.1%. The equivalent numbers for the English Wikipedia were 29.1% and 53.0%.

We knew that if we created the exact same figure as figure 8.2, but showed the distribution of actual contributor-contribution distances *not* averaged over each user, we could get some idea as to the answer to the question. In other words, instead of showing the distribution of contributors' mean contribution distances, this new figure would show the distribution of distances from all contributions to their respective contributors. Since power users are responsible for so many of these contributions, if they had a different geographic behavior, we would see drastic changes in the figure. For instance, if power users tended to contribute more locally, then this new figure would have a much greater slope on the left side and/or have a much larger y-intercept (and 100-km intercept), reflecting a more locally produced repository. However, if geographic contribution behavior is not correlated with activity level, the new figure would be roughly the same as figure 8.2.

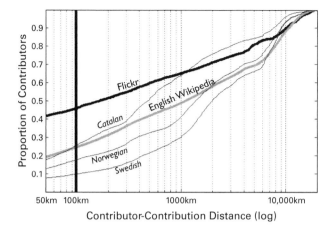

Figure 8.3
The localness of repositories as a whole. This figure is the same as figure 8.2, but not averaged by user. The lack of major differences between these two figures told us that user activity level was not heavily correlated with geographic contribution behavior.

As it turns out, the cumulative distribution function (CDF) barely changes (figure 8.3). In the words of our paper, "figure [3] demonstrates that the spatial contribution behavior is relatively independent of number of contributions. If it were not, we would see a significant difference between figures [2] and [3]. For instance, ~47 percent of Flickr photos are taken within 100 km from their photographer (figure [3]), while we saw that ~53 percent of photographers take photos within 100 km on average (figure [2])." (Hecht and Gergle 2010a: 231).

Stepping back for a moment, after we generated figures 8.2 and 8.3, it became clear to us that neither of the viewpoints on the localness of geographic user-generated content discussed in the introduction seemed to be on the mark. While geographic user-generated content was far from definitively local, it was not definitively touristic or nonlocal either. Our evidence suggests that, like so many other academic debates, the answer lies somewhere in the middle.

Perhaps more interesting was the large difference between Flickr and all of the Wikipedias in both figures. This difference led us to suggest what we called a "spatial content production model," or SCPM (lovingly called a "scopum" around the lab). We reasoned that in Flickr's case, uploading geographic content more or less requires one to have visited the location of the subject of contribution, and therefore Flickr is going to be a more local repository. We call Flickr's SCPM the "you have to be there" model. On the other hand, Wikipedia displays something of a "flat-earth" (Friedman 2005) SCPM. More formally, Wikipedia exhibits a degree of "time-space compression" (Harvey 1991) in which distance matters less, at least at a structural level. In Wikipedia, anyone anywhere can contribute to any article about anywhere, assuming they are contributing in a language in which they are fluent and the community accepts the contribution. In this light, it is somewhat remarkable that Wikipedians do display substantial local editing behavior, even if it is less substantial than in Flickr's case. From a technology-design perspective—something very important to the field of human-computer interaction, which is our primary subfield of computer science—we hypothesized that a community wishing to garner more local content may want to enforce a Flickr-like SCPM model, and we suggested several ways of doing so in the paper.

However, to really understand SCPMs, we felt we needed a more detailed look at the geographic contribution behavior of the users in our data set, something that went beyond distance averages. The most immediate step would be looking at the "spatial footprint" of contribution behavior. In other words, if we mapped the contributions of each contributor relative to the location of the contributor, what kind of patterns would we find? Indeed, this was the subject of our final research question.

RESEARCH QUESTION: What is the area of the "spatial footprint" of contributors of user-generated content? At a high level, the analytical approach here is simple: study the point pattern of each contributor's contributions and generate summary statistics of these patterns. There are any number of statistics we could have chosen: number of countries in which a user edits other than their home country, metrics capturing the average straight-line distance from a centroid, and so on. However, we felt that determining the area of the region defined by the point pattern and some coefficient of the clustering of the pattern would be a more

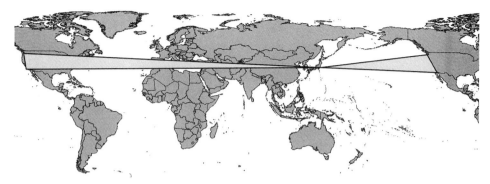

Figure 8.4
A sample of the challenges of global-scale spatial analysis on the surface of the Earth.

formal way of attacking this question. In theory and at local scales, both are easy and well defined. However, when one considers the shape of the Earth—once again, that pesky Earth!—it becomes much more difficult. At issue in particular is longitude -180/180, which is more colloquially known as the International Date Line. It creates a situation in which one can draw many possible enclosing regions for point patterns that split across this line (figure 8.4).

Consider a Wikipedia editor who edits three articles: "Seattle," "San Diego," and "Tokyo." Two polygons can be constructed from the corresponding spatial points that constitute the three articles. Starting from the point in Tokyo, the polygon on the left is the one that results from connecting the latitude and longitude coordinates while moving west. However, notice if you move to the east, the resulting polygon is smaller (and is thus more accurate). This is the simplest case of this phenomenon. There may be hundreds of points spread across the International Date Line.

Another challenge had to do with finding an acceptable clustering coefficient statistic that would work. Without getting too mired in details, various aspects of this research question eliminated the use of the standard statistics typically taught in a geostatistics class. In the end, we had determined that Ripley's K, a spatial analysis statistic from epidemiology, was suitable for our needs. But wait! By the time we figured this out, it was too late. The "Great Scoop" had occurred.

The "Great Scoop"

Unlike many disciplines, computer science's main publication venues are conference proceedings—the vast majority of which have rigid submission deadlines. Several weeks before the submission deadline for our paper, we were still working diligently to solve the spatial footprint puzzle. It was while somewhat anxiously searching the literature for help on a particular part of that puzzle that we encountered a paper published just days earlier that claimed to have solved the puzzle and performed the exact same analysis on English Wikipedia contributors!

The singlehandedly most distressing part of this discovery was that we felt the authors had done a rather sloppy job with their geographic analyses. They had not considered the methodological problems that we had spent weeks trying to solve. In other words, they performed their analyses as if the world was flat. In fact, they even reported their results in latitude and longitude squared! This is something akin to reporting results in feet squared when the units are constantly changing, as they did when they were historically based on the size of the current King's foot. Because most computer scientists are not versed in geographic analyses, these mistakes made it through the peer review process of a respectable publication venue.

We were thus confronted with a rather large problem: do we continue pushing toward finding a solution to the spatial footprint problem, or do we cut our losses and focus only on the distance problem, for which analysis was already more or less complete? If we found significantly different results than the authors of the published paper, this would form a useful contribution. However, if we found roughly the same results, it would be much more difficult to argue for the novelty of our contribution, even if the analysis was technically more accurate.

In the end, we decided that the increased risk due to the scooping tipped the scales in the balance of abandoning the spatial footprint analysis and focusing instead on getting the distance analysis right and written up well. In other words, given the relatively short timeline left before the submission due date, we decided to focus on the part of the analysis that made a guaranteed significant contribution toward answering our primary research question about the localness of user-generated content. A paper that contributed a methodology for doing more formal geographic user-generated point patterns analysis could wait for another day.

The dénouement

As is often the case with being "scooped," we were initially quite upset. In retrospect, we have come to view the scooping and the subsequent refocusing of the paper to be a blessing in disguise. By the time we discovered the other paper, any spatial footprint results we could have produced would likely have been rushed. Narrowing the research down to only the distance-based analysis raised the quality of the contribution significantly, although it shortened the length of the paper.

Overall, there were three lessons we (especially the graduate student half of our team) learned from "The Great Scoop." The first is that scooping happens. It is simply a hazard of working in a rapidly advancing area of research, and one should be prepared for it. This experience prompted conversations with friends and colleagues in the extremely active field of bioengineering, and they relayed far more harrowing scooping stories. Second, when scooping does occur, it is usually not as disastrous as it initially appears. Chances are that the research one is working on has something novel outside of what has been uncovered in the other paper. Third, when working on a research question that has not yet been addressed in the literature, a complete answer to the question is not necessary to make a valuable research contribution.

Conclusion (a.k.a. "Nagging Worries")

Throughout the production of our paper, and even after its acceptance and publication (Hecht and Gergle 2010a), we have continued to be bothered by a number of validity-related worries. Of course, we translated these worries into prose in the form of limitations in the published work, but as scientists these are things we feel we must eventually address in order to sleep well at night. For therapeutic (on our part) and educational (on your part) purposes, we will expand upon them here, if only both to demonstrate and admit that well-received and published work can still have open questions.

At the root of our validity concerns is the use of the term "local." What does it mean for a contributor to be "local"? Is localness purely a spatial phenomenon, or is it a spatio*temporal* phenomenon? Brent lived in Albany, California, for the first 18 years of his life, but now lives in Chicago. Does that mean when he edits the Wikipedia page for "Albany,

California" he is no longer a local contributor? Is Darren a local contributor to the "Carnegie Mellon University" page, which is about the school where he earned his PhD, but not a location that he visits often now? Even when we ignore this critical issue, we are faced with the question of thresholds. How far away from a picture taken in the Rogers Park neighborhood of Chicago does the photographer have to live for that photo to be a "nonlocal" contribution of user-generated content? The next neighborhood? The next city? The next county? How can we incorporate a more fluid notion of localness into our analyses and discussions?

Even though it was clear to us that the term "local" implies at least some spatiotemporal element, we decided to assume it was a purely geographic phenomenon for the purposes of our paper. We addressed this in the limitations section. We also discuss it every time we present this work.

A second concern has to do with the choice of some of our measures and metrics. We are still disappointed with the use of straight-line distance as a proxy for localness. It is common sense that straight-line distance serves as a crude metric for localness, and the discipline of geography has studied the fascinating nuances of this phenomenon for decades. For instance, five miles in Chicago means something quite different in terms of "localness" than five miles in the middle of nowhere, Texas, or five miles across hamlet-dotted rural Germany. The same can be said when considering border phenomena; one mile in Palo Alto, California, is very different from one mile across the Palo Alto–East Palo Alto border. Our worries were allayed, however, by the "first real data" part of this research project. As with all research in new areas, we needed to start somewhere, and using more sophisticated proxies for localness could be the subject of future research. For better or worse, we can also fall back on the fact that there is a substantial literature in computer science that uses straight-line distance as a primary distance metric for social science and social science–like research (Backstrom, Sun, and Marlow 2010; Crandall et al. 2009; Eisenstein et al. 2010; Wing and Baldridge 2011).

We are also not satisfied with the quality of IP geolocation. One way to augment our paper would be to do a smaller-scale analysis that looked at "user pages" on Wikipedia (analogous to profile pages) for indications on where each contributor is from. These pages are far from standardized, and data collection would thus involve a massive amount of hand coding. Another approach would be to marry a survey-based approach with our mining approaches to help estimate the error present in the profile data. Lastly, there is the possibility that IP geolocation may get a lot better in the next couple of years (Wang et al. 2011). When we or others follow up on this project, this would be a top-priority task and if the findings are the same, would go a long way toward informing our large-scale analysis. This is also an interesting example of how much default settings of a system matter. Flickr asks users their geographic location, and while not required, many supply it. There is no equivalent formal field for Wikipedia user pages, and thus the service does not have any systematic information on this data point.

Wikipedia provides an additional source of heartburn in that we are limited regarding the claims we can make about the *content* of Wikipedia pages. Because we only looked at number of edits, we have no idea if these edits had any lasting effect on the content of the page. It could be that local edits are being drowned out or that they are having a disproportionately important effect. We also do not know if they are simply corrections of typographical or spelling errors having little to do with the substance of the entries. This is clearly something that should matter and is near the top of our list for future work in the area.

As is the case with most research projects, we only could handle the validity issues we could, and discuss the rest in the limitations section of the paper. In closing, it is our hope that this chapter provides some guidance for your adventure down the often pothole-laden road that is social science research, particularly that on the interdisciplinary fringe. We also hope that readers interested in geographic topics or methods are able to apply some of the suggestions we make and learn from some of our mistakes—and not in the "Oh, I read about someone else that had this problem, too" after-the-fact way, but rather in the prescient "We shouldn't do that because … " way.

Notes

1. Roughly speaking, these are the folks who are trying to help computers understand pictures and videos.

2. For the interested reader, we have also written on using geographic methodologies in virtual communities research (Hecht and Gergle 2011). That chapter provides a more detailed look at Internet-oriented geographic methods and is written for social scientists interested in studying virtual communities.

3. You will also see the term *volunteered geographic information* bandied about, typically in the geography literature. These two terms roughly mean the same thing. However, in good academic form, we should include the disclaimer that they have subtle differences that are outside the scope of this chapter.

4. WikAPIdia has morphed into a new, more powerful, and broader software library called WikiBrain, which is a collaboration between Brent Hecht (now a professor at the University of Minnesota) and Shilad Sen at Macalester College. WikiBrain can be downloaded at wikibrainapi.org.

5. CSV stands for comma-separated values. This is a file format that has numerous values, each of which is separated by a comma (e.g., value1, value2, value3, …).

6. http://wiki.dbpedia.org/Datasets#h18-17.

7. Recent research has suggested that much more accurate IP geolocation is possible (Wang et al. 2011), an exciting possibility for research in this space.

8. http://www.maxmind.com/app/geolitecity.

9. http://web.archive.org/web/20100203234322/http://www.maxmind.com/app/geolite_city_accuracy.

10. Garbage in, garbage out (or GIGO) is a computer science axiom that basically states that if you feed flawed data into a program to be processed, the resulting output will also be flawed.

11. Restrictions on GPS units were lifted on May 1, 2000, so that civilians (as opposed to just the military) could have access to the level of GPS accuracy we enjoy today. See http://www.pocketgpsworld.com/GPS-Selective-Availability-lifted-10-years-ago-9500.php.

12. Wikipedia has recently solved this problem (for now), and full English Wikipedia histories can be downloaded at http://dumps.wikimedia.org/enwiki. You'll likely need terabytes of disk space, however, in order to decompress the files.

13. http://meta.wikimedia.org/wiki/Toolserver.

14. http://web.archive.org/web/20100705000834/https://wiki.toolserver.org/view/Account_approval_process.

15. http://www.flickr.com/services/api.

16. For local-scale research, things get more complicated, a topic that we cover in our virtual communities book chapter (Hecht and Gergle 2011).

17. http://www.colorado.edu/geography/gcraft/contents.html.

References

Backstrom, L., E. Sun, and C. Marlow. 2010. Find me if you can: Improving geographical prediction with social and spatial proximity. 19th International World Wide Web Conference. Raleigh, NC.

Crandall, D. J., L. Backstrom, D. Huttenlocher, and J. Kleinberg. 2009. Mapping the world's photos. 2009 International World Wide Web Conference (761–770). Madrid, Spain.

Eisenstein, J., B. O'Connor, N. A. Smith, and E. P. Xing. 2010. A latent variable model for geographic lexical variation. Conference on Empirical Methods in Natural Language Processing (1277–1287). Boston.

Friedman, T. L. 2005. *The World Is Flat: A Brief History of the Twenty-first Century*. New York: Farrar, Straus and Giroux.

Gabrilovich, E., and S. Markovitch. 2007. Computing semantic relatedness using Wikipedia-based explicit semantic analysis. Twentieth Joint Conference for Artificial Intelligence. Hyderabad, India.

Goodchild, M. 2010. Spatio-temporal constraints on social networks: Position paper. Specialist meeting on spatio-temporal constraints in social networks. Santa Barbara, CA.

Goodchild, M. F. 2007. Citizens as sensors: The world of volunteered geography. *GeoJournal* 69 (4): 211–221. doi:.10.1007/s10708-007-9111-y

Goodchild, M. F., M. Yuan, and T. J. Cova. 2007. Towards a general theory of geographic representation in GIS. *International Journal of Geographical Information Science* 21 (3): 239–260.

Harvey, D. 1991. *The Condition of Postmodernity: An Enquiry into the Origins of Cultural Change*. New York: Wiley-Blackwell.

Hecht, B., and D. Gergle. 2009. Measuring self-focus bias in community-maintained knowledge repositories. Fourth International Conference on Communities and Technologies. State College, PA.

Hecht, B., and D. Gergle. 2010a. On the "localness" of user-generated content. ACM Conference on Computer Supported Cooperative Work. Savannah, GA.

Hecht, B., and D. Gergle. 2010b. The tower of Babel meets Web 2.0: User-generated content and its applications in a multilingual context. 28th International Conference on Human Factors in Computing Systems (291–300). Atlanta, GA: Association for Computing Machinery. doi:.10.1145/1753326.1753370

Hecht, B., and D. Gergle. 2011. A beginner's guide to geographic virtual communities research. *Handbook of Research on Methods and Techniques for Studying Virtual Communities: Paradigms and Phenomena*, 333–347. New York: IGI Global.

Hecht, B., and E. Moxley. 2009. Terabytes of Tobler: Evaluating the first law in a massive, domain-neutral representation of world knowledge. Ninth International Conference on Spatial Information Theory (88–105). Berlin: Springer-Verlag.

Hecht, B., L. Hong, B. Suh, and E. H. Chi. 2011. Tweets from Justin Bieber's heart: The dynamics of the "location" field in user profiles. 29th ACM Conference on Human Factors in Computing Systems.

Helft, M. 2009. November 16. Online maps: Everyman offers new directions. *The New York Times*.

Jones, C. B., and R. S. Purves. 2008. Geographical information retrieval. *International Journal of Geographical Information Science* 22 (3): 219–228.

Priedhorsky, R., J. Chen, S. K. Lam., K. Panciera, L. Terveen, and J. Riedl. 2007. Creating, destroying, and restoring value in Wikipedia. 2007 International ACM Conference on Supporting Group Work (259–268). Sanibel Island, FL: Association for Computing Machinery. doi:.10.1145/1316624.1316663

Wang, Y., D. Burgener, M. Flores, A. Kuzmanovic, and C. Huang. 2011. Towards street-level client-independent IP geolocation. 8th USENIX Symposium on Network Systems Design and Implementation. Boston.

Whittaker, S., L. Terveen, W. Hill, and L. Cherny. 1998. The dynamics of mass interaction. ACM 1998 Conference on Computer Supported Cooperative Work (257–264). Seattle.

Wing, B. P., and J. Baldridge. 2011. Simple supervised document geolocation with geodesic grids. Proceedings of the 49th Annual Meeting of the Association for Computational Linguistics (pp. 955–964). Portland, OR.

9

The Art of Web Crawling for Social Science Research

Michelle Shumate and Matthew S. Weber

In the first chapter of Robert Pirsig's book *Zen and the Art of Motorcycle Maintenance* (1974), the main character contrasts his view of motorcycle maintenance with that of his friend John.

It seems natural and normal to me to make the use of the small tool kits and instruction booklets supplied with each machine, and keep it tuned and adjusted myself. John demurs. He prefers to let a competent mechanic take care of these things so that they are done right ... I could preach the practical value and worth of motorcycle maintenance till I'm hoarse and it would make not a dent in him. After two sentences on the subject his eyes go completely glassy and he changes the conversation or just looks away. He doesn't want to hear about it. (10–11)

On the subject of Web crawlers, we have often been subject to both suspicions about the mechanics of the machines that perform these tasks and glassy looks as we discuss the intricacies of their inner workings. There is a very small group indeed that is willing to discuss the benefits and limitations of crawling three versus four levels away from the main directory. Even fewer are willing to discuss the benefits of "packaged" Web crawlers versus building your own. And just like motorcycle mainte-nance, there is a great deal of know-how that develops as you work with Web-crawler technology that is not easily summed up in the available technical manuals.

Web crawlers are a class of technologies that copy data from websites and organize that data into particular formats. For example, we have used Web crawlers to collect text from websites for subsequent analysis, to collect authorship information from news websites, and to collect all of the hyperlinks from particular sections of websites. There are thousands of these programs currently available, and you could, with a little techni-cal assistance, create your own version of one.

The purpose of this chapter is twofold. First, we make an impassioned argument that you should not leave the details of your Web crawler to a computer programmer, just as you should not turn your motorcycle over to a trained mechanic. There are research benefits to knowing the inner workings of your tools and dangers in not knowing exactly how they work. Second, we will review some of the "know-how" of Web crawlers and, in doing so, reveal some of the unresolved debates, even between the two of us, about the appropriate ways to operate and fix them. This chapter is not a technical manual for Web crawler maintenance, but instead an insider's guide based upon experience and reflection. You do not need to be a programmer to run a Web crawler, but you should be at least a little curious about the ways the tool you are using works. While we know some of our arguments might easily be resisted as too technical, we found there is a certain satisfaction in demystifying the technologies that are increasingly at the core of social science research.

Background

Before we dig into the nuts and bolts of Web crawling, we would like to share a bit about our experiences with the technology and how it is that we both became engrossed in this line of research.

Michelle: I discovered the art and science of hyperlink analysis while at my first job after my doctoral work. For my dissertation, I had spent a considerable amount of time entering various types of interorganizational relationships among international nongovernmental organizations (NGOs) from the *Yearbook of International Organizations* into a database. As part of that data-entry work, I had a set of URLs for organizational websites, and I began thinking about how I could use that website data to write a research paper. It was 2003, and my first start at the topic was to begin to hand-code with the help of two willing graduate students and a few of the websites for analysis. Hand-coding means to use the techniques derived from content analysis (Neuendorf 2002) to manually identify and record each hyperlink. I quickly realized that my background and experience in content analysis was not going to be sufficient. It was difficult to keep track of where I was in a website and even harder to record systematically all of the hyperlinks. There were too many errors in the process, and the reliability scores I was getting from the two graduate students were really bad.

So, I began to do searches for hyperlinks in academic journals and discovered Jackson's (1997) and Rogers and Marres's (2000) work on hyperlink analysis. While neither work was necessarily a guide to *how* one might use a Web crawler, they gave me the courage to continue and led me to begin to think theoretically about what hyperlinks might mean in comparison to the other types of interorganizational relations that I had investigated.

I learned about Web crawlers, starting with SocSciBot and Issuecrawler, by reading the manuals, scouring the SOCNET listserv, and trial and error. I hope in writing this chapter to save some scholars from the extensive investment in time and energy that all of that took me. However, you cannot avoid a certain amount of trial and error when learning about Web crawlers. Because I am a self-taught Web analyst, I learned the inner workings of prepackaged Web crawlers by making mistakes and then trying to fix them. Some researchers mistakenly believe that the use of a prepackaged Web crawler means that you do not need to understand how crawlers work, as long as they do work. However, once I began to dive into the analysis of tens of thousands of Web pages that were produced by adjusting a crawler setting I did not understand—only to discover I did not want any of them—the necessity of understanding the inner workings of my tools became clear.

For me, the first of these lessons came from trying to crawl the set of URLs from the *Yearbook of International Organizations* project. I quickly realized that some of the organizations were using a subdirectory on another organization's Web server for their NGO's website. This meant that, using the standard crawler settings, all of the data were counted twice in my crawl, once for the organization that hosted the main directory and once for the subdirectory. If I was not careful in cleaning my data for analysis, I would have never realized that the default setting would have led to inaccurate findings (and possibly to having to publish a retraction or correction later).

Matthew: From the early days of Web 2.0, I have experimented with different programming technologies. I worked my way through college programming websites as a side business. During my graduate studies, I became interested in the Web as a research tool after taking a doctoral seminar on social network analysis. During that course, I came across Turner and colleagues' (2005) early work mapping social interaction on USENET, and it was clear to me that the same type of methods could be used to map information flow and social interaction on the Web.

Although I knew a bit about programming, I knew very little about Web crawling. At first, I relied on painstaking hand crawling for a study that examined how hyperlinks are used to structure information flow between newspaper websites. Despite the labor involved, this research design worked. As I developed my research further, I wanted to examine how the U.S. media industry as a whole had adapted to and evolved within the online business environment. This developed into my dissertation project: I conducted a longitudinal study of the evolution of the U.S. news media industry, in which I examined how organizations adapted online linking patterns over time, and how they established connections with other organizations via hyperlinks. This type of online research builds, in part, on a growing area of research examining patterns of hyperlinking as a way to map and analyze trends in groups and organizations (Adamic and Adar 2001; Halavais 2008).

During this time, I visited the Oxford Internet Institute and learned about longitudinal analysis of Web content conducted in partnership with the Internet Archive. I thought, "Could I do something similar for my dissertation work?"

The Internet Archive is a nonprofit organization that hosts a vast repository of archived Web pages (for an overview, see Ankerson in this volume). After searching for tools and consulting with peers, it became clear that no good software existed that would employ the Internet Archive's data to investigate the research questions I wanted to answer. With the support of my university, I launched a two-year project to develop a custom Web crawler to interface with the Internet Archive. The result of this work was a custom tool, History Crawl (Weber and Monge 2011a), that could be used to extract historical networked data from the Internet Archive—that is, data showing the relationship of websites captured in the archive to each other. Using the crawler, I was able to extract a 10-year longitudinal data set for my dissertation research.

I learned a lot about how to design a successful research study using Web crawlers, largely through the many missteps that are natural in any new process. There is a thriving support community for programmers and researchers, making it easy to seek help from others. Although I can read and write computer programs such as Python, Java, and Ruby at a basic level, I do not consider myself a programmer by any means, and my consultations with programmers were essential. I believe that most researchers are capable of understanding basic code, and I recommend introductory texts such as the *For Dummies* series. Even a cursory understanding will help with most tasks.

Now that we have presented our history with Web crawling, in the following sections we will outline a number of questions that we view as critical for a first entrée into this area of research.

Key Questions

How do you think theoretically about website data?

<u>Michelle</u>: Too many studies that I have reviewed over the years might be characterized as lovely descriptions of a set of data that researchers found they could easily collect, without much thought given to the theoretical, heuristic, or practical value of such a study. As with any research, the first stage of Web analytic research is to conceptualize the study. In my view, this is where many studies fail—at the outset. While Web crawlers can collect vast quantities of textual and intertextual information, as a researcher you must determine what is significant before you begin.

When I began naively to research hyperlinks back in 2003, I thought of them as being like other networks based on communication flow. In this view, an organization "sends" a hyperlink (or in a slightly more nuanced view, it sends Web users) from their website to another organization's website by making a hyperlink. However, over time and with the help of some anonymous reviewers, I began to reconceptualize what hyperlinks meant. Instead of flow networks, hyperlinks in my view are representational networks (Pilny and Shumate 2012; Shumate 2010; Shumate and Dewitt 2008; Shumate and Lipp 2008). There is nothing being sent from one organization to another by placing a hyperlink on a website. Instead there is, within very particular domains (e.g., NGOs devoted to the same cause), an affiliation that is being stated. The "recipient" of the hyperlink may or may not be aware of its existence.

When considering interpersonal networks or information networks, social network scholars worry about situations like "overload": the state of a particular node being too central to the network and therefore receiving too much information. Yet with hyperlink networks, because no message is being sent, there is no overload potential as a result of being a highly central website in the hyperlink network.

This conceptualization of the hyperlink is revolutionary. To put this another way, unlike most other kinds of links, hyperlinks have no direct cost. As such, power-law (Barabási 2003; Barabási, Albert, and Jeong 2000) effects are more prevalent in hyperlink networks. Put another way, patterns of hyperlinking may be more likely to produce profoundly asymmetric relationships than flow networks. For example, consider one of the most popular websites on the Internet, Amazon.com. Lots of websites link to particular books on Amazon to encourage people to buy or reference the book. You could go on your personal website today and add a link to Amazon.com. However, your link does not cost Amazon anything. It may or may not receive additional website traffic. It is likely not even aware of the hyperlink. Because there is no additional cost to Amazon, it does not make sense for the company to try to constrain the number of hyperlinks it receives, and it is highly unlikely that very popular websites will hyperlink to all of the sites that hyperlink to them. Instead, social influence processes, amplified by advertising and others' visible hyperlink behavior, drive some websites to be the recipients of many hyperlinks.

The hard work of theoretical conceptualization must occur and be logically tested in each new domain where network analysis is applied, including discussion board threads, the mining of email and newspaper articles for relationships, and studies of Web-based content. Without such conceptualization, no matter the sophistication of the Web crawling (or data mining), a study is likely to be perceived as misguided or as just a technical exercise.

What makes social-scientific Web analysis different from a purely structural or systems perspective, as is often done in physics, is a robust conceptualization in regards to either or both creator and audience. The point is not simply describing the structure of the networks that exist.

In a similar vein, selecting a domain of media to examine is an important choice. As noted by Thelwall, Vaughan, and Björneborn (2005) as well as Burnett and Marshall (2003), the Internet is rich with varied activities and actors, and the search for a universal theory or explanation of Internet-based content is likely to be unfruitful. As they illustrate, crawling the entire Web is likely to produce an incoherent network filled with a mix of actors doing very different things. The choice of domain in Web analysis means three levels of choice in my view: (a) the actors I am studying, (b) the scope of the study, and (c) the specific activities in which these actors engage (e.g., commerce, producing news, discussion, collective action, hyperlinking).

In research involving Web crawling, these choices are more complicated than they appear.

(1) Who is really acting? Is it someone acting on behalf of an organization, an individual, or an automatic update programmed long ago?

(2) How do I select actors appropriate for my study? In the case of network or interaction studies, snowball or other network-based sampling methods are likely to be more appropriate than probability sampling techniques, but such a choice has obvious trade-offs, because without probability sampling it is hard to make the case that your findings are broadly representative of a real population. What temporal boundaries should I use, and how frequently should I observe? Because online research offers access to all kinds of data, there are more possibilities here than ever before. However, with all of these data available, the absence of robust theoretical or methodological guidelines becomes more evident.

(3) Similarly, activities that may be examined are boundless. However, there are likely conceptual differences between the meanings of various activities, and so researchers must consider carefully the implications of these choices. For example, consider the difference between hyperlinking and following someone on Twitter. A hyperlink can be placed on a website, and no additional cost is born by either the target or the creator of the hyperlink. However, if you choose to follow someone on Twitter (assuming you leave notifications in the default mode), you will receive updates as often as the target posts them. Therefore, the follow link in Twitter has costs and indicates a path of information flow. To consider both creating hyperlinks and Twitter follow links as the same type of activity, even though both are creating links, does not make sense. The nature of the activity under

investigation should lead you to some logical conclusions about the structure of the network and to consider different theories that are likely to apply to the activity.

In short, before you even begin to delve into the various methodological choices you must make, these choices must be grounded in a strong conceptualization of the study.

Matthew: My first step in tackling Web analytic research is to outline formally the research question I plan to address. This includes taking a first look at previous literature, thinking about analytic techniques I plan to use, and brainstorming the type of data that I will want to collect. As I start to draft an outline, I begin to think about the process of crawling, and I sketch out a plan for collecting data.

I agree with Michelle that once you are sure Web-based data are appropriate for your study, a key step is to establish the theoretical framing of the Web content, especially hyperlinks. Michelle argues that hyperlink networks are representational networks denoting a relationship of affiliation between organizations, but I do not believe that this is always the case. There are different kinds of hyperlinks. Although hyperlinks are not necessarily "sent" from one organization to another, they may in fact direct a user's experience. For instance, the Huffington Post curates content from a host of websites. Hyperlinks direct users back to the original story, guiding a user from one website to another. This "sending" of users is, I would argue, quite similar to other kinds of flow networks.

As new technological standards are developed on the Internet, researchers need to use caution when thinking of hyperlinks as only representing relationships or affiliations. New standards for hyperlinking are always being developed, such as the resource development framework and HTML 5 (Hickson 2011). Both are intended to increase the amount of metadata on the Web, potentially embedding descriptive information into hyperlinks beyond simply directional guidance or relational structure (Marlow et al. 2006). Semantically enabled search infers meaning from search terms and can integrate data, allowing users to search more accurately for the answer to questions such as "Which Major League Baseball pitchers won more than five games in the 2008 season?"

In addition, on social networking platforms such as Twitter and Facebook, networks exist through friend lists and contact lists instead of hyperlinks. These lists are links between people, and they represent a different type of network altogether, although it is one that can be studied by Web crawling to examine the formation of social relationships and issues such as social capital in friendship networks (Ellison, Steinfield, and Lampe 2007).

Research Protocol?

<u>Matthew</u>: Beyond hyperlinking, it is important to consider what other content could be important to capture. Many websites are media-rich, and it is possible to extract large bodies of text, photos, and video from them. Extracting additional content increases the amount of time required to crawl websites. This is worthwhile when there's a clear research interest in this type of content, but otherwise unnecessary. When I crawled media organizations' websites, I extracted pages that were hyperlinked to one another, but I didn't collect full websites. If I had wanted to look at hyperlinking within the site, or changes in the type of content over time, then it would have been important to collect entire sites.

You should decide whether or not you even need to crawl the Web yourself to obtain the Web data you need for a study. There are many public data sources available that contain Web data. For instance, Yahoo!'s Webscope Program (http://webscope.sandbox.yahoo.com) has made a number of data sets available to academic researchers free of charge, including hyperlink data, information from Yahoo!'s question-and-answer site, and metadata from websites. If Twitter data are of interest, the Library of Congress is working to archive the collected corpus of tweets. It is currently unclear how these data will be made available, but a number of universities are working to establish research protocols for accessing this database.

It is also important to think about the tools available. Is there a preexisting package that can be used, or is it time to use a custom Web crawler? Think about the type of data to be extracted, and how much. Some of the basic questions to be answered include the following.

(1) How many websites will be crawled (i.e., scope)? Some prepackaged crawlers have limitations on the number of sites or the rate at which one can crawl. For instance, Michelle mentioned SocSciBot, which is an easy-to-use Web crawler that can handle the majority of basic Web crawls. SocSciBot is designed to output to Pajek, which is

a specialized network analysis package, and automatically eliminates a number of elements from crawls, including JavaScript. This limits the range on analyses that can be performed and may restrict data validity by eliminating certain pages.

(2) How deep into a given site does the crawl need to go (i.e., depth)? That is, are the links that occur only on the main landing page of a website of interest, or does the research call for both content and links?

(3) What languages are the websites in? Custom crawlers are flexible and can be adapted to handle a wide array of languages, whereas prebuilt crawlers often do not process foreign characters. I learned this lesson when I was studying global media organizations and ended up with a collection of websites written with Japanese characters; I was able to recode my crawler to process these sites properly.

I believe that existing packages are adequate for the majority of projects researchers will encounter. Why, then, would you design your own Web crawler? When I set out to crawl the Internet Archive, it was necessary to create a custom crawler because the archive uses a set of storage protocols that are unique to that site. Custom crawlers, however, have a number of other advantages. They allow crawling to be more efficient by specifying in advance the exact data that will be extracted. This can increase the speed of crawling significantly. Custom crawling also allows a high level of control over the output format. For example, if you would like to analyze your data in UCINET (a basic network-analysis package), you could program the custom crawler to output a link list that can easily be imported into the UCINET program. I designed my Web crawler to output all crawled fields to a SQL database that I can manipulate as needed. It was not the most efficient solution, but it gave me lots of flexibility for conducting future studies.

Most of my experience has been with the Python programming language. It is a powerful and efficient programming language, and there are many preexisting modules of code that are free to use, which means that you do not actually need to know a significant amount of coding to use it. Modular components can be assembled piecemeal to suit the needs of a research project. There are even a number of open-source crawlers written in Python that one can download and modified as needed. These are hybrid crawlers; they require customization, but are largely prebuilt. One that is currently popular is Scrapy.[1] The open-source software community at Sourceforge.net maintains a complete and up-to-date list.

According to Domaintools.com, a Web registry tracker, there are more than 125 million active Web domains as of December 2010.[2] That does not take into account the hundreds or even thousands of Web pages that can exist within a single domain. Therefore, a key step in Web crawling is delineating the domain names that will produce the Web data I plan to extract. Am I interested in crawling a preset list of domain names, or do I plan to start with a seed list and crawl out through the network of connected sites? Are there top-level domains (.com, .edu, .org, etc.) that I plan to include and exclude? What about country domains (.cz, .us, .jp, etc.)? In my experience, a seed list of 75 websites crawled outward three steps can quickly build to a list of more than 100,000 websites.

Michelle: Once you have determined the process for selecting the websites of interest, even more nuanced choices must be made about what types of data are most relevant. For example, I may be interested in the "main" pages of an organization's website. However, determining what "main" means and accounting for variation across websites takes time. For example, when I was crawling NGO websites, some sites contained one or two Web pages and others contained over 5,000 pages, a significant variation in potential depth. The amount of text then becomes a confounding variable in the study, and practical decisions had to be made about the depth that would be most appropriate.

Depending on the composition of the websites across the organizations of interest, two, three, four, or even five levels away from the main directory may be the most appropriate choice. However, there are times in which no decision rule makes sense. For example, when I was working on corporate social responsibility statements from Fortune 500 companies, I tried using a crawler to look for Web pages within the website that contained various different search terms but failed. Then I tried identifying specific areas of the website where the needed text might be and having the Web crawler pull text from those subdomains, but realized I was getting too much text that was irrelevant. Finally, I ended up visiting every website and identifying the relevant sections manually. There was too much variation in the format, depth, and categorization of these messages to automate the process.

<u>Matthew:</u> You want to think through these choices carefully ahead of time. Executing a large crawl can take a month. One of the worst is spending that month running a crawl only to realize that you forgot a key attribute for the analysis. Additional attributes, however, exponentially increase the amount of time needed for crawling, data formatting, and analysis.

When possible, it can be very helpful to use secondary data sources for studies as well. When I studied the evolution of news media organizations in online environments, I spent a substantial amount of time interviewing online editors and business managers in order to contextualize my work. When this type of secondary source is feasible, it increases the power of data substantially because it adds another level of meaning to crawled data.

<u>Michelle:</u> I spend a good deal of time thinking about the ways my data need to be formatted in order to analyze the data set most efficiently. For hyperlinks, I create a file that lists the website crawled in column 1 and the website hyperlinked in column 2. For text, I generally strip rich formatting and HTML code in favor of raw text files, as long as I am primarily interested in the textual content only. I make the choice for ease of use with computerized content analysis programs such as Crawdad (Corman and Dooley 2006) and the desire to avoid purchasing a large amount of storage. However, if you are interested in doing the types of analyses that rely on images as they appear in the original Web pages, then raw text files would not be a good choice. For comment lists or conversations, identifying conversation threads may be of particular importance. Thinking about these things ahead of time will save hours of work trying to reformat the data later.

<u>Matthew:</u> I take a different approach. I almost always store my data in databases so that I can easily extract data in a variety of formats (spreadsheets, text files, network formats). Structured query language (SQL) is a standard programming language used to request information from databases, and there are a number of good software packages that support SQL (Navicat is one that I have used quite a bit).

Data must be verified for accuracy and reliability. The Web is a great data source, but it is also a murky space filled with dead links, dead websites, and plenty of pornography. I am always amazed how quickly a simple Web crawl manages to capture all three of these with even the best of filters. One simple measure of accuracy is to take a subset of websites (a percentage of the original crawl) and hand crawl the data. By comparing the hand crawl data against the Web crawl, it is possible to assess what was intended versus what was extracted unintentionally. Measures of data reliability will also help to assure reviewers when submitting articles for publication. For instance, compare the percentage of websites capture by a hand crawl against the percentage of websites captured by a crawler for the same URLs. A significance test of the difference may also help support the reliability of the data.

Privacy and the Institutional Review Board

<u>Michelle:</u> There are at least three kinds of pitfalls relating to the protection of human subjects that have to be addressed in a study like this in order to satisfy your ethical obligations and the institutional review board at your university. The first is legal. Many people are interested in researching Facebook; however, the website has a very strict statement of rights and responsibilities that is violated when one collects data about individuals and their use of the site without their explicit consent. Some researchers collect and later post these data anyway and run into problems with Facebook later (e.g., Traud, Mucha, and Porter 2012). In contrast, social network sites that are part of Google's OpenAPI make some data publicly available. The second concern is technical. When I crawl a website, I email the Web administrator explaining what I am doing and giving them the option to tell me to stop. In addition, one should take special care not to overload servers or take up bandwidth that creators of websites in developing countries are unlikely to be able to afford. I refer the interested reader to Thelwall and Stuart's (2006) paper on the ethics of Web crawling, which provides a more in-depth discussion of these issues, including how robots.txt files can be handled. The final privacy/human subjects issue involves collecting data where individual users could be identified, and they *may* have some expectation of privacy. While private information on the Internet is an illusion, if you needed to log in to a website to see user profiles or have the option of adjusting privacy settings, this means that users have the impression that some of their

information will be private. In such cases, I believe that informed consent should be sought before attempting to collect this information. Institutional review boards around the country are becoming savvier to some of the ways in which IP addresses and logs can be linked back to specific users, and the use of such information could be an infringement of the privacy rights of your participants. At minimum, Web crawling research projects that can be linked to individuals (rather than organizations) should be subject to review by the institutional review board, even if you only need to submit an application for exemption.

Matthew: Because I deal primarily with organizational data, I have been fortunate in my interactions with institutional review boards. I am generally able to gain exempt status for my studies. However, since I often use interviews in tandem with Web crawling, I often have to de-identify both sets of data to protect interview subjects or organizational identities. This is a time-consuming process; the researcher must create a master list and assign a numerical identification code to each website. This can then be used to code the interview data. It is possible to create automatic filters to do this when custom crawlers are used. The interview data I collect often contain information that could be sensitive to the organization, and therefore confidentiality is an important step. For instance, when I interviewed one executive at a major media organization, he talked to me about lessons learned from the past, and in doing so revealed information about a forthcoming product that had not been publicly announced. It was imperative that I kept this material private.

Depending on the type of research an individual is doing, this is a critical process, and researchers should be particularly careful when dealing with social network data and websites that belong to individuals. In 2008, Harvard University announced the release of a wave of data on the use of Facebook.com by approximately 1,700 students (see Lewis et al. 2008). The data were anonymous, but were quickly identified as belonging to students at Harvard. The Harvard data set was identified largely because of its attributes (such as the size of the school and language used in the codebook). This serves to highlight the sensitive nature of online data. Although digital traces and network data often contain unique signatures that can be used to trace data back to its source, simple identifying characteristics should also be considered. If a researcher is dealing with a small sample pool, attributes such as the number of pages within a single domain may be enough to identify the original URL and/or organization.

Completing a Web Crawl

Michelle: When I taught a colleague to use SocSciBot for the first time, I was reminded about the many surprises that await social science researchers when using such tools. It takes a lot longer than most people realize. My colleague thought that he could set up a Web crawl of 300 Web domains with a 5,000 Web page maximum per site to begin at 5:00 p.m. as he was leaving work and that it would be done when he returned. In fact, that first website was still being crawled when he got into work the next morning. In order to be respectful of webmasters, a delay between crawling a certain number of Web pages, called a pause, is built into crawling software so that the speed of the crawl is usually limited (a.k.a. rate limiting, described below). This means that a sample of 200–300 domains can take a month to crawl, if nothing goes wrong.

However, things always go wrong. Even the most robust crawlers will hit a snag and freeze, or some unrelated computer update will run and restart the computer. Web crawling is often like having a new puppy. I grade some papers, I check on how the Web crawling is going. I prep a lecture or review an article for a journal, and then I check on the Web crawler's progress. Graduate students I have trained to do this often end up saying that conducting a survey is a lot less work.

Finally, researchers should expect to interact with their IT professionals. In the first semester when I arrived at the University of Illinois, where I was doing some of this work, the Internet access in our building kept crashing (which, of course, was messing up my Web crawling). In a meeting about an unrelated topic, the head of the building's IT complained that someone had set up an unauthorized router in the building and that they were seeing some highly unusual Web traffic from a Web crawler. I was the guilty party. Always one to ask for forgiveness instead of permission, I had set up both a router and a crawler in my basement lab (the fact that it was in a back basement room is likely the only reason they had not caught me). I confessed, remedied the router issue, and notified them about the Web crawler. You may want to ask for permission first, or at least notify your system administrator that an unusual pattern of Web traffic is heading their way.

Matthew: Expect to be overwhelmed. In an organizational research study I conducted on the newspaper industry, I started with a seed sample of 76 websites and, with preliminary filtering, ended up with a network of 25,628 domains (the full network, counting individual Web pages, was close to half a million pages). The crawl itself took five months to complete, and filtering took an additional month. After applying specific filters, the data I actually planned to analyze was reduced to 2,977 domains. I intentionally collected a larger data set by design in order to map the ecosystem as a whole and to create a source for future research. At the time this seemed like a good idea, but given the lengthy crawling process that it required, I would not do it again without a specific, pressing research need.

The study above is an extreme case, as the research project described was overwhelmingly large in scale, but I learned a number of helpful lessons from it. I set up virtual network computing (VNC) on the computer hosting the crawler, and it proved to be a lifesaver. VNCs allow a user to connect to and control another computer from their own. My crawler was hosted at the University of Southern California, but I worked remotely most of the time. I was able to log into the host machine via VNC and check for errors. I still had to be on site on occasion to deal with errors, but this setup allowed for considerable freedom. Short Web crawls can be run from a home computer or laptop, but for larger studies it is helpful to have a dedicated machine. For this project, I used three computers that crawled simultaneously, and the custom crawler was designed to then aggregate the simultaneous crawls into a common database.

Web crawling can return a tremendous amount of data, and for the researcher this can create a serious storage issue. When I collected my dissertation data, I ended up with more than 500GB of raw data. I had a number of choices at that point with regard to storage. On the one hand, physical hard drives are relatively inexpensive. Currently a 1 Terabyte drive can be purchased for roughly $100. In my case, that was the perfect solution, because it provided me with enough space for storage and was kept locally, which satisfied IRB concerns regarding the privacy and security of data (local storage is perceived to be more secure than cloud storage). When I have worked with smaller data sets or subsets, I have found that it is relatively easy to work with online storage sites such as Dropbox. A 1TB online storage drive costs roughly $6 a month, and Windows Live Sky Drive offers 15GB for free. Traditional hard drives are more secure and faster, but should be backed up and are subject to failure. The first drive I used for my dissertation data failed after three months, and I had to replace it; luckily, I had a backup! Online solutions generally cost the same but offer more flexibility. When using online solutions, it is also necessary to think through security issues and ensure data are protected.

Lastly, be polite when crawling. Be courteous to websites. Rate-limiting refers to the number of times a given IP address is allowed to access a Web page. For large crawls, it is not realistic to contact every website, but rate limits should be obeyed, even if a site does not mandate limits. Twitter.com, for instance, specifies that anonymous IP addresses are rate-limited to 150 requests per hour. There is a form that can be filled out to increase the rate limit to 350 requests per hour. OpenSocial does not clearly define rate limits for its APIs, but one should be careful to crawl at a reasonable rate. Excessive crawling can actually make a crawler look like a virus attack or a hacker attack, resulting in one's access being restricted or denied. If a researcher will be crawling one site extensively, it is worthwhile to be in touch with the owners of the domain and the site administrators. For instance, when I worked with the Internet Archive, my research was made possible only by working directly with the Internet Archive's research group. I sought their approval before starting the project, and was careful to obey their requested crawler rate limits.

What to Do with All These Data

Michelle: Depending upon the Web crawler I chose and the types of data I have to analyze, I use some secondary utility programs to get the data into the format I need. For example, if the Web crawler has downloaded thousands of HTML documents, I may need an HTML detagger—a program that transfers everything into plain text for further content analysis. When I am interested in performing hyperlink analysis that investigates the connections between different Web domains, I need a utility program to truncate the URLs in my data set. (That is, I need to omit any unnecessary details on the right side of the URL and leave the domain names intact.) While utility programs can make such preprocessing easier, I have always found that I needed to spend at least a few days double-checking these processes and further cleaning my data. When creating rules to reformat thousands of entries, there are usually exception cases that I do not anticipate and then have to fix manually.

Matthew: When it comes to formatting data and transferring them for analysis, I believe there is a significant advantage in using a custom Web crawler. When a researcher uses someone else's package, and someone else's detagger, the researcher is working within another programmer's parameters. This is fine in many instances, but for academic purposes it does not always meet the needs of a research project.

When I was working on the HistoryCrawl project, I worked with a programmer to develop a number of filters that removed spam and unwanted links from the data set, and then outputted the data in multiple formats so that I could import that into a number of different programs for analysis and visualization. This is not an easy process; the first few times we ran the filters, the program was set to stop every time it encountered a website it did not know how to handle. With over 100,000 websites in the data set, it was a time-consuming process to check every error and create a rule for categorizing the site.

The end result, however, was that I ended up with 10 years of data on tens of thousands of websites. But that was also the problem. I planned to do a significant amount of network analysis. Although the basic network analysis package, UCINET, can handle 32,767 nodes, it slows down notably with more than a few thousand. And if a researcher wants to look at longitudinal data, it is even more difficult because of the necessary computing power. More recent programs such as RSiena, which utilize the R open-source statistical program, can handle larger data sets (up to 3,000 domains longitudinally). These types of constraints are another reminder of the importance of thoroughly thinking through one's desired analyses before beginning a crawl.

The Write-Up

Matthew: When I wrote my dissertation, my description of the crawling and filtering process took up enough text to fill a journal article. I am not able to reference a manual in order to provide readers with technical details. This is particularly problematic when explaining the choices that I have made in data collection and analysis; these choices are the result of both theoretical questions and technical limitations imposed by the type of crawl I conducted.

In the short run, I have accepted, like Michelle (see below), that many of these details have to be reduced to one-sentence descriptions and generic terms. Without a reference manual to source, I include a one-page appendix outlining the general structure of the crawler in order to provide more detail. Here I am able to reference sources for specific components that were used in the crawler and explain some of the critical choices that were made. I have had to balance between simplifying my findings and educating readers about a powerful research tool.

Working with large data sets, it is also important to think about how to describe the data. In my study examining the flow of information in online networks (Weber and Monge 2011b), I had to find a balance between describing the general network structure and characterizing the role of individual websites in producing and transmitting information. Visualizations are useful for macro-level descriptions, particularly when dealing with network data. Descriptive data are critical, especially when key statistics can be compared to well-established benchmarks. Online metrics such as average number of links, number of megabytes per Web page, and number of times a Web page is updated per year all help to describe the overall nature of the data set. This data can easily be balanced with specific findings and other relevant data.

<u>Michelle</u>: One of the biggest challenges I had when first writing up my research on hyperlink networks was how much technical detail to include. The first drafts of my method section were around 15 pages, which obviously includes too many details. My first conference-submitted versions came back with comments like "this is a technical methods piece," a clear sign that I was again introducing too many technical details of Web crawlers into my method section. The compromise I have found when using preexisting crawlers is to be sure to select one with a great technical manual and reference that manual. In doing so, I have sacrificed replicability for readability, which is not an ideal compromise. I have tried, when allowed, to insert footnotes with more technical details. However, the standard methods section does not permit explanation of many of the

tacit choices that have to be made when cleaning Web crawling data, or mucking with a Web crawler that cannot deal with a particular site. Unfortunately, many of those details get washed away in concise statements like "after cleaning the data, the results yielded ... " or "for all but two of the websites in the sample, ..." There is little space for rationale and even less space for explaining the mechanics of Web crawler maintenance.

Conclusion

Through the preceding dialogue, we have outlined many of the central issues that scholars in the social sciences must address when conducting Web analytic research. As is clear from our exchange, there is no set process for this type of research. In fact, we found that we sometimes had opposing perspectives regarding many of the key points. Scholars choosing to pursue this type of research will find that it is a wide-open research domain. As such, there are many with years of experience in Web crawler maintenance who are willing to offer advice when the unexpected happens.

We hope that the interested reader, like the main character in Pirsig's novel, has come to appreciate the necessity and perhaps wisdom in understanding the mechanics of Web crawlers. There are many decisions to be made, and all of them have implications for the quality and impact of the research we conduct.

Notes

1. See https://github.com/scrapy/scrapy.
2. A domain refers to a root URL such as Google.com, Illinois.edu, or Duke.edu.

References

Adamic, L. A., and E. Adar. 2001. You are what you link. Paper presented at the 10th Annual International World Wide Web Conference, Hong Kong.

Barabási, A.-L. 2003. *Linked: How Everything is Connected to Everything Else and What It Means.* New York: Plume.

Barabási, A.-L., Albert, R., and Jeong, H. 2000. Scale-free characteristics of random networks: The topology of the world-wide Web. *Physica A: Statistical Mechanics and its Applications 281* (1–4): 69–77.

Burnett, R., and P. D. Marshall. 2003. *Web Theory: An Introduction*. New York: Routledge.

Corman, S. R., and K. J. Dooley. 2006. *Crawdad Text Analysis System 2.0*. Chandler, AZ: Crawdad Technologies.

Ellison, N. B., C. Steinfield, and C. Lampe. 2007. The benefits of Facebook "friends:" Social capital and colleges students' use of online social network sites. *Journal of Computer-Mediated Communication 12* (4): 1143–1168.

Halavais, A. 2008. The hyperlink as an organizing principle. In *The Hyperlinked Society: Questioning Connections in the Digital Age*, ed. J. Turow and L. Tsui. Ann Arbor, MI: The University of Michigan Press.

Hickson, I. 2011. HTML5. Retrieved from http://www.w3.org/TR/html5.

Jackson, M. 1997. Assessing the structure of communication on the World Wide Web. Journal of Computer Mediated Communication, 3 (1). http://onlinelibrary .wiley.com/doi/10.1111/j.1083-6101.1997.tb00063.x/full.

Lewis, K., J. Kaufman, M. Gonzalez, A. Wimmer, and N. Christakis. 2008. Tastes, ties and time: A new social network dataset using Facebook.com. *Social Networks 30* (4): 330–342.

Marlow, C., M. Naaman, d. boyd, and M. Davis. 2006. HT06, tagging paper, taxonomy, Flickr, academic article, to read. Paper presented at the Hypertext 2006 conference, New York.

Neuendorf, K. A. 2002. *The Content Analysis Guidebook*. Thousand Oaks: Sage.

Pilny, A., and M. Shumate. 2012. Hyperlinks as extensions of offline instrumental collective action. *Information Communication and Society 15* (2): 260–286. http://www.tandfonline.com/doi/abs/10.1080/1369118X.2011.606328.

Pirsig, R. 1974. *Zen and the Art of Motorcycle Maintenance*. New York: Bantam Books.

Rogers, R., and N. Marres. 2000. Landscaping climate change: A mapping technique for understanding science and technology debates on the World Wide Web. *Public Understanding of Science (Bristol, England)* 9: 141–163.

Shumate, M. 2010. Knowledge management systems and work teams. In *Communication and Organizational Knowledge: Contemporary Issues for Theory and Practice*, ed. H. Canary and R. McPhee, 191–208. New York: Routledge.

Shumate, M., and L. Dewitt. 2008. The North/South divide in NGO hyperlink networks. *Journal of Computer-Mediated Communication 13*: 405–428.

Shumate, M., and J. Lipp. 2008. Connective collective action online: An examination of the hyperlink network structure of an NGO issue network. *Journal of Computer-Mediated Communication 14*: 178–201.

Thelwall, M., and D. Stuart. 2006. Web crawling ethics revisited: Cost, privacy and denial of service. *Journal of the American Society for Information Science and Technology 57*: 1771–1779.

Thelwall, M., L. Vaughan, and L. Björneborn. 2005. Webometrics. *Annual Review of Information Science & Technology 39* (1): 81–135.

Traud, A. L., P. J. Mucha, and M. A. Porter. 2012. Social structure of Facebook networks. *Physica A 391* (16): 4165–4180. arXiv1102.2166.

Turner, T. C., Smith, M. A., Fisher, D., and Welse, H. 2005. Picturing Usenet: Mapping computer-mediated collective action. *Journal of Computer Mediated Communication 10* (4), 7.

Weber, M., and P. Monge. 2011a. *HistoryCrawl* [computer software]. Los Angeles: University of Southern California.

Weber, M., and P. Monge. 2011b. The flow of digital news in a network of sources, authorities, and hubs. *Journal of Communication 61* (6): 1062–1081.

10

Big Data, Big Problems, Big Opportunities: Using Internet Log Data to Conduct Social Network Analysis Research

Brooke Foucault Welles

Used children's bookstore: that is my exit plan. If this PhD does not work out, I will leave and open a used children's bookstore. It will have low shelves stocked with "already loved" children's books, little stools where kids can sit and read, story hours, and lattes for moms and dads. I am not sure if the bookstore will ever be anything more than a fantasy, but in the darkest hours of my dissertation, it gave me great comfort to imagine what I would do when I quit and left my PhD work behind.

It is not that I dislike my research topic. I like it a lot. I study online friendship, using social network analysis techniques to examine and model server-side logs of online interaction in order to determine how people select a relatively small number of friends among the hundreds or thousands of anonymous strangers they meet in places like virtual worlds and online games. Understanding how people come to know one another via computer-mediated communication is something I have been interested in for a long time. And, as more and more people go online to socialize, I think my dissertation topic is becoming increasingly important, and the results have interesting implications for researchers and practitioners alike. I enjoy the type of research that I do, and I genuinely want to know the answers to my research questions.

So why, then, did I have this fantasy about opening a bookstore? And why did I consider walking away from my research and my life as a PhD student three times, once so seriously that I even scouted retail real estate in order to find a suitable site for the bookstore? If you are at all familiar with social network analysis, you may be expecting a chapter about the difficulties of collecting network data or dealing with missing data, which are very real challenges that most network analysts face (Wellman 2007). But not me. I have mountains of data, more data than I could ever possibly use (see Williams and Xiong 2009 for a discussion of how to work with companies to obtain such data). In fact, the type of research I do is often called "big data" research because the volume of data I have to work with is so very large. Along with a small but growing group of network researchers, I use data extracted from logs of Internet behavior to study the network relationships among people, organizations, and resources (e.g., Ahmad et al. 2011; Hansen, Shneiderman, and Smith 2010; Hughes and Palen 2009; Livine et al. 2011; Shen and Williams 2011). Specifically, I study friendship networks in the virtual world Second Life, examining if and how the configuration of friendship links between people in Second Life resemble those found offline in places like schools and neighborhoods (Foucault et al. 2009; Foucault Welles, Van Devender, and Contractor 2010).

Unlike many researchers who toil away conducting surveys in schools and community centers in order to study friendship networks, my data were handed to me on a silver platter (or, rather, a silver hard drive). I have around 3 terabytes of data about Second Life users and their friendships from server-side logs of online behavior that were given to my research group by Linden Labs, the company that owns Second Life. I am exceedingly lucky to have these data, as they likely saved me years of work, and they are not generally easy to come by (Williams and Xiong 2009).

And yet, my research has not been without challenges, some, ironically, caused by having so much data. Three stages of my research presented challenges that seemed so insurmountable at the time that I nearly gave up altogether. In this chapter, I will detail those challenges and offer advice on how others might avoid similar setbacks, or at least manage them without seriously considering opening a bookstore instead. As big data research involving large-scale analysis of logs of Internet behavior becomes more popular, I hope that the insights and advice in this chapter will save other researchers some time and heartache, and help to keep their exit plans squarely in the realm of fantasy rather than reality.

Crisis No. 1: The IRB

Anyone conducting research involving human subjects at an American university must first seek approval from the school's Institutional Review

Board (IRB), whose mandate is to ensure that participants' rights are protected. I knew about IRBs before I began my work and was prepared to go through the long process of applying for permission to conduct my research. Warned by friends who had already secured IRB approval for their work, I was ready to defend my research decisions, deal with complicated application procedures, comply with seemingly bureaucratic requests, and go through several rounds of revisions before my application was approved. I was not, however, prepared for what actually happened.

In order to understand my IRB experience, you first need to understand a bit more about my data set. For my research, I use server-side records of user behavior in the virtual world Second Life. These data were automatically and unobtrusively collected by Linden Labs, the company that owns the game Second Life. Linden Labs has kept complete records of every user action, interaction, and transaction since Second Life was launched. The company gave me approximately 3 terabytes of data from nine months in 2006 that include a small number of demographic and game usage variables for six million Second Life users (identified by a user identification number), as well as the in-world friendships and group memberships for those users.

In my IRB application, I requested permission to analyze the network of friendships among the 6 million users in my data set, examining how things like user gender, age, and popularity in Second Life influenced how those friendships formed. I explained how the data would be stored, how users' identities would be kept anonymous, and how results would be reported to protect privacy. As I sent in my application, I was fairly confident that my application would be approved without a problem.

Four weeks later, to my great dismay, I received an email informing me that my application was denied because I did not have consent forms from my users. There was no request for revisions, no instructions on how to handle this situation. Nothing. The email from my IRB informed me that I could not proceed with my research until I tracked down all 6 million users in my data set and collected signed forms giving permission to use and analyze their data from them.

I panicked. By requiring consent forms, the IRB had effectively shut down my research program. There was no way I could even identify the users in my data set, much less contact them and get signed consent forms.

I honestly had not even thought about consent forms before they asked. After all, Linden Labs owned the data set and freely gave it to me. But having the data set was not enough—I needed permission to view and use it. No permission, no research, no dissertation, no PhD. At the time, I could not see a way out of this situation, and the open-a-children's-book-store-exit-plan began to look more and more appealing. I started scouring the Internet for used children's books. I even wrote down the contact phone number for an empty retail location in my neighborhood.

Happily, I never called that number. As you may have guessed, I eventually did secure IRB approval to use my data. It turns out that the initial denial stemmed largely from the IRB reviewer's misunderstanding about big-data research. Generally speaking, IRBs are well versed in a variety of research methods, and many of these methods offer useful templates for the ethical treatment of subjects in most research settings. However, this was not the case for me. My IRB had never before reviewed a study involving big data, and it rejected my application because its staff did not understand how such extensive data could be collected from users without interacting with them directly. The reviewer, referencing research protocols with which she was familiar, assumed that I must have distributed a survey to the users in order to collect the data, and therefore ought to have consent forms from each user. It never occurred to her that there might be another way to gather information about Second Life users.

With any luck, moving forward, research involving big data logs will become increasingly commonplace. Until then, it may well be that when you propose such a study, it will be among the first using such techniques that your IRB has ever reviewed. Based on my experience, my best advice for researchers seeking IRB approval for studies involving logs of Internet behavior is to get to know someone at your local IRB and start talking to that person on the phone. Better yet, consider inviting the person for coffee and a friendly research chat. When my application was simply an anonymous request in the queue, it was easy to reject because it did not appear to conform to the tenets of ethical research. But, as soon as I developed a relationship with my IRB reviewer and explained to her (face to face), what I was trying to do, she was full of useful suggestions about how to explain my research so that it could be approved.

IRB reviewers are not in the business of thwarting research—just the opposite, actually—but it is their responsibility to make sure that human subjects are protected. If they do not understand your study and the nature of your data (which they likely will not), they will ask lots of questions and make seemingly unreasonable demands in the name of research ethics. While it is possible to work these issues out through formal IRB submissions and electronic communication, it will be much faster and less anxiety-provoking if you explain things face-to-face. In my experience, IRB reviewers typically find this kind of research pretty exciting, and once they have understood what I am trying to do, they have been happy to shepherd my applications through the review process. If you can develop rapport with your IRB reviewers and remain polite and calm when you interact with them, you will likely find they are quite helpful to you as well.

In addition to developing relationships with your IRB reviewers and helping them understand the research you intend to do, there are a few specific things you can do that will help move along your IRB approvals for projects involving logs of Internet behavior. First, whenever possible, get your data with permission from the company that owns the website or application you are studying. Scraping data from a website or using bots to collect data (that is, using a computer program to collect data automatically from the Internet for you) in an online game falls into a very gray area, ethically speaking. You have no way to demonstrate that subjects could reasonably be aware that they might be participating in research, or that they had the opportunity to opt out if they did not want to participate (two important tenets of the ethical treatment of human subjects). A letter of support from a game company or website owner, ideally coupled with a terms of service agreement to demonstrate that your data were collected knowingly and with consent can go a long way. Armed with a letter from Linden Labs, and a copy of Second Life's terms of service, I was able to obtain a waiver of informed consent for the users in my data files, on the grounds that they consented to having data collected about their actions when they created their accounts and that they were given the option to withdraw consent by discontinuing account creation.

If at all possible, it is also important to keep personally identifying information out of your data set. This includes things like real-world names, email addresses, or other contact information, and, to a lesser extent, screen names, account IDs, and demographic information such as age, sex, and race. The best way to ensure that your data are free of identifying information is never to collect or request such information in the first place. There are plenty of interesting questions that can be answered without identifying individual users, and if you choose one of those questions, your IRB application will be infinitely easier.

Of course, there are also questions that require some identifying information to answer. In my own research, it is important to be able to track individual users across several data logs and know basic demographic information about them (age, gender, zip code, etc.) The best way I have found to handle this situation is to ask the game company to encrypt account IDs before they send them, or, if that is not possible, I encrypt account IDs as soon as I get them and destroy the key so there is no way to for me or anyone else to decrypt them in the future. This can be achieved simply and inexpensively by asking a friend to perform a simple transformation to your data, such as adding an integer to a numerical user ID, or adding characters to user IDs that are strings (letters or combinations of letters and numbers). If you know someone with computer programming skills, that person will be able to help you perform more complicated transformations using something called a hash function (essentially a small program that transforms each user ID according to a specific formula), or you can also purchase software that can help you encrypt your data. Once my data are encrypted, I use the encrypted IDs (rather than the original, more identifiable IDs) to track the users in my data set. This strategy allows me to keep track of individual users, but makes it impossible for me or anyone else to tie the data back to any personally identifiable information.

Crisis No. 2: Working with Big Data

Becoming a computer programmer (sort of)
Armed with IRB approval and a bevy of interesting research questions, I set out to begin analyzing my data. I sat down at my computer, opened my favorite social network analysis program, and promptly realized I did not actually have any data to work with. Worse yet, I did not know where the data were, or how to get them. Undaunted, I sent an email to the senior software developer in my research lab and asked him to send me the data. He replied, politely explaining that the data were not available

to be "sent," and besides, even if he could send them, they would not fit on my hard drive. Hopelessly naïve about big data sets at the time, I was utterly confused, and not sure if the software developer was being difficult, or if I was missing something.

It turned out to be the latter. Once again, you will need a bit of context to understand what went wrong. Before I began working with my Second Life data set, I had imagined that it would be similar to other large data sets I had worked with in the past. I had quite a bit of experience with data management and analysis software, and had completed projects that involved analyzing several thousand lines of data using software such as Microsoft Excel and SPSS. However, I was not at all prepared to work with big data, including my own data set, which was several orders of magnitude larger than anything I had worked with in the past. Instead of thousands of lines of data, I had millions. Instead of gigabytes of data, I had terabytes. Not only could I not open the data using a program that I was familiar with, the hard drive on my relatively high-end computer (for its time) was about thirty times too small to even hold the data set, much less manipulate it.

Although the hard drives on desktop computers are getting larger all the time, so too are Internet log data sets, and if you intend to work with big data, you should anticipate running into data-management challenges. Internet log data are unlike most types of data that social scientists use. Like my data, log data often come in the form of gigantic text files containing gigabytes of messy, tab-delimited data. These data will need to be edited, sorted, and transferred to a database before you can even begin to use them. If you are very lucky, someone will have already done this work for you. If not, it will be well worth your money to hire someone who knows how to set up databases to help you. A badly organized database will cost you a lot of time and aggravation, and a well-organized database will make it easier for you to access the data you need efficiently. Unfortunately, unless you have a computer science background, setting up large databases is a specialized skill, and not one you are likely to be able to pick up quickly.

Once your data are organized into a database, you may be alarmed to discover that the database can only be accessed via specialized computer code. I sure was. Like many social scientists, my experience writing computer code is limited, and I find the whole idea of computer programming fairly intimidating. So, when I discovered that I would need to write computer code in order to get my data, I did what many social scientists might do—I panicked. It was not a crisis of bookstore-opening proportions, but I did spend a lot of time whining to anyone who would listen that I did not want to have to get a degree in computer science in order to do social science research.

Of course, this turned out to be unnecessary. While setting up a large database is quite difficult, learning how to access data stored in a well-organized database is fairly straightforward. My data are stored in a database that could be accessed using a computer programming language called Structured Query Language, or SQL. In order to get data for analysis, I use SQL to write "queries," which are short programs that describe the data you would like to retrieve. So, for example, I might write a query asking the database to give me a list of all of the friendships between users who created accounts in 2007. The database would then create a text file containing only the subset of the data that met the criteria I described in the query.

Although I was initially intimidated by the idea of writing these queries, I was relieved to discover that queries follow a very standard format that can easily be modified once you have the basic formula in place. So, rather than learning to write queries from scratch, I asked a computer scientist friend to make me "formula cards" that contained SQL queries for the types of data I most often wanted to retrieve. For example, the vast majority of my queries involve retrieving lists of friendships between users who have certain characteristics (such as having created accounts in 2007, being female, or having spent at least 30 minutes using Second Life). So, my friend created a formula card containing the query for retrieving lists of friendships limited by certain characteristics, and when I wanted to retrieve data, I was able simply to plug in the name of the characteristic I was interested in, rather than write the whole query from scratch.

If you are not lucky enough to have a computer scientist friend who can help you, all is not lost. There are several introductory books that teach beginners how to write SQL queries. I found Morelan's "Joes 2 Pros" materials to be among the most accessible for true novices (Morelan 2009). Or, if you are not inclined to learn to query databases yourself, you can hire someone to do it for you. If you are a student working toward a degree, you may want to check with your advisor to be sure this is acceptable practice, and, if it is, you will need to plan ahead to include this related cost in your research budget. Rates for computer programmers vary by location, but you should expect to pay at least several hundred dollars for qualified help.

The importance of codebooks

Regardless of whether you learn to query the database yourself, or pay someone else to do it for you, your ability to access the data will be contingent on having a high-quality codebook that details what data you have, how they are stored, and what each variable means. I was very lucky that Linden Labs provided a good codebook for my data, and any confusion over variable names and values had already been clarified by students who had worked with the data before I started. However, I can easily see how a bad codebook could bring down a research program, so I cannot stress this enough: *make sure you have a high-quality, detailed codebook for your data.*

If you extract the data yourself, this means carefully documenting the data as they are gathered from the online world. If someone else gives a ready-made data set to you, then you may receive a workable codebook to go along with it (it is a good idea to request this when you ask for the data in the first place). If you do not get a codebook, you may have to work with someone at the organization that provided the data set to decipher cryptic data labels and create a codebook on your own. Or, if you are unlucky, you may be forced to slog through the data on your own to figure out what all the variables and figures mean. In any case, before you can successfully work with data, you will need to produce a codebook that includes the names of the variables, what they mean, and how each variable is represented.

A good codebook should include the form of the data (numeric, text, date, etc.), how many cases were collected, what values should be expected for each case, and what row or column in your database holds the data. For instance, consider the following (hypothetical) codebook:

Database overview—This database contains records for approximately 5 million players of My Favorite Game collected on May 1, 2011. Each row (n = 4,998,927) represents a unique player, and each column represents a unique variable. There are 45 variables for each player.

Column 1—UserID: a unique 16-character string consisting of numbers and letters assigned when players create new accounts.

Column 2—User_Sex: a single letter (M/F) representing the sex of the user, as self-reported at account creation.

Column 3—Account_Create_Date: an 8-digit number (MMDDYYYY) representing the month, day, and year the account was created.

...

This codebook clearly spells out how much data you have (4,998,927 rows by 45 columns), how the data are stored (players in rows and variables in columns), what each column is called, and what kind of data you can expect to find in each column. It also explains what each variable means, along with some information about how it was collected. This last bit is more important than it may first appear. Although it may be perfectly clear to you what each variable name means when you first collect or receive the data set, you may be surprised how quickly you forget after your data are gathered. I cringe to think about the amount of time I have wasted trying to remember what the variable name "BinLogMin" means. Do yourself a favor and be meticulous with your documentation up front. Hargittai, in *Research Confidential* (2009: 3–4), lists additional reasons for why such detailed documentation is absolutely essential to every project.

Sampling your data

Data and codebook in hand, I faced one final challenge before I could begin my analysis: sampling. The problem was not that I was surprised to discover I needed to sample my data in order to analyze them; I always knew I would need to sample my data in order to extract a network that could be analyzed reasonably. If you are a big-data researcher, and you thought you would be performing network analyses on your whole data set, I have some bad news for you. With the exception of calculating some very basic descriptive network statistics, it is impossible to analyze a network that is larger than about 5,000 nodes, and it is fairly challenging to analyze anything larger than 1,000 nodes. To be clear, by impossible, I do not mean difficult for someone in your position. I mean actually impossible.[1] Most predictive network analyses are extremely computationally intensive, and even using state-of-the-art machinery, it can take several hours or even days to analyze networks of 1,000+ nodes. Analyzing networks of millions of nodes would literally take thousands of years given current computational resources, and if you are writing a dissertation or on the tenure clock, or simply a mere mortal, you do not have that kind of time.

No, the problem was that none of the established network-sampling techniques worked for my particular data set. And it is very likely that none will work for you either. You see, until very recently, network data were collected by hand, and the resulting networks were small and manageable. It is only because of the widespread proliferation of online networks that network analysts have had access to big data and begun to develop techniques for sampling smaller networks out of big networks of millions or billions of nodes. As a result, there are only a few established techniques for taking network samples, and even these techniques are not well developed for large, online data sets (e.g., Clauset 2005; Newman 2006; Salganik and Heckathorn 2004; Zhang et al. 2011). So, like me, you may find that the established techniques will not work. In my case, established sampling procedures such as random sampling, snowball sampling, and computational subnetwork detection were either too time-consuming, or they produced samples that were unsuitable for analysis.

So, I was forced to develop my own sampling procedures. It is hard for me to offer general advice if you find yourself in a similar situation, because the sampling technique you use will depend heavily on your research topic and questions. However, I would encourage you to anticipate having difficulty taking network samples, and to allot extra time for this phase of your research. I spent a long and frustrating year trying out different sampling procedures until I settled on one that was suitable for my research.

Ultimately, what worked for me was to draw heavily on offline friendship network studies, where researchers most often collected data within classrooms or neighborhoods. When it came time to take my sample, I found an organizational unit inside Second Life (groups) that resembled a classroom in the offline world. Of course, online groups do not have every characteristic of offline classrooms, but for my purposes they are sufficiently close to serve as a suitable proxy for sampling. As you begin your quest for the perfect sample, you may find it useful to draw upon existing literature on your topic of interest, modeling as closely as possible the "sampling" techniques used by researchers who used them to collect data by other means. Although they may not discuss it in these terms, those researchers all did some sort of network sampling when they decided where and from whom to collect their data, and you may be able to find proxies in your own data that approximate those choices.

Crisis No. 3: The Mapping Principle

Happily, after I sampled my data, my research project proceeded without incident for quite some time. I analyzed my networks, wrote up the results, and sent them out for publication. And then I got back my first set of reviews. Rejection.

Two reviewers were fairly enthusiastic about my project, offering small suggestions for improvement while generally agreeing that it was good work. But the third reviewer tore it apart. Although the reviewer thought my research was interesting and the methods were sound, he or she rejected the premise that I was studying friendship at all, saying that I had no evidence that the network phenomena I observed were representative of actual friendship, as we understand it in the offline world.

Naturally, my first reaction was to assume that the reviewer was a buffoon who had clearly missed the point of my paper. The problem was, the reviewer was right. I did not have any evidence that I was studying real friendship. Worse yet, I did not have any data that could provide such evidence. It seems almost absurd to complain about not having enough data when you already have more data than anyone could use in a lifetime. But complain I will. I would love to be able to tell you whether or not the "friendships" I study are authentic friendships, as we would understand them in the offline world, or something more like acquaintances or contacts that are called "friends" through an accident of online game design. But there is simply no way for me to know this. If I had information about what people were saying to one another, or whether or not they trusted one another, I might be able to craft an argument about the authenticity of the so-called friendships that I study, but I do not have these data and probably never will.

I am not sure I can fully convey the depth of crisis that this realization spurred. I felt like an idiot. Since the beginning of my dissertation research, I had claimed to be studying online friendship, when all along I was actually studying something else entirely. I wondered how it was possible, at this late stage in my project, that I was only just discovering that *I was not researching what I thought I was researching.* Although I was nearly done with my dissertation research, I seriously considered walking away yet again. After all, if a reviewer who spent a few hours with my research already knew more than I did after spending nearly two years on it, I was clearly not cut out for this line of work. Maybe used children's bookstore owner was the right line of work for me after all.

But, it turns out that this sort of misunderstanding is quite common among researchers who study online behavior. In his 2010 call to action, Williams (2010) urges virtual worlds researchers to think critically before making claims about the extent to which behaviors observed online map to similar behaviors in the offline world (he calls this "the mapping principle"). In some cases, when people study online behavior, they are interested simply in describing what happens online. However, in my research, and in many other cases, we would also like to make interesting connections to the offline world as well; using online data as a kind of Petri dish for predicting what might happen under similar circumstances when people interact face-to-face. And it is no wonder why. As online data sets become increasingly available, it is often easier and cheaper to study Internet-based interactions than it is to study similar interactions offline.

But, as I learned the hard way, you must never assume that online behavior maps perfectly to offline behavior and vice versa. Although some researchers are meticulous about demonstrating that behaviors map before they draw conclusions about the offline world based on online observations (i.e., Ahmad et al. 2011; Burt 2010; Castronova et al. 2009), most are not. Indeed, researchers have been burned by modeling behaviors in online worlds, only to discover that they bear little resemblance to the offline world (Balicer 2007; Lofgren and Fefferman 2007).

For me, reconsidering the true nature of my research and resisting the temptation to draw inferences about real friendship based on my observations about online friendship has been one of the biggest struggles in my research. Although for some users, in some cases, online friendship is quite similar to offline friendship, for many, online friendship represents a superset of social relationships that includes real friends, acquaintances, business associates, and so on. The effort required to make and keep a friend in the online world is often significantly lower than in the offline world, and so the mapping between online and offline friendship is weak at best. It took a bad review and a lot of heartache for me to discover this, but you may be able to avoid similar problems if you do a bit more thinking about your research questions and the mapping principle up front.

Choosing the right research questions

You may be able to avoid the whole mapping issue if you choose research questions that you can answer using the data that you have. When I began my research project, I was primarily interested in how online social relationships develop. Somewhere along the way, I was seduced by the idea of friendship, probably because my data contained a relationship called "friendship." This may not have been a problem if I had either been diligent about remembering I was not studying friendship as it exists in the offline world (rather, an online relationship called "friendship"), or if I had checked to be sure that I had data that could be used to demonstrate that my "friendship" data represented actual friendships (such as information about communication, trust, or another quality associated with friendship relationships.) But I did not do either of these things, and I paid the price later on in the form of a rejected paper.

Luckily for me, it was not impossible to undo my mapping problem and salvage most of my work. After much thinking, I realized that I needed to abandon the idea that I was studying friendship, and return to my original research question about online social relationships. I had wandered so far down the "friendship" path that it took me a long time to become comfortable with the idea that I was not studying friendship in the classic sense, but something called "friendship" that exists in a specific context among a specific group of people. At first, I spent a lot of time apologizing for the shortcomings in my data, and fretting about all of the interesting questions I could not answer. But eventually, I realized that, with fairly minor revisions to the literature review and framing of my project, I could refocus on the topic I was actually studying: the dynamics of online social relationships.

The problem with big data is that, when you have so much data, it is easy to be seduced into thinking that you can answer any and every question, without the constraints typical of social science research. But, of course, that is not true. You will be able to answer many questions with your data, but not all of them. Save yourself some heartache and choose questions that lend themselves well to the sorts of data you have. I wish I had spent more time looking through my codebook before I dove headlong into a study that I mistakenly thought was about friendship. If I had really considered the variables I had to work with, I would have realized I could not study friendship, in the traditional sense. But I also would have realized the wealth of interesting questions about social relationships that I *could* study using the data I already had, and that many of those questions were well aligned with my original research interests.

If you have already started your research, I would encourage you to take a moment to verify that you have the data you need to answer the question you think you are working on. If you are just coming up with research questions, spend some time with your codebook. Make lists of variables and connections between users that seem interesting to you. Then, go back to your research interests and generate questions using the variables and connections in your lists. Although data should never drive hypotheses in social science research (hypotheses should be theory-driven), when you have very large data sets to work with, it makes sense to let the data inspire your research questions. If you do so, and choose answerable questions up front, you may be able to avoid entirely the types of mapping issues I encountered.

Determining whether your data map

Even if you do use your data to drive your research questions, if those questions involve comparing online and offline networks, you will need to establish that your online networks reasonably map to their offline counterparts before you can generalize claims from your research to the offline world. There are several different ways you can do this. First, you must engage directly with the community you study. That means that if you study networks on Twitter, then you have to tweet. If you study World of Warcraft, you have to play the game. You may not need to be a power user or the best player, but there is no way for you to understand the dynamics of an online network unless you are part of it. Create an account and spend some time getting to know the game or service you study, and tell your boss/advisor/partner/parents that you are doing this in the name of science. As you use the game or service, you will come to know the subtleties of the network, and you will be better positioned to determine whether the behaviors you study map to the offline world.

In addition to playing the game or using the service you study, you may be able to compare directly the online networks you study to similar networks in the offline world to see if structural features align. Ahmad and colleagues (2011), for example, were interested in whether online criminal activity (in the form of goldfarming in online games) could be used to make predictions about the behaviors of offline criminal networks, such as drug-dealing gangs. Before they endeavored to make any predictions, they first verified that online goldfarming networks had many structural similarities to offline drug-dealing networks, and then restricted their predictions to matters dealing with network structure (Ahmad et al. 2011).

Of course, such comparisons require that suitable offline data exist, which may not always be the case. So, instead, another possibility is to compare the behavior of actors in your network to behaviors we would expect to find if they were in the offline world. Burt (2010) did this when he examined the behavior of brokers, or individuals who occupy a position of power because they connect otherwise unconnected groups of people, in Second Life networks. He discovered that brokers in Second Life shared many of the characteristics of brokers in the offline world (for instance, they were more likely to start successful groups), and concluded that Second Life may be a suitable platform for studying brokerage behaviors such as leadership tendencies, popularity, and power in groups.

If you are very lucky, you may be able to stage experiments or find naturalistic experiments that allow you to observe if changes in online worlds produce the results we would expect to find if similar changes happened in the offline world. Castronova and colleagues (2009) were able to examine whether macroeconomic behavior in the online game Everquest 2 followed predictable offline-world growth patterns via a naturalistic experiment. Occasionally, due to computational limitations, very popular online games run out of space for new users. When this happens, the game companies add new game servers to allow more players to join the game. Generally speaking, each game server represents an isolated "world" and players cannot transfer resources between servers. So, by observing economic transactions on a brand new game server, Castronova and colleagues (2009) were able to track how a new economy grew over time. They discovered that new game servers followed predictable patterns of growth in gross domestic product and inflation and concluded that online games may be a suitable proxy for studying economic behavior.

Regardless of how you establish whether your online data map to the offline world, there will always be limitations on the extent to which you can generalize your online results to make predictions about offline behavior. In some cases, when you are only interested in making claims about the online world, this may not be a problem. However, if you would like to generalize beyond the online context you study to the offline world, it is important that you first confirm the behaviors you study map appropriately. As I have discovered, it makes your research stronger, not weaker, to acknowledge the limits of your data and results, and predictions about online behavior can be every bit as valuable as predictions about similar behavior offline. So, if your data can tell us little about the offline world (as is the case with my research), draw conclusions about online behavior instead of trying to force your data to map to the offline world. Journal and grant reviewers will see through bad mapping, and your otherwise outstanding research will have a much harder time seeing the light of day if you try to extend your conclusions too far.

Conclusion

Whether you began your research because you were interested in big data, network analysis, online behavior, or all of the above, you have an exciting road ahead of you. Doing network research using big data is no panacea, and you will face unique challenges, many of which will require you to invent new techniques and research methods. Some of the challenges may seem so insurmountable that you may consider walking away from your research altogether.

However, as I hope this chapter has illustrated, that is rarely ever necessary. Even big problems have solutions, and if you manage to work through these problems, the rewards will be great. Although network analysts are just beginning to use big data, as these data sets and methods for analyzing them become increasingly available, this type of research will only grow in popularity. Further, as more and more interactions take place online, studies of Internet behavior are becoming increasingly valued in the social sciences. Because you have chosen to take on the difficulties of working within an emerging area, you will have the opportunity to make significant methodological, theoretical, and practical contributions with your research; perhaps more so than your peers who have chosen to do research using more established techniques in more traditional settings. This means that you will have your pick of interesting questions to work on and that you may be able to write papers about areas of your research, including methods and data management techniques, that those working in more traditional areas have difficulty publishing in.

So, make your exit plan and take comfort in fantasizing about it when you run into trouble. But hopefully, with a bit of time, patience, and careful planning, you will never need to act on that plan. Instead, I expect you will quickly discover that you are at the forefront of a new and important research area, and you will be well positioned to become one of very few experts on using network analysis of big data to understand social behavior.

Acknowledgments

I would like to thank my advisor, Noshir Contractor, dissertation committee members Darren Gergle and Barton Hirsch, and SONIC lab members Yun Huang, Mengxiao Zhu, York Yao, and Anne Van Devender for coaching me through many of the challenges discussed in this chapter. My dissertation research was funded by grants from Northwestern University, the National Science Foundation (#NSF-IIS 0729505), and the Army Research Institute (#W91WAW-08-C-0106).

Note

1. The one exception to this may be a special class of network modeling that involves using computers to generate large-scale hypothetical networks based on a set of known rules. This technique is popular among economists and physicists, but rarely used by social scientists, who are most often trying to establish theories to explain observed social behavior, rather than examining what would happen to a network over time when certain rules dictate how nodes interact.

References

Ahmad, M. A., Keegan, B., Williams, D., Srivastava, J., and Contractor, N. 2011. What can gold farmers teach us about criminal networks? *XRDS Crossroads 17* (3): 11–15.

Balicer, R. D. 2007. Modeling infectious diseases dissemination through online role-playing games. *Epidemiology 18* (2): 260–261.

Burt, R. S. 2010. Structural holes in virtual worlds. Unpublished manuscript. Chicago, IL.

Castronova, E., D. Williams, Y. Huang, C. Shen, B. Keegan, and R. Ratan. 2009. As real as real? Macroeconomic behaviour in a large-scale virtual world. *New Media & Society 11* (5): 685–707.

Clauset, A. 2005. Finding local community structure in networks. *Physical Review E: Statistical, Nonlinear, and Soft Matter Physics 72* (2): 026132.

Foucault, B., M. Zhu, Y. Huang, Z. Atrash, and N. Contractor. 2009. Will you be my friend? An exploration of adolescent friendship online in Teen Second Life. Paper presented at the 59th Annual Conference of the International Communication Association.

Foucault Welles, B., A. Van Devender, and N. Contractor. 2010. Is a "friend" a friend? Investigating the structure of friendship networks in virtual worlds. Paper presented at the Conference on Human Factors in Computing Systems.

Hansen, D., B. Shneiderman, and M. A. Smith. 2010. *Analyzing Social Media Networks with NodeXL: Insights from a Connected World.* Burlington, MA: Morgan Kaufmann.

Hargittai, E. 2009. Research Confidential. The University of Michigan Press. Ann Arbor, MI.

Hughes, A., and L. Palen. 2009. Twitter adoption and use in mass convergence and emergency events. *International Journal of Emergency Management 6* (3/4): 248–260.

Livine, A., M. P. Simmons, E. Adar, and L. A. Adamic. 2011. The party is over here: Structure and content in the 2010 election. Paper presented at the Fifth International AAAI Conference on Weblogs and Social Media, Barcelona, Spain.

Lofgren, E. T., and Fefferman, N. H. 2007. The untapped potential of virtual game worlds to shed light on real world epidemics. *The Lancet Infectious Diseases 7* (9): 625–629. doi: .10.1016/S1473-3099(07)70212-8

Morelan, R. A. 2009. *Beginning SQL Joes 2 Pros: The SQL Hands-On Guide for Beginners.* BookSurge Publishing.

Newman, M. E. J. 2006. Finding community structure in networks using the eigenvectors of matrices. *Physical Review E: Statistical, Nonlinear, and Soft Matter Physics 74* (3): 036104.

Salganik, M. J., and D. D. Heckathorn. 2004. Sampling and estimation in hidden populations using respondent-driven sampling. *Sociological Methodology 34* (1): 193–240.

Shen, C., and D. Williams. 2011. Unpacking time online: Connecting Internet and massively multiplayer online game use with psychosocial well-being. *Communication Research 38* (1): 123–149.

Wellman, B. 2007. Challenges in collecting personal network data: The nature of personal network analysis. *Field Methods 19* (2): 111–115.

Williams, D. 2010. The mapping principle, and a research framework for virtual worlds. *Communication Theory 20* (4): 451–470.

Williams, D. and L. Xiong. 2009. Herding Cats Online: Real Studies of Virtual Communities. In E. Hargittai (Ed.) *Research Confidential*. University of Michigan Press. Ann Arbor, MI. 122-140.

Zhang, B., D. Krackhardt, R. Krishnan, and P. Doreian. 2011. Extracting subpopulations from large networks. Paper presented at the INSNA Sunbelt Social Networks Conference http://www.ml.cmu.edu/current_students/DAP_BZhang.pdf

11

When Should We Use Real Names in Published Accounts of Internet Research?

Amy Bruckman, Kurt Luther, and Casey Fiesler

"John" is one of the most established members of Newgrounds, an online community of artists, programmers, and musicians with over 5 million registered members as of January 2015.[1] In February 2004, John organized an event called a "time trial challenge" in which animators collaborated over the Internet to complete short movies in less than three days. The event was a huge success. Over the next 12 months, John led 12 more challenges, each more popular than the last, with the finale attracting nearly half a million views—at a time when YouTube was only a few weeks old. More importantly, John had started a phenomenon: the community animation project, or "collab." Rarely seen before the time trial challenges, collabs were now crowding out all other discussions on the Newgrounds forums, with nearly a hundred new collabs begun in August 2006 alone. In 2007, the community celebrated "John Day" with more than 25 tribute animations created in his honor. By 2010, John had led or participated in nearly 50 collabs watched by tens of millions of viewers. That same year, Newgrounds hired him as a full-time community manager and animator.

John's real name is Luis Castañon. Considering his creative accomplishments, we argue that anonymizing him in our research accounts of his work would be unethical. In studying the Internet today, the popular conception of "human subjects research" is fundamentally outdated. Our basic assumptions need to be rethought for an age where we are studying people who deserve credit for their work, and who are entitled to respond to our representations of them.

In this chapter, we will first briefly review the history of the notion of "human subjects research." Next, we will explore why that paradigm needs to be rethought. This is further complicated by the intriguing relationship between real names and pseudonyms, and by the presence of minors online. Finally, we will provide practical advice for researchers working with research participants—when to ask whether research subjects wish to be credited by name, and when *not* to credit them by name even if they request it.

If our participants are credited by name, it follows that they are likely to find accounts of themselves in print, and have comments on those accounts. We will argue that participants are entitled to respond to our representations of them before publication, and discuss the benefits and costs of this approach.

The History of Human Subjects Research

During World War II, researchers in Nazi Germany used humans in horrific experiments that today we would not allow to be performed on animals. The Nuremberg Code (1949) was drafted in the wake of The Nuremberg War Trials. However, problems still existed in the ethics of human subjects research. Most notably, in the Tuskegee syphilis experiments, 400 African-American men with syphilis were monitored for 40 years (1932–1972) without being told of their disease (History of Research Ethics, 2010). When this atrocity came to light, a commission was created that led to the creation of the Belmont Report (1979). The Belmont Report remains the primary statement of principles of ethical research on human subjects today. It lays out three main principles, paraphrased here.

1) Respect for persons:
   a) treat people as ends in themselves, not means to an end.
2) Beneficence:
   a) do not harm, and
   b) maximize possible benefits and minimize possible harms.
3) Justice:
   a) Distribute the burdens and benefits of research equally across society.

In the United States, U.S. Code Title 46 contains the laws regulating federally funded human subjects research. Most universities in the United

States apply these regulations to all research they conduct, even though technically the rules only apply to federally funded work. The laws do not apply to research conducted at corporations or by private individuals, and obviously do not apply outside the United States.

What is a "human subject"? U.S. Title 46 (2009) says:

"(f) *Human subject* means a living individual about whom an investigator (whether professional or student) conducting research obtains (1) Data through intervention or interaction with the individual, or (2) Identifiable private information." (U.S. Title 46.102.f)

But what is "private information"? The code continues:

Private information includes information about behavior that occurs in a context in which an individual can reasonably expect that no observation or recording is taking place, and information which has been provided for specific purposes by an individual and which the individual can reasonably expect will not be made public (for example, a medical record). Private information must be individually identifiable (i.e., the identity of the subject is or may readily be ascertained by the investigator or associated with the information) in order for obtaining the information to constitute research involving human subjects. (ibid.)

The notion of "private information" is a fundamental component of the definition of a human subject; however, that does not mean that such information needs to be hidden. Title 46 states that research should only be approved if "when appropriate, there are adequate provisions to protect the privacy of subjects and to maintain the confidentiality of data" (ibid.).

The question this leaves, then, is when is it "appropriate" to protect the privacy of subjects? This brings us back to the core principles of the Belmont Report, which states that we should not harm subjects (or at least minimize the chance of harm). The traditions of human subjects research have their roots in medical and psychological research. Just as medical records are kept confidential, it is appropriate to protect volunteers for medical and psychological research by disguising their identities in published accounts. However, these ideas translate less well to other forms of research.

In our study of Luis Castañon, failing to give him credit for his work would be harming him. Therefore, we are ethically obligated to give him credit for his work using his name, if the study contains no information that would be damaging to him, and if he chooses to be identified.

From "Subjects" to "Participants"

So far we have provided a simple critique of the prevailing norms of anonymizing subjects in written accounts. Anonymizing can do harm, and
hence sometimes is inappropriate. Probing deeper, however, we might
draw into question the fundamental notion of the speaking researcher
and silent subject. Anthropologist Renato Rosaldo writes:

> The Lone Ethnographer's guiding fiction of cultural compartments has crumbled.
> So-called natives do not 'inhabit' a world fully separate from the one ethnogra-
> phers 'live in.' Few people simply remain in their place these days. When people
> play 'ethnographers and natives,' it is ever more difficult to predict who will put
> on the loincloth and who will pick up the pencil and paper. More people are doing
> both, and more so-called natives are among the ethnographer's readers, at times
> appreciative and at times vocally critical. (Rosaldo 1993: 45)

Rosaldo studied Ilongot headhunters in a rural area of The Philippines
through their transition from tribal society to increasing assimilation into
"modern life." Certainly members of tribal cultures not literate in English
were unlikely to have access to ethnographic accounts of their practices.
Yet even in the extreme example of people at a preindustrial stage of
development, one might begin to ask the question: are the "natives" entitled to respond to our representations of them? The Belmont Report's
first principle of respect for persons is grounded in Kant's second formulation of the categorical imperative—that one must always treat people as
ends in themselves, rather than as means to an end (Kant 1964/1785).
They are not a means to the end of better research results; they are intelligent, autonomous beings with dignity. To treat people as ends in themselves suggests that they are entitled to respond to our representations of
them.

In the social science of 50 years ago, it was unthinkable to consider
that our participants might respond to our representations of them. They
had no access to our written accounts and were presumed to have no
interest in perusing them, as well as insufficient background knowledge
to make sense of research reports in any case. Some of these assumptions
may have been false then. They are all clearly false now, for most research.

The Internet plays a key role in research, even if we are not doing Internet research. The Internet increasingly gives our participants (even Ilongot
ones) the ability to access our accounts of them. When the research topic

Figure 11.1
Research participants post their own recording of our interview, and comment on its benefits to them (http://web.archive.org/web/20080703163157/http://rubber ninja.newgrounds.com/news/post/25437).

is behavior on the Internet itself, we have even more reason to believe our research is accessible to our participants.

Treating people as ends in themselves also suggests that they might want to be repaid for the time invested in being a study subject by learning something from their experience. This is supported by the Belmont Report's principle of justice, suggesting that we should equitably share the costs and benefits of research. Figure 11.1 is an example of participants benefiting from participating in one of our studies, and discussing this openly online.

In this light, traditional research practice seems colonial: the enlightened researcher comes to investigate the ignorant savages. A postcolonial view suggests that the natives are not ignorant and have a right to respond to our representations of them. Further, their insights may substantially improve our accounts. It is true that the defamiliarized (etic) perspective of the outsider can lead to insights not possible from a native/insider (emic) point of view. But the etic point of view can be substantially enhanced by first-class participation of informants. In other words, sometimes the natives know exactly what is going on. Even if we may ultimately choose to discount their contributions or objections, we would never do so lightly, and need at least to give them the opportunity to speak.

Although we use the words "subject" and "participant" somewhat interchangeably, the word "participant" is preferred because it conveys a sense of people's agency. If one can make a coherent argument that Ilongot tribe members should be treated as participants rather than subjects, the argument is even more compelling for Internet users. The participants in our studies of the Internet are more than capable of finding our research reports. Research reports are more and more available online for free and not locked away in expensive subscription journals. Our research participants not only can, but likely will, find our reports and respond to them. From a purely pragmatic perspective, we need to get into the habit of assuming from the start that they will respond, and plan how to make their response a productive contribution to the research process.

Enter Jerry Springer

Where this gets murky is in the case of unflattering portraits of the participants. Research cannot be all sunshine and brilliant, creative videos. Sometimes things are darker, and unflattering accounts are both useful and necessary. To the extent that a portrait may anger or embarrass informants, the researcher has a tough choice. Showing the portrait to the informants may jeopardize a future research relationship with them, if any is desired. Depending on circumstances, the unflattering information could potentially harm the subjects, or could help them by drawing attention to something important. If the research participant is given the opportunity to offer their opinion of something unflattering, that response must be viewed critically (as all informant accounts must). It can be difficult to separate defensive behavior from valid objections to the legitimacy of the account. Thus, sharing accounts with informants pre-publication can be both a boost and threat to the validity of our accounts.

A simple policy for dealing with the new speaking subject would be to say: name them by name if they request it. However, unflattering accounts complicate the situation. Many people are fond of publicity. They will reveal extremely negative private information about themselves just for the opportunity, for example, to be on television. This happens routinely on television shows like *The Jerry Springer Show*, where guests talk openly about highly embarrassing behaviors, and shows like *COPS*, where people give permission to air footage of themselves being arrested (Calvert 2000). This phenomenon also occurs in Internet research (Cherny 1999).

Just because someone asks for his or her real name to be used does not mean doing so is wise. The decision is ultimately a judgment call for the researcher, complicated by the fact that we often do not know our participants well enough to judge whether naming them would harm them. Given a conflict between participants' wishes and what seems prudent for them, researchers sometimes need to err on the side of caution and anonymize participants against their wishes.

To override the conscious choice of a subject is a somewhat uncomfortable exercise of power. However, being sensitive to power relations does not mean pretending such relations do not or should not exist. Ignoring someone's wishes is not something one does lightly, but sometimes it may be advisable or even necessary. Our consent form makes it clear that while we ask for the subjects' wishes regarding identification, we cannot guarantee that we will be able to identify them by name even if they request it.

In Luther's studies of animators (Luther and Bruckman 2008), we have had no problematic cases to date. However, we will see in a later section that in Fiesler's studies of fan writers and remixers, things get more complicated.

Think of the Children

If rational adults sometimes make questionable choices about their desire to be identified by name, what about children? In the United States, teens are more likely than adults to share content online (Lenhart et al. 2010), and many of the creative projects we encounter online are produced by young people. However, the question of how to identify (or anonymize) children's names legally and ethically adds a new layer of complexity to the discussion.

Our first study of Newgrounds included a set of interviews with members of collabs about their experiences with online leadership. In planning this study, we soon realized that most collab members were teenagers or even younger. We became convinced that we should interview some of these young people for our study. Not only did they represent most of the people working on collabs, but we were fascinated to learn how children could work together over the Internet to create some truly impressive movies and games.

For U.S.-based academic researchers who work with children, special consent procedures are typically needed. The state of Georgia, where we are based, defines a child as anyone younger than 18. Legally, children are not able to consent for themselves, and their ability to enter contracts is limited. As a result, the institutional review board (IRB) at our university, which oversees all human-subjects research in compliance with federal regulations, generally requires researchers to collect two forms from child-participants: a "minor assent form" signed by the child and a "parental consent form" signed by the parent.

In conducting our interviews, we followed this standard procedure with one exception. The end of both forms included a question asking if the child wanted his or her real name used in our papers. Our expectation was that this question would prompt parent and child to reflect on the consequences of potentially creating a permanent, Google-able link between the child's identity and his or her contributions to Newgrounds. This extra reflection seemed especially important for sites like Newgrounds, which, for example, boasts a dedicated category for fecal-themed submissions (Newgrounds, n.d.) and provided the fodder for a critical analysis of racist 9/11-themed Web animations (Van Buren 2006). The risk of long-lasting negative exposure for creators of offensive or puerile material is real. On the other hand, controversial submissions on Newgrounds are often among the most popular, attracting hundreds of thousands of downloads, and it is often said in the entertainment industry that "there is no such thing as bad publicity." Indeed, some of our interviewees were students or aspiring artists who sought to use their Newgrounds portfolios as a springboard to a professional career in animation.

For this study, every child-parent pairing requested we use the child's real name where possible. But if a disagreement had occurred—for example, the parent requested anonymization but the child did not—we would have anonymized the child in every case, regardless of the preference mismatch. No one should be forced to be identified for participation in research, even if Mom says so.

The decision of whether to take credit for one's creations and statements is not likely one that a child is equipped to make on his or her own. What seems like a great idea at age 12 may turn out much less prudent a decade later. For our interviews, we would have insisted on the added protection of parental consent even if our IRB had not required it, since parents are better equipped than we are to judge the relative risks and benefits of anonymization for their child. If we think using real names could benefit a child in our study, we must secure parental permission to do it.

The corollary of this argument is that if for some reason we do not wish to seek parental consent, we must also give up the hope of letting that child use his or her real name. For example, it would be nearly impossible for researchers to create a large online community for children if each child needed to scan or fax documented proof of permission before signing up. In these situations, we and other researchers have typically sacrificed the child's ability to be identified for the greater good of being able to use the website at all. For instance, the registration page for MIT's Scratch programming community does not provide a "Name" field, instructs registrants to pick a username that is *not* their full name, and hides location information for anyone younger than 18. Scratch boasts over 5 million registered members (as of January 2015), mostly children, who have created more than 7 million projects—numbers hard to imagine if signing up required parental consent for children.[2] Similarly, in developing Pipeline, our software for organizing collabs, we hide most profile information (including names) for users under 18. These anonymization procedures mitigate the need, at least from the IRB's perspective, for written parental consent, but the cost is that these young content creators are denied the ability to associate their names with their work.

In conducting ethical research, we must do all we can to protect participants' identities from harm while respecting their desire for credit, but we can only do so much. Children in practice make these decisions without parental involvement every time they post content online. Newgrounds, for example, allows contributors to list their real name, in addition to username, alongside their submitted movies and games, which are then indexed by search engines. In this way, these authors are already permanently linked to their Newgrounds creations. This caveat extends beyond the special case of children; all of our participants, regardless of age, had the possibility of being identified with their online work prior to our study. When we use their names in our papers, we are only solidifying a bond that already exists.

Mark Twain and the Problem of Pseudonyms

In many studies of online activity, anonymizing subjects in any meaningful way is impractical. In particular, the "regulars" (Kim 2000) of a site are often easily recognizable to all site participants. It is often necessary to disguise the name of the site being studied in order to disguise research participants. However, it does not provide a great deal of protection to refer to "a large Internet auction site"—people will know you are talking about eBay. If you write about the most active user of a website that provides technical news to a tech-savvy crowd, a significant number of people will know that you are talking about Slashdot founder Rob Malda, a.k.a. CmdrTaco. (Or perhaps we are really talking about Digg founder Kevin Rose, but people leap to assume we are talking about Malda.) Not just founders but core regular members of Internet sites often become de facto public figures, and hence difficult-to-impossible to disguise in published accounts. We have written elsewhere (Bruckman 2002) about the challenges of disguising material in published accounts when that is necessary and the range of practical strategies available. We note here that if CmdrTaco wants to be identified in our account, it makes things a whole lot easier.

Just as Rob Malda could easily be identified by referring to him as the most active user of Slashdot, he could just as easily be identified by referring to him as CmdrTaco. In early Internet research it was common for researchers to disregard pseudonyms as identities and quote them directly in published research rather than anonymizing (Frankel and Siang 1999). However, pseudonyms are now typically treated as persistent identities worthy of the same ethical considerations as real names. One reason for this is that pseudonyms can be broken (e.g., by searching online for CmdrTaco and finding his real name associated with it; Bruckman 2002). Another is that pseudonyms on the Internet often carry as much weight in terms of identity and reputation as real names do. Therefore, in communities of creators, the same considerations for credit that we describe for real names should also be applied to pseudonyms.

In addition to Newgrounds collabs, another context in which we are studying online creativity is that of remix artists and fan creators. The latter includes fans of television shows, books, or other media who create stories, artwork, and videos based upon those existing sources. There are vast networks online of people creatively expanding the boundaries of *Harry Potter* and *Star Trek* and sharing these works with one another. We have been exploring this space as part of a larger research project on social norms around copyright in online communities and have observed that the issue of credit and anonymity is complicated by pseudonyms.

Writers have often published under "pen names" for a variety of reasons. In English-language literature, George Eliot and Mark Twain are two of a myriad of examples.[3] Fan communities had a long tradition of pseudonymity even before they were connected on the Internet, when stories and art were distributed in fanzines and at conventions. Accounts of fan culture have described the risks associated with participation (Bacon-Smith 1992; Jenkins 1992). Some of these exist because of the prevalence of eroticism and homosexual themes in fan fiction; fan creators might fear anti-obscenity laws, hold sensitive employment positions such as teachers, or face opposition from family members. Other reasons have nothing to do with the appropriateness of content; for example, those who aspire to write commercially are often told that publishers do not take fan fiction writers seriously. Still others are concerned about potential copyright entanglements. Beyond issues of risk, some fan creators use pseudonyms that echo some aesthetic or convention in their genre, or, as pseudonyms become more common, others may adopt them simply because pseudonyms have become a norm of the community. This tradition still exists today, and in fact there are highly ingrained norms within the community against "outing" fans by connecting their pseudonyms with real names (Fiesler 2008). Despite the lack of "real" names, social networks of fan creators can be closely knit, and these constructed identities are just as important as their "real life" ones (Busse 2006).

Our ongoing research in this space involves interviews with fan creators, and a consideration of the creative work itself is relevant to issues of copyright and norms. As with our study of animators, we planned to offer our participants the option to have their real names included in any publications in which we mention their work. However, from previous studies we knew that fan creators are often uncomfortable providing us their real names even under a seal of confidentiality and prefer to be known entirely by their pseudonyms. Rather than considering the issue of real names to be moot, we decided simply to treat their preexisting pseudonyms in the same manner as real names. Therefore, when we give them the option to waive anonymity, we ask *what* name they would want to be referred to in our publications in place of a fake pseudonym.

It is not the case that by eschewing the use of real names, creators are suggesting that they do not want credit for their work. Within fan communities, the desire for recognition among their peers is an important part of the culture and influences norms of attribution not only with source material but also with each other (Fiesler 2008). To be a BNF or "big name fan" is something to aspire to and comes with increased recognition within the community, often reserved for the most popular artists or writers (Busse 2006). Just as the name CmdrTaco carries a great deal of weight within Slashdot, there are writers and artists within fan communities who are influential without anyone knowing their real names. It is entirely reasonable that these creators would still want credit for their work in our publications, and that they would want it tied to their established creative identity. Even one of our participants who is "out" with her real identity in fandom—she testified in front of Congress about copyright issues as related to fan-created videos—maintains a pseudonym for disseminating her creative work because that is how she is known. This pseudonym is how she collects social capital within the community, just as lasting recognition for literary achievement is associated with Mark Twain rather than Samuel Clemens.

Within the space of "people doing creative things online," the norms of different communities can diverge widely when it comes to values surrounding identity and credit (Luther et al. 2010). The example of fandom taught us that the choice between real names and anonymization, while often better than nothing, is too simplistic for some communities. Allowing participants to indicate *how* they want to be identified, if at all, can be as important as *whether* they are identified.

The Practical Details

Most of the ideas discussed in this chapter are made concrete in the consent forms that must be approved by our ethics boards and distributed to our participants. To give people the opportunity to express their wishes for anonymization, consent forms for most of our studies now include this language:

Using Your Name
In some cases, people we interview are proud of things they have done online (for example, creative projects) and would like to have their name listed in our published reports. If you would like to request that we use your name if possible, please check the box below. We will not be able to use your name if we feel there is anything that might embarrass you in our report. For most people, using a fake name is the right choice, so you do not need to check the box, but you may if you wish.

Please use my name if possible (optional): [ ]
    What name would you like us to use? (optional) _____

The text in this example applies specifically to interviews, but this is equally relevant to most forms of quantitative and qualitative data collection.

Luis Castañon was one of seventeen participants in our study of leadership in online creative collaboration. Of those seventeen participants, sixteen opted to use their real names in our papers (Luther and Bruckman 2008). We have been surprised by how many of our subjects want their real names used, and also by the fact that to date this practice has generated no problems and few questions. That is likely because this new model of giving people credit for their work is not a contrivance—it is more logical and intuitive for research participants than the outdated model of a vulnerable human subject who needs to be anonymized for protection.

We offer this option in most but not all of our consent forms. To cite an extreme example, we obviously did not provide this option to participants in our study of the use of mobile and social computing by survivors of domestic violence (Dimond, Fiesler, and Bruckman 2011). Other cases can be a more difficult decision. However, since the wording of the form allows us to use their real names, but does not require it, in most cases the wording is now included in our human subjects protocols.

Where possible, we allow participants to respond to our accounts of them before publication. Luis Castañon reviewed a draft of this chapter. We take the opinions of our participants as seriously as possible, but also view their accounts critically and consider the possibility that their insider point of view could be misleading.

Power and Paradigm Shifts

It would be naïve to suggest that power relations between researchers and participants have shifted in any fundamental way. Although the ordinary blogger's voice now sometimes rises above the din, the truth remains that professional researchers are much more likely to be heard. And for the most part, that is as it should be. In theory at least, the researcher has special training that gives him or her a more insightful view of observed phenomena. Users are becoming creators of content on the Internet, but that does not mean all voices can or should be heard at equal volume.

Nevertheless, something has changed. Our research participants have voices, and they will respond to our representations of them—whether we like it or not. There are no simple answers here—issues of minors online, potentially embarrassing accounts of people's activities, and content that people may later come to regret complicate the management of names and pseudonyms considerably. However, our basic mind-set about the nature of our undertaking needs to shift. The people whose online activities we chronicle are not anonymous "subjects," but "participants" in a collaborative process between researcher and participant in making sense of this new medium.

Notes

1. http://www.newgrounds.com.

2. https://scratch.mit.edu/statistics.

3. See http://en.wikipedia.org/wiki/List_of_pen_names for a list of additional examples.

References

Bacon-Smith, C. 1992. *Enterprising Women: Television Fandom and the Creation of Popular Myth*. Philadelphia: University of Pennsylvania Press.

Bruckman, A. 2002. Studying the amateur artist: A perspective on disguising data collected in human subjects research on the Internet. *Ethics and Information Technology 4* (3): 217–231.

Busse, K. 2006. My life is a WIP on my LJ: Slashing the slasher and the reality of celebrity and Internet performances. In *Fan Fiction and Fan Communities in the Age of the Internet*, ed. K. Hellekson and K. Busse, 207–224. Jackson, North Carolina: McFarland & Company.

Calvert, C. 2000. *Voyeur Nation: Media, Privacy, and Peering in Modern Culture.* Boulder, CO: Westview Press.

Cherny, L. 1999. *Conversation and Community: Chat in a Virtual World.* Stanford, CA: CSLI Publications.

Dimond, J., C. Fiesler, and A. Bruckman. 2011. Domestic violence and information communication technologies. *Interacting with Computers 23* (5): 413–421.

Fiesler, C. 2008. Everything I need to know I learned from fandom: How existing social norms can shape the next generation of user-generated content. *Vanderbilt Journal of Entertainment and Technology Law 10* (3): 729–762.

Frankel, M. S., and S. Siang. 1999. Ethical and legal aspects of human subjects research on the Internet. Washington, DC: American Association for the Advancement of Science. http://www.aaas.org/sites/default/files/migrate/uploads/report2 .pdf.

History of Research Ethics. 2010. http://www.unlv.edu/research/ORI-HSR/ history-ethics

Jenkins, H. 1992. *Textual Poachers: Television Fans and Participatory Culture.* London: Routledge.

Kant, I. 1964. *Groundwork for the Metaphysics of Morals.* Trans. H. J. Patton. New York: Harper & Row. (1785).

Kim, A. J. 2000. *Community Building on the Web.* Berkeley, CA: Peachpit Press.

Lenhart, A., K. Purcell, A. Smith, and K. Zickuhr. 2010. Social Media and Young Adults. Pew Internet and American Life Project. http://www.pewinternet .org/2010/02/03/part-3-social-media/#content-creation-sharing-remixing- blogging-and-more. Retrieved May 7, 2015.

Luther, K., and A. Bruckman. 2008. Leadership in online creative collaboration. In Proceedings of the 2008 ACM Conference on Computer Supported Cooperative Work, 343-352, New York: Association for Computing Machinery.

Luther, K., N. Diakopoulos, and A. Bruckman. 2010. Edits and credits: Exploring integration and attribution in online creative collaboration. In Proceedings of the 28th International Conference on Human Factors in Computing Systems, 2823–2832, New York: Association for Computing Machinery.

Newgrounds. (n.d.) "Scat." http://www.newgrounds.com/collection/scat. Retrieved May 7, 2015.

Nuremberg Code. 1949. The trials of war criminals before the Nuremburg Military tribunals under Control Council Law No. 10. Retrieved from http://www .hhs.gov/ohrp/archive/nurcode.html.

Rosaldo, R. 1993. *Culture and Truth: The Remaking of Social Analysis.* Boston, MA: Beacon Press.

The Belmont Report. 1979. Washington, DC: U.S. Department of Health, Education, and Welfare.

United States Title 46. 2009. Protection of human subjects. http://www.hhs.gov/ohrp/humansubjects/guidance/45cfr46.html.

Van Buren, Cassandra. 2006. Critical analysis of racist post-9/11 Web animations. *Journal of Broadcasting & Electronic Media* 50 (3): 537–554. doi:10.1207/s15506878jobem5003_11.

Contributors

Megan Sapnar Ankerson is assistant professor in the communication studies department at the University of Michigan. Her research and teaching interests involve new media and visual culture, Web history, software studies, and media aesthetics.

danah boyd is the founder and president of Data & Society, a New York City–based research institute. She is also a principal researcher at Microsoft Research and a visiting researcher at New York University. Her research examines the intersection of technology and society. Her recent book, *It's Complicated: The Social Lives of Networked Teens*, has received widespread praise from scholars, parents, and journalists.

Amy Bruckman is professor and associate chair in the School of Interactive Computing in the College of Computing at Georgia Tech. She does research on online collaboration. She both studies existing systems and creates new ones designed to encourage users' creative collaboration. Bruckman received her PhD from the MIT Media Lab in 1997, and a BA in physics from Harvard University in 1987.

Casey Fiesler will be faculty in the Department of Information Science at the University of Colorado Boulder beginning in Fall 2015, following completion of a PhD in Human-Centered Computing from the School of Interactive Computing at Georgia Tech. She is interested in the interaction between computing, norms, ethics, and law. Her dissertation research focuses on the role that copyright law plays in online creative communities. She also holds a law degree from Vanderbilt University, with specialized coursework in intellectual property and Internet law.

Brooke Foucault Welles is assistant professor in the department of communication studies at Northeastern University. Broadly, she is interested in how social networks shape and constrain behavior, with a particular emphasis on how new media change the role that networks play in our daily interactions. Foucault Welles' recent work focuses on how people come to recognize resources within their online social networks and leverage them to achieve personal, organizational, and social goals.

Darren Gergle is professor in the departments of communication studies and electrical engineering and computer science (by courtesy) at Northwestern University, where he directs the CollabLab: The Laboratory for Collaborative Technology. His research interest is in developing a theoretical understanding of the role that visual information plays in supporting communication and group interactions. A key component of his work is the application of social and cognitive psychology theory to the design, deployment, and evaluation of computing technologies.

Eric Gilbert is assistant professor in the School of Interactive Computing at Georgia Tech. He and his lab focus on building and analyzing social media. His work is supported by grants from Yahoo!, Google, Samsung, Facebook, the National Science Foundation, and DARPA. He has also founded several social media sites, and his work has received four best paper awards and two nominations from the Association for Computing Machinery's SIGCHI.

Eszter Hargittai is Professor in the Communication Studies department and Faculty Associate of the Institute for Policy Research at Northwestern University, where she heads the Web Use Project. Her work looks at inequalities in Internet use, focusing on how differences in people's Web-use skills influence what they do online in domains such as health, political participation, job searching, the sharing of creative content, and privacy management. She writes a professionalization column called Ph.Do for *Inside Higher Ed.*

Brent Hecht is assistant professor of computer science and engineering at the University of Minnesota. With interests that lie at the intersection of human-computer interaction, geography, and big data, his research centers on the relationship between big data and human factors such as culture. A major focus of his work involves volunteered geographic information and its application in location-aware technologies.

Aron Hsiao is a PhD candidate in sociology at the New School for Social Research and a theorist of computing, technology, and culture. His academic research is focused on big data and mobile devices as phenomena integral to, and resulting from, ethnomethods and ethnomethodological data. His longtime presence in the technology and culture space includes collaborations with eBay, the Annenberg Center for Global Communication Studies, Media Tenor International, The Pragmatic Programmers, and the big data analytics firm Terapeak. He is also the author of several books on open-source technologies.

Karria Karahalios is associate professor in the computer science department at the University of Illinois, Urbana-Champaign, where she heads the Social Spaces group. Her primary research areas are graphics, visualization, and human-computer interaction.

Paul Leonardi is the Duca Family Professor of Technology Management at UC–Santa Barbara, where he also serves as the Investment Group of Santa Barbara Founding Director of the Master of Technology Management Program. His research, teaching, and consulting focus on helping companies create and share knowledge more effectively. He is interested in how implementing new technologies and harnessing the power of informal social networks can help companies take advantage of their knowledge assets to create innovative products and services.

Kurt Luther is assistant professor of computer science at Virginia Tech. His research interests include human-computer interaction, social computing and crowdsourcing, and creativity support tools. He is also interested in connections to the digital humanities, especially history. He holds a PhD in human-centered computing from Georgia Tech and a BS from Purdue University.

Virág Molnár is assistant professor of sociology at the New School for Social Research. Her research explores the intersections of culture, politics, social change, and knowledge production, with special focus on urban culture and transformations of the built environment. She has written about the relationship between architecture and state formation in socialist and postsocialist Eastern Europe, the post-1989 reconstruction of Berlin, and the new housing landscape of postsocialist cities.

Christian Sandvig is Steelcase Research Professor and associate professor in Communication Studies, the School of Information, and the Institute for Social Research at the University of Michigan. He is also a Faculty Associate of the Berkman Center for Internet & Society at Harvard University. His research investigates digital information infrastructures and public policy.

Aaron Shaw is assistant professor in the department of communication studies at Northwestern University and a faculty associate of the Berkman Center for Internet and Society at Harvard University. He studies collective action, collaboration, and mobilization online. His work addresses the organizational factors that determine whether peer production communities (like Wikipedia) succeed or fail; mobilization and engagement in online systems; and the dynamics of participation in online communities.

Michelle Shumate is associate professor in the communication studies department and the director of the Network for Nonprofit and Social Impact at Northwestern University. She investigates the dynamics of interorganizational networks designed to impact large social issues. She focuses on developing and testing theories to visualize, understand, and enable effective interorganizational networks in a variety of contexts including nongovernmental organization (NGO)-corporate partnerships, NGO collaboration networks, and named cross-sector networks that include NGOs, businesses, and government organizations.

Matthew S. Weber is assistant professor in the School of Communication and Information at Rutgers University. His research examines organizational change and adaptation, both internal and external, in response to new information communication technology. His recent work focuses on the transformation of the news media industry in the United States in reaction to new forms of media production. Matthew utilizes mixed methods in his work, including social network analysis, archival research, and interviews.

Index